ISBN 1434829014
EAN-13 9781434829016

©2006-2008 Jeffry A Borror / *Continuux LLC*

Published by *Continuux LLC*
6 Lounsbery Rd, Bedford Corners, New York, 10549, USA

All rights reserved. No part of this book may be reproduced in any form or by any means, without permission in writing from the author.

The author and publisher of this book have used their best efforts in preparing this book, including development, research and testing of the examples given herein. The author and publisher make no warranty of any kind, expressed or implied with regard to the documentation or programs contained in this book.

2008 Printed in the United States of America

Cover image: Victory Angel in Plaza Francia, Buenos Aires, Argentina

q
FOR MORTALS

A Tutorial In q Programming

JEFFRY A. BORROR

Continuux LLC

CONTENTS

ACKNOWLEDGMENTS	xvii

OVERVIEW	**1**
0.0 The Evolution of *q*	1
0.1 Philosophy	1
0.2 Mathematical Functions Refresher	3
0.3 Getting Started	6
0.3.1 Starting *q*	6
0.3.2 Variables	6
0.3.3 Whitespace	7
0.3.4 The *q* Console	8
0.3.5 Comments	8
0.3.6 Assignment Value	9
0.3.7 Order of Parsing	10
0.4 Sample *q* Program	10

**CHAPTER 1	ATOMS**	**12**
1.0 Overview	12
1.1 Integer Data	13
1.1.1 int	13
1.1.2 short and long	13
1.2 Floating Point Data	14
1.2.1 float	14
1.2.2 real	15
1.2.3 Scientific Notation	15
1.3 Binary Data	16
1.3.1 boolean	16
1.3.2 byte	16
1.3.3 Binary Data is Numeric	17
1.4 Character Data	17
1.4.1 char	17
1.4.2 symbol	18

1.5 Temporal Data	19
1.5.1 date	19
1.5.2 time	20
1.5.3 datetime	20
1.5.4 month	21
1.5.5 minute	21
1.5.6 second	22
1.5.7 Constituents and Dot Notation	22
1.6 Infinities and NaN	25
1.7 Null Values	26
1.7.0 Overview of Nulls	26
1.7.1 Binary Nulls	27
1.7.2 Numeric and Temporal Nulls	27
1.7.3 Character Nulls	28
**CHAPTER 2	LISTS**	**29**
2.0 Overview	29
2.1 Introduction to Lists	29
2.1.1 List Definition and Assignment	29
2.1.2 count	30
2.2 Simple Lists	31
2.2.1 Simple Integer Lists	31
2.2.2 Simple Floating Point Lists	31
2.2.3 Simple Binary Lists	32
2.2.4 Simple Symbol Lists	33
2.2.5 Simple char Lists and Strings	33
2.2.6 Entering Simple Lists	33
2.2.7 Lists of Temporal Data	34
2.3 Empty and Singleton Lists	34
2.3.1 The General Empty List	34
2.3.2 Lists with a Single Item	35
2.4 Indexing	36
2.4.1 Index Notation	36
2.4.2 Indexed Assignment	37
2.4.3 Indexing Domain	38
2.4.4 Empty Index and Null Item	38
2.4.5 Lists from Variables	40
2.5 Joining Lists	41
2.6 Lists as Maps	42

2.7 Nesting	43
2.7.1 Depth	43
2.7.2 Pictorial Representation	43
2.7.3 Examples	44
2.8 Indexing at Depth	46
2.8.1 Repeated Item Indexing	46
2.8.2 Notation for Indexing at Depth	47
2.9 List Indexing	48
2.9.1 Retrieving Multiple Items	48
2.9.2 Indexing via a Simple List	49
2.9.3 Indexing via a General List	50
2.9.4 Assignment with List Indexing	51
2.9.5 Juxtaposition	52
2.9.6 Find (?)	53
2.10 Elided Indices	53
2.10.1 Eliding Indices for a Matrix List	53
2.10.2 Eliding Indices for a General List	54
2.11 Rectangular Lists and Matrices	56
2.11.1 Rectangular Lists	56
2.11.2 Matrices	57
2.11.3 Two and Three Dimensional Matrices	57
2.11.4 Matrix Flexibility	59
**CHAPTER 3	PRIMITIVE OPERATIONS**	**60**
3.0 Introduction to Functions	60
3.0.1 Function Notation	60
3.0.2 Primitives, Verbs and Functional Notation	60
3.0.3 Item-wise Extension of Atomic Functions	61
3.1 Operator Precedence	62
3.1.1 Traditional Operator Precedence	62
3.1.2 Left of Right Evaluation	63
3.1.3 A Gotcha of Left of Right Evaluation	63
3.1.4 Rationale for No Operator Precedence	64
3.2 Match (~)	64
3.3 Relational Operators	66
3.3.1 Equality (=) and Inequality (<>)	66
3.3.2 Not Zero (not)	67
3.3.3 Ordering: <, <=, >, >=	69
3.4 Basic Arithmetic: +, -, *, %	71

3.5 Maximum (|) and Minimum (&) 75
3.6 Exponential Primitives: sqrt, exp, log, xexp, xlog 76
    3.6.1 sqrt 76
    3.6.2 exp 76
    3.6.3 log 77
    3.6.4 xexp 77
    3.6.5 xlog 78
3.7 More Primitives: div, mod, signum, reciprocal, floor, ceiling and abs ... 78
    3.7.1 div and mod (Modulus) 78
    3.7.2 Sign (signum) 79
    3.7.3 reciprocal 79
    3.7.4 floor 80
    3.7.5 ceiling 81
    3.7.6 Absolute Value (abs) 81
3.8 Operations on Temporal Values 82
    3.8.1 Internal Format of Temporal Types 82
    3.8.2 Basic Operations 83
    3.8.3 Day Counts and Time Counts 83
3.9 Operations on Infinities and Nulls 86
    3.9.1 Producing Infinities 86
    3.9.2 Producing NaN 87
    3.9.3 Basic Arithmetic on Infinities and Nulls 88
    3.9.4 Type Promotion 89
    3.9.5 Equality 89
    3.9.6 Match 91
    3.9.7 not 91
    3.9.8 neg 92
    3.9.9 Comparison 92
    3.9.10 Maximum and Minimum 94
3.10 Alias (Advanced) 94
    3.10.1 Alias and Double assignment 94
    3.10.2 Dependencies 96

CHAPTER 4 | FUNCTIONS 98

4.0 Overview 98

4.1 Function Specification 98
    4.1.1 Function Definition 98
    4.1.2 Function Notation and Terminology 99
    4.1.3 Implicit Parameters 101
    4.1.4 Anonymous Functions 102

4.1.5 The Identity Function (::)	102
4.1.6 Functions are Nouns	103
4.2 Local and Global Variables	**103**
4.2.1 Local Variables	103
4.2.2 Global Variables	104
4.2.3 Local and Global Collision	105
4.3 Amend (:)	**105**
4.3.1 Amend in C Language	106
4.3.2 Simple Amend	106
4.3.3 Amend with Lists	107
4.4 Projection	**108**
4.4.1 Function Projection	108
4.4.2 Verb Projection	109
4.4.3 Multiple Projections	110
4.5 Lists and Functions as Maps	**111**
4.5.1 Similarity of Notation	111
4.5.2 Item-wise Extension of Atomic Functions	112
4.5.3 Indexing at Depth and Ragged Arrays	112
4.5.4 Projection and Index Elision	114
4.5.5 Out of Bounds Index	114
4.6 Creating Strings from Data	**115**
4.7 Adverbs	**116**
4.7.1 each-both (')	116
4.7.2 Monadic each	118
4.7.3 each-left (\:)	120
4.7.4 each-right (/:)	120
4.7.5 Cartesian Product (,/:\:)	120
4.7.6 Over (/)	122
4.7.7 Scan (\)	123
4.7.8 each-previous (':)	123
4.7.9 Pay No Attention to the *k* behind the Adverbs	124
4.8 Verb Forms of Indexing and Evaluation	**126**
4.8.1 Verb @	127
4.8.2 Verb Dot (.)	128
4.9 Functional Forms of Amend	**131**
4.9.1 Apply (@) for Dyadic Functions	131
4.9.2 Apply (@) for Monadic Functions	133
4.9.3 Dot (.) for Dyadic Functions	134
4.9.4 Dot (.) for Monadic Functions	135

CHAPTER 5 | CASTING AND ENUMERATIONS — 137

- 5.1 Types and Cast — 137
  - 5.1.1 Basic Types — 137
  - 5.1.2 type — 137
  - 5.1.3 Type of a Variable — 139
  - 5.1.4 Cast ($) — 139
  - 5.1.5 Creating Symbols from Strings — 141
  - 5.1.6 Parsing Strings to Data — 142
  - 5.1.7 Coercing Types — 143
- 5.2 Creating Typed Empty Lists — 143
- 5.3 Enumerations — 144
  - 5.3.1 Traditional Enumerations — 144
  - 5.3.2 Data Normalization — 145
  - 5.3.3 Enumerations — 147
  - 5.3.4 Working with an Enumeration — 147
  - 5.3.5 Updating an Enumeration — 149
  - 5.3.6 Appending to an Enumeration — 149
  - 5.3.7 Resolving an Enumeration — 151
  - 5.3.8 Type of an Enumeration — 151

CHAPTER 6 | DICTIONARIES — 153

- 6.0 Overview — 153
- 6.1 Dictionary Basics — 153
  - 6.1.1 Definition — 153
  - 6.1.2 Lookup — 155
  - 6.1.3 Dictionary vs. List — 156
  - 6.1.4 Lookup with Verb @ — 157
  - 6.1.5 Uniqueness of Keys — 158
  - 6.1.6 Non-simple Domain or Range — 158
  - 6.1.7 Extracting a Sub-Dictionary by Key — 159
- 6.2 Operations on Dictionaries — 160
  - 6.2.1 Amend and Upsert — 160
  - 6.2.2 Reverse Lookup with Find (?) — 161
  - 6.2.3 Removing Entries — 162
  - 6.2.4 Primitive Operations — 163
  - 6.2.5 Join — 164
  - 6.2.6 Arithmetic Operations — 166
- 6.3 Column Dictionaries — 169
  - 6.3.1 Definition and Terminology — 169
  - 6.3.2 Simple Example — 169

6.3.3 Accessing Values	170
6.3.4 Rows and Columns	171
6.3.5 Column Dictionary with a Single Column	171
6.4 Flipping a Dictionary	172
6.4.1 Transpose of a Column Dictionary	172
6.4.2 Flip of a Column Dictionary	173
6.4.3 Flip of a Flipped Column Dictionary	173

CHAPTER 7 | TABLES — 175

7.0 Overview	175
7.1 Table Definition	175
7.1.1 Table is the flip of Column Dictionary	175
7.1.2 Table Display	176
7.1.3 Table Definition Syntax	177
7.1.4 Table Metadata	179
7.1.5 Records	181
7.1.6 Flipped Column Dictionary vs. List of Records	181
7.2 Empty Tables and Schema	183
7.3 Basic select and update	184
7.3.1 Syntax of select	184
7.3.2 Displaying the Result	185
7.3.3 Selecting Columns	185
7.3.4 Basic update	186
7.4 Primary Keys and Keyed Tables	186
7.4.1 Keyed Table	186
7.4.2 Simple Example	187
7.4.3 Keyed Table Specification	188
7.4.4 Accessing Records of a Keyed Table	188
7.4.5 Retrieving Multiple Records	189
7.4.6 Reverse Lookup	190
7.4.7 Components of a Keyed Table	191
7.4.8 Tables vs. Keyed Tables	191
7.4.9 Compound Primary Key	194
7.4.10 Retrieving Records with a Compound Primary Key	195
7.4.11 Key Lookup with txf	196
7.5 Foreign Keys and Virtual Columns	197
7.5.1 Definition of Foreign Key	197
7.5.2 Example of Simple Foreign Key	197
7.5.3 Resolving a Foreign Key	198
7.5.4 Foreign Keys and Relations	199

7.6 Working with Tables and Keyed Tables	200
7.6.1 First and Last Records	200
7.6.2 Find	201
7.6.3 Primitive Join (,)	202
7.6.4 Coalesce (^)	204
7.6.5 Column Join	205
7.7 Complex Column Data	206
7.7.1 Simple Example	206
7.7.2 Operations on Compound Column Data	208
7.7.3 Compound Foreign Key	209
7.8 Attributes	210
7.8.1 Sorted (`s#)	211
7.8.2 Unique (`u#)	213
7.8.3 Parted (`p#)	213
7.8.4 Grouped (`g#)	214

CHAPTER 8 | QUERIES: q-sql — 216

8.0 Overview	216
8.1 Insert	217
8.1.1 Basic Insert	217
8.1.2 Alternate Forms	219
8.1.3 Repeated Inserts	219
8.1.4 Columnar Bulk Insert	220
8.1.5 Table Insert	220
8.1.6 Insert into Keyed Tables	220
8.1.7 Insert into Empty Tables	221
8.1.8 Insert and Foreign Keys	222
8.2 The select and exec Templates	224
8.2.1 Syntax	224
8.2.2 The where Phrase	226
8.2.3 The select Phrase	227
8.2.4 The by Phrase	228
8.2.5 The exec Template	229
8.2.6 Using distinct with select and exec	231
8.2.7 Using each in where	232
8.2.8 Nested where	233
8.2.9 select[n]	234
8.2.10 fby	235
8.3 The update Template	237
8.3.1 Basic update	237

8.3.2 update-by	239
8.4 upsert	240
8.5 delete	241
8.6 Grouping and Aggregation	243
8.6.1 SQL Aggregation	243
8.6.2 Grouping without Aggregation	243
8.6.3 Aggregation without Grouping	245
8.6.4 Grouping with Aggregation	245
8.6.5 Using Uniform and Aggregate Functions	246
8.6.6 Using each	246
8.6.7 Using ungroup	247
8.7 Sorting	249
8.7.1 xasc	249
8.7.2 xdesc	250
8.8 Renaming and Rearranging Columns	251
8.8.1 xcol	251
8.8.2 xcols	252
8.9 Joins	254
8.9.1 Equijoin on Foreign Key	255
8.9.2 Inner Join	256
8.9.3 Pseudo Join	257
8.9.4 Ad hoc Left Join	258
8.9.5 Plus Join	261
8.9.6 Union Join	262
8.9.7 Asof Join	263
8.10 Parameterized queries	264
8.11 Views	267
8.11.1 View	267
8.12 Functional Forms	268
8.12.1 Functional select	269
8.12.2 Functional exec	271
8.12.3 Functional update	272
8.12.4 Functional delete	272
8.13 Examples	273
8.13.1 The Table Schemas	273
8.13.2 Creating the Tables	274
8.13.3 Basic queries	276
8.13.4 Meaty Queries	280
8.13.5 Remote Queries	284

CHAPTER 9 | EXECUTION CONTROL — 286

9.0 Overview — 286

9.1 Control Flow — 286
- 9.1.1 Basic Conditional Evaluation — 286
- 9.1.2 Extended Conditional Evaluation — 287
- 9.1.3 Vector Conditional Evaluation — 290
- 9.1.4 if — 291
- 9.1.5 do — 291
- 9.1.6 while — 291
- 9.1.7 Return and Signal — 293
- 9.1.8 Protected Evaluation — 294

9.2 Debugging — 295

9.3 Scripts — 296
- 9.3.1 Creating and Loading a Script — 297
- 9.3.2 Special Notations — 297
- 9.3.3 Passing Parameters — 298
- 9.3.4 Example — 300

CHAPTER 10 | I/O — 301

10.0 Overview — 301

10.1 Data Files — 301
- 10.1.1 File Handle — 301
- 10.1.2 Using hcount and hdel — 302
- 10.1.3 Using set and get — 302
- 10.1.4 Using hopen and hclose — 303
- 10.1.5 Using Dot Amend — 303
- 10.1.6 Writing Splayed Tables — 304

10.2 Save and Load on Tables — 305

10.3 Text Data — 308
- 10.3.1 Writing (0:) and Reading (read0) Text Files — 308
- 10.3.2 Using hopen and hclose — 308
- 10.3.3 Prepare Text (0:) — 309

10.4 Binary Files — 310
- 10.4.1 Writing (1:) and Reading (read1) — 310
- 10.4.2 Using hopen and hclose — 310
- 10.4.3 Reading Text Files as Binary — 311

10.5 Parsing File Records — 311
- 10.5.1 Fixed Length Records — 312

10.5.2 Variable Length Records	314
10.6 Interprocess Communication	315
10.6.1 Communication Handle	316
10.6.2 Connection Handle	316
10.6.3 Message Format	317
10.6.4 Synchronous Messages	319
10.6.5 Asynchronous Messages	320
10.6.6 Message Handlers	321
10.6.7 Handling Close	323
10.6.8 Http Connection Handler	324

CHAPTER 11 | WORKSPACE ORGANIZATION — 325

11.0 Overview	325
11.1 Contexts	325
11.1.1 Context Notation	325
11.1.2 Reserved Contexts	326
11.1.3 Working with Contexts	327
11.1.4 A Context is a Dictionary	328
11.1.5 Expunging from a Context	329
11.1.6 Functions and Contexts	329
11.1.7 Saving a Context	331
11.1.8 Loading a Context	331
11.1.9 Namespaces (Advanced)	331

CHAPTER 12 | COMMANDS AND SYSTEM VARIABLES — 333

12.1 Command Format	333
12.1.1 Tables (\a)	333
12.1.2 Console (\c)	334
12.1.3 Web Console (\C)	334
12.1.4 Change O/S Directory (\cd *path*)	334
12.1.5 Directory (\d)	335
12.1.6 Functions (\f)	335
12.1.7 Load (\l)	336
12.1.8 Offset (\o)	336
12.1.9 Port (\p)	336
12.1.10 Precision (\P)	337
12.1.11 Seed (\S)	338
12.1.12 Timer (\t)	338
12.1.13 Elapsed Time (\t *expr*)	339
12.1.14 Timeout (\T)	340
12.1.15 Variables (\v)	340

12.1.16 Workspace (\w) 340
12.1.17 Week Offset (\W) 340
12.1.18 Expunge Handler (\x) 341
12.1.19 Date Format (\z) 341
12.1.20 Operating System (*text*) 341
12.1.21 Interrupt (Ctrl-C) 342
12.1.22 Terminate (\) 342
12.1.23 Exit *q* (\\) 343

12.2 System Variables 343
    12.2.1 IP Address (.z.a) 343
    12.2.2 Dependencies (.z.b) 343
    12.2.3 Global Date (.z.d) 344
    12.2.4 Local Date (.z.D) 344
    12.2.5 Startup File (.z.f) 344
    12.2.6 Host (.z.h) 344
    12.2.7 Process ID (.z.i) 345
    12.2.8 Release Date (.z.k) 345
    12.2.9 Release Major Version (.z.K) 345
    12.2.10 License Information (.z.l) 345
    12.2.11 O/S (.z.o) 346
    12.2.12 Process Close (.z.pc) 346
    12.2.13 Process Get (.z.pg) 346
    12.2.14 Process HTTP Get (.z.ph) 346
    12.2.15 Process Input (.z.pi) 347
    12.2.16 Process Open (.z.po) 347
    12.2.17 Process HTTP Post (.z.pp) 347
    12.2.18 Process Set (.z.ps) 347
    12.2.19 Self (.z.s) 348
    12.2.20 Global Time (.z.t) 348
    12.2.21 Local Time (.z.T) 348
    12.2.22 Timer Expression (.z.ts) 349
    12.2.23 User (.z.u) 349
    12.2.24 Value Set (.z.vs) 349
    12.2.25 Handle (.z.w) 350
    12.2.26 Command Line Parameters (.z.x) 350
    12.2.27 GMT (.z.z) 350
    12.2.28 Local Date and Time (.z.Z) 351

12.3 Command Line Parameters 351
    12.3.1 Console (-c) 351
    12.3.2 Web Browser Console (-C) 352
    12.3.3 Offset (-o) 352
    12.3.4 Port (-p) 352
    12.3.5 Print Digits (-P) 352
    12.3.6 Timer (-t) 352

12.3.7 Timeout (-T)	352
12.3.8 Workspace Size (-w)	353
12.3.9 Week Offset (-W)	353
12.3.10 Date Format (-z)	353

APPENDIX A | BUILT-IN FUNCTIONS — 354

A.0 Overview	354
A.1 String Functions	354
A.1.1 like	354
A.1.2 lower	356
A.1.3 ltrim	356
A.1.4 rtrim	356
A.1.5 ss	357
A.1.6 ssr	357
A.1.7 string	357
A.1.8 sv	360
A.1.9 trim	361
A.1.10 upper	362
A.1.11 vs	362
A.2 Mathematical Functions	363
A.2.1 acos	363
A.2.2 asin	364
A.2.3 atan	364
A.2.4 cor	365
A.2.5 cos	365
A.2.6 cov	366
A.2.7 cross	366
A.2.8 inv	367
A.2.9 lsq	367
A.2.10 mmu	368
A.2.11 sin	368
A.2.12 tan	369
A.2.13 var	369
A.2.14 wavg	370
A.2.15 wsum	371
A.3 Aggregate Functions	371
A.3.1 all	372
A.3.2 any	372
A.3.3 avg	372
A.3.4 dev	373
A.3.5 max	374
A.3.6 med	374

- A.3.7 min — 375
- A.3.8 prd — 375
- A.3.9 sum — 376

A.4 Uniform Functions — 377
- A.4.1 deltas — 377
- A.4.2 differ — 378
- A.4.3 fills — 379
- A.4.4 mavg — 380
- A.4.5 maxs — 381
- A.4.6 mcount — 382
- A.4.7 mdev — 382
- A.4.8 mins — 382
- A.4.9 mmax — 383
- A.4.10 mmin — 384
- A.4.11 msum — 384
- A.4.12 next — 384
- A.4.13 prds — 385
- A.4.14 prev — 386
- A.4.15 rank — 386
- A.4.16 ratios — 387
- A.4.17 rotate — 389
- A.4.18 sums — 389
- A.4.19 xbar — 390
- A.4.20 xprev — 391
- A.4.21 xrank — 392

A.5 Miscellaneous Functions — 393
- A.5.1 Conditional Append (?) — 393
- A.5.2 asc — 393
- A.5.3 bin — 394
- A.5.4 count — 396
- A.5.5 cut — 397
- A.5.6 cut (_) — 398
- A.5.7 desc — 401
- A.5.8 distinct — 401
- A.5.9 drop (_) — 402
- A.5.10 eval — 403
- A.5.11 except — 404
- A.5.12 exit — 404
- A.5.13 fill (^) — 405
- A.5.14 find (?) — 406
- A.5.15 flip — 408
- A.5.16 getenv — 410
- A.5.17 group — 410
- A.5.18 iasc — 411

A.5.19 identity	412
A.5.20 idesc	412
A.5.21 in	413
A.5.22 inter	413
A.5.23 join (,)	415
A.5.24 join-each (,')	417
A.5.25 list	418
A.5.26 md5	419
A.5.27 null	419
A.5.28 parse	420
A.5.29 random (?)	422
A.5.30 raze	423
A.5.31 reshape (#)	425
A.5.32 reverse	426
A.5.33 setenv	427
A.5.34 sublist	427
A.5.35 system	428
A.5.36 take (#)	429
A.5.37 til	431
A.5.38 ungroup	434
A.5.39 union	435
A.5.40 value	436
A.5.41 where	438
A.5.42 within	439

APPENDIX B   441

ERROR MESSAGES   441

B.1 Runtime Errors	441
B.2 Parse Errors	442
B.3 System Errors	442
B.4 License Errors	443

REFERENCES   444

INDEX   445

q FOR MORTALS

ACKNOWLEDGMENTS

Every book is a substantial endeavor requiring the assistance and support of many. First and foremost in this case are the folks at Kx Systems. Janet Lustgarten's encouragement got things started. Niall Dalton was instrumental in getting the publication process kicked off and imposed a coherent organization on the first draft. Arthur Whitney, the *q* god, provided concise answers to desperate *q* prayers. Above all, Simon Garland patiently answered endless questions with tact and wit.

Many others provided suggestions and corrections along the way. Rich Wagner ratified my initial vague idea. Jude Skowron and Howard Stein were the guinea pigs who used early drafts to learn *q*. Jamie Grant provided much-needed insight into lesser-known *q* features. Alexander Belopolsky provided corrections to early drafts. Attila Vrabecz and his encyclopedic knowledge always kept me honest. Dennis Shasha proofed the entire text and provided many insights. Charles Skelton provided valuable support. Steven Apter's iconoclastic *no stinking loops* was an inspiration.

The text has been used as the basis for courses in *q* programming. Thanks to Maria Buckley and the initial victims in Barclays Capital Markets in London. A special thanks to Lyndon Adams and the folks at Citigroup Global Markets as well as Chris Lo and the team at JP Morgan, both in London, who really shook things out. Cheers.

To all the others who contributed suggestions and corrections but are not listed, I am nonetheless grateful.

Catherine Schikkerling did a great job converting the constantly changing word processing document to the online format as initial versions went up on the Kx site. And she firmly kept me on track through this publication process.

Finally, special thanks to Omar who overlooked all the time I spent with my laptop.

OVERVIEW

0.0 THE EVOLUTION OF q

The *q* programming language and its database kdb+ were developed by Arthur Whitney. Released by Kx Systems, Inc. in 2003, the primary design objectives of *q* are expressiveness, speed and efficiency. In these, it is beyond compare. The design tradeoff is a terseness that can be disconcerting to programmers coming from more verbose database programming environments e.g., C++, Java or C#, combined with SQL (Structured Query Language). While the *q* programming gods revel in programs resembling an ASCII core dump, this manual is for the rest of us.

q evolved from APL (A Programming Language), which was first invented as a mathematical notation by Kenneth Iverson at Harvard University in the 1950s. APL became one of the first computer languages when it was introduced by IBM as a vector programming language, meaning that it was able to process lists of numbers in a single operation. It became successful in finance and other industries that required heavy number crunching.

Since *q* is a vector processing language by birth, it is well suited to performing complex calculations quickly on large volumes of data. What's new in *q* is that it can also process large volumes of data very efficiently in the relational paradigm. Its syntax allows select expressions that are similar to SQL 92, and its collection of built-in functions forms a rich superset of those in SQL 92.

There is also some LISP (List Processor) in *q*'s genes. In fact, the fundamental data construct of *q* is a list. The notation and terminology are different, but the functionality is there and is arguably simpler. For those so inclined, writing compilers is a snap in *q*.

q also shows the influence of functional programming and while it is not purely functional, it is arguably as functional as C++, Java and C# are object-oriented.

0.1 PHILOSOPHY

A proficient *q* developer thinks differently than in conventional RDBMS (Relational Database Management Systems) programming environments such as C++, Java and C#, henceforth referred to as **verbose programming**. In order to get you into the correct mindset, we summarize some of the potential discontinuities for the *q* newbie.

There are three major data-related issues in verbose database programming:

- Business objects must be mapped to a completely different representation — e.g., tables — for persistence. It takes considerable effort to get the object-relational transfer correct — witness the complexity of EJB.

- Business objects must be mapped to another representation for transport, usually some binary or XML form that flattens reference chains.

- Performing data manipulation such as selection and aggregation is best done in stored procedures on the database server. Complex numeric calculations are best done away from the database on an application server.

Much of verbose programming design is spent getting the various representations correct, and much of verbose programming code is spent marshalling resources and synchronizing the different representations. These issues disappear in *q*.

In Memory Database: One way to think of kdb+ is as an in-memory database with persistent backing. The form in which entities are held in memory is virtually identical to the way they are stored on disk and transported. Since data manipulation is performed in memory with *q*, there is no separate stored procedure language. This is somewhat akin to disconnected record sets in ADO.NET, but there is no separation between the language used to construct the table objects (C#) and that used to manipulate the data in the tables on disk (SQL).

Interpreted: *q* is interpreted instead of compiled. During execution, data and functions live in an in-memory workspace. Iterations of the development cycle tend to be quick because all information needed to debug is available in the workspace. *q* programs are stored and executed as scripts. In addition, *q* functions can be created as strings and executed dynamically, so it is possible to write self-modifying code.

Ordered Lists: Because classical SQL is based on unordered sets, the order of rows in a table is not defined. In *q*, ordered lists are the foundation of all non-trivial data structures, so table rows have an order. This makes processing large volumes of time series data easy and fast. Very fast.

Evaluation Order: While *q* is written left-to-right, expressions are evaluated right-to-left or, as the *q* gods prefer, left **of** right, meaning that the function or operator to the left executes on what is to the right of it. There is no operator precedence, so parentheses are rarely needed to resolve operation order.

Table Oriented: All objects abandon, ye who enter here. In contrast to the languages mentioned above, *q* does not implement such concepts of object-oriented programming as classes, inheritance and virtual methods. Instead, *q* builds complexity through the construction and mapping of ordered lists, which are actually sequences or vectors in mathematical parlance. The higher-level constructs for data manipulation in *q* are dictionaries and tables. A function in *q* can be named globally in the workspace, or defined anonymously within another function. Variables can be global or local to a function.

Column Oriented: SQL tables store data in rows and an operation applies to a field one row at a time. *q* stores tables as columns and applies an operation to an entire column vector.

Types: *q* is a strongly typed, dynamically checked language, but its typing is less cumbersome than many typed languages. Each variable has a value of well-defined type and type promotion for operations is automatic. A variable's type is not explicitly declared; instead, the type of a variable name reflects the value assigned to it. Lists that have been assigned with a homogenous data type will not accept or promote other types.

Null Values: In classical SQL, the value NULL represents missing data for a field of any type. In *q*, types have separate null values. Infinite and null values can participate in arithmetic and other operations with reasonable results.

Integrated I/O: I/O is done through handles that act as functional windows to the outside world. Once such a handle is set up, retrieving the handle's value results in a read and passing a value to the handle is a write.

0.2 MATHEMATICAL FUNCTIONS REFRESHER

In order to understand *q*, it is important to have a clear grasp of the basic concepts and terminology of mathematical functions. There is no shortcut. In fact, nearly all the constructs of *q* can be understood as function mappings. The following refresher may help those who are unfamiliar or rusty with mathematical functions.

In mathematics, a *function* associates a unique output value with each input value. The collection of all input values is the *domain* of the function and the *range* is the collection from which the output values are chosen. A function is also called a *map* (or *mapping*) from the domain to the range.

The output value that a function f associates to an input value x is read **f of x**. More verbosely, we say that the output is the result of applying f to the input parameter(s), or that the output value is f evaluated at x. In mathematics and most programming languages, the output value of a function is represented with the function name to the left of its arguments. The arguments are usually enclosed in matching parentheses and are separated by commas or semicolons.

There are two basic ways to define a function: an algorithm or a graph. You can specify an algorithm as a list of formulas that perform a sequence of operations on an input value to arrive at the corresponding output value. For example, we define the squaring function, over the domain and range of real numbers, to assign as output value the input value times itself. Alternatively, you can define a function by explicitly listing all input-output associations. The collection of associated inputs and outputs is the *graph* of the function.

As you will no doubt recall from many bucolic hours in high-school math class, a function defined by formula can always be converted to a graph by feeding in input values, cranking out the associated outputs, and collecting the results into a table. In general, there is no explicit formula to calculate the values for an arbitrary input-output graph. If it is possible to define a function via a formula, this is usually the preferred way to specify it since it is compact, but there is no guarantee that the formula will be easy or quick to compute.

Here are the two forms for the squaring function over the domain of integers 0 through 3, as you might recall them from school:

```
f(x) = x²              I    O
                       -    -
                       0    0
                       1    1
                       2    4
                       3    9
```

When graphing a function, we normally think of the I/O table as a list of (x,y) pairs:

```
(0, 0)
(1, 1)
(2, 4)
  ...
```

However, it can also be viewed as a pair of columns in which there is a positional correspondence between the input column and the output column:

```
0 —> 0
1 —> 1
2 —> 4
   ...
```

The latter perspective will prove very useful.

The number of arguments to a function is called its *valence*. Some valences are common enough to have their own terminology. A function of valence 1 (i.e., defined by an algorithm that has one parameter) is said to be *monadic*. An example is `neg(x)` that takes a number and returns the negative of the number (i.e., -1 times the number).

A function of valence 2 (i.e., two parameters) is said to be *dyadic*. An example is `sum(x, y)` that takes two numbers and adds them to get the result. A function with no parameters is *niladic*; for example, a function with no arguments that returns the constant 3.

Given functions `f` and `g` for which the range of `g` is (contained in) the domain of `f`, the *composite* of `f` and `g`, denoted `f·g`, is the function obtained by chaining the output of `g` into `f`. That is, the composite assigns to an input x the output value `f(g(x))`. Pictorially, we can see that the composite chains the output of `g` into the input of `f`,

```
      g            f
x ———> g{x} ———> f(g(x))
```

The domain of the composite is the domain of `g` and its range is the range of `f`.

A *recursive* function is a function over an enumerable domain — usually the positive integers — whose definition has a special form. It is defined on some initial value; then for other values, it is defined in terms of previously defined values. In the most common case, a recursive function is defined explicitly for the input value 0 (the *initial case*) and its value for any $n>0$ is specified in terms of its values up to $n-1$. Often, but not always, the value for n is defined in terms of its value for $n-1$ only. In some situations the initial case will correspond to 1 instead of 0. Many definitions and operations on lists in *q* will be presented recursively.

Important

In the remainder of this document, we shall use the term *map*, or *mapping*, to refer to a mathematical function and will always mean a *q* function when we write **function** without a modifier.

We hope this trip down mathematics memory lane is not new territory for you. If it is, we strongly advise that you linger here until you're comfortable with the material before proceeding. There is no escaping the fact that *q* is a language whose foundation is mathematical functions. If you build on shaky ground, your understanding will certainly collapse under the weight of what is to come.

0.3 GETTING STARTED

0.3.1 Starting *q*

The installation places the *q* executable in $HOME/q (or $QHOME) on Unix-based systems, or in the \q directory on the c: drive on Windows.

Start a *q* session by typing q on the command line. You should see a new window with the Kx Systems copyright notice followed by a *q* command line. You will see a leading q) on the command line. This is the *q console*. Type 6*7 and press Enter to see the result:

```
q)6*7
42
q)
```

> **Important**
>
> In this manual, to increase readability we shall omit the *q* prompt in all our snippets, showing the input you type as indented and the response as left justified.

```
    6*7
42
_
```

Here, _ represents the blinking cursor awaiting your next input.

0.3.2 Variables

A *variable* is a symbolic name that is associated with some *q* entity. Declaring a variable and assigning its value are done in a single step with : called amend (or assign). Note that assignment does not misuse = as many languages do. To assign variable a the integer value 42 write:

```
    a:42
```

A variable name must start with an alpha which can be followed by alpha, numeric or underscore. Some folks read the assignment operation succinctly as **gets**.

Naming Recommendations:

- Choose a name long enough to make the purpose of the entity evident, but no longer. The purpose of a name is to communicate to another reader. Long names may not make code easier to read. For example, **chkDsk** is clearer than **cd** but is no less clear than **checkDisk**.

- Use verbs for operators and functions; use nouns for data.

- Be consistent in your use of abbreviations. Be mindful that even obvious abbreviations may be opaque to readers whose native language is different than yours.

- Be consistent in your use of capitalization, such as initial caps, camel casing, etc. Pick a style and stick to it.

- Do not use names such as **int**, **float** or other words that have meaning in *q*. While not reserved, some carry special meaning when used as arguments for certain *q* operators.

- Use contexts for namespacing.

- Refrain from using the underscore character in *q* names. If you insist on using underscore in names, do not use it as the last character. Expressions involving the built-in _ operator and names with underscore will be difficult to read.

0.3.3 Whitespace

In general, *q* permits, but does not require, whitespace around operators, separators, brackets, braces, etc. You could also write the above expression as:

```
a : 42
```

or,

```
a: 42
```

Because the *q* gods prefer compact code, you will see programs with no superfluous whitespace... none, zilch, zip, nada. In order to help you get accustomed to this terseness, we use whitespace mainly in juxtaposition and after semicolon and comma separators. You should feel free to add whitespace for readability where it is permitted, but be consistent in its use or omission. We will point out where whitespace is required or forbidden.

0.3.4 The q Console

Once you type your preferred version of the above assignment into the *q* console (which you should do now), the only response you will see is the cursor awaiting input on the next line. To see the value of a, type its name and press Enter:

```
    a:42
    a
42
```

You may wonder why the *q* console does not echo the value of a specification. This is simply a design feature of the *q* console.

> **Note**
>
> One noticeable change in release **2.4** of *q* is the console display of lists, dictionaries and tables. For those accustomed to the *k*-like display in **2.3**, the console representation of complex data types in **2.4** is that of the show function. See the section on .z.pi in **Chapter 12** on how to alter the console display.

0.3.5 Comments

In *q*, the forward-slash character (/) is used to indicate the beginning of a comment. So / instructs the interpreter to ignore anything to the end of the line.

> **Note**
>
> At least one whitespace character must separate / from any text to the left of it on a line.

In the following example, no definition of b is processed, so an error occurs:

```
    a: 42/ nothing here counts b:6*7
    b
`b
```

And the following generates an error:

```
a:42/ intended to be a comment
'
```

> **Recommendation**
>
> The *q* gods have no need for explanatory error messages or comments since their *q* code is always correct and self-documenting. Mortals spend hours poring over cryptic *q* error messages such as the ones above. Moreover, many mortals eschew comments in misguided misanthropic coding machismo. Don't.

0.3.6 Assignment Value

A variable is not explicitly declared or typed. Instead, the value assigned to a variable carries the type. In our example, the expression to the right of the assignment is syntactically an integer value, so the name a is associated with a value of type int. (The *q* types will be covered in **Chapter 1**.)

The fact that variables are not declared before assignment means that an assignment can be interpreted either as the initial assignment or as a re-assignment, depending on the context. It is perfectly permissible to reassign a variable with a value of different type. Once this is done, the name will reflect the new type of the value assigned to it.

> **Warning**
>
> You can unintentionally change the type of a variable with a wayward assignment. Or you can inadvertently reuse a variable name and wipe out any data in the variable. An undetected typo can result in data being sent to a black hole. Be careful to enter variable names correctly.

Some verbose languages permit only a variable name to the left of an assignment. In *q*, as in C, an assignment carries the value being assigned and can be used as part of a larger expression. So we find:

```
   1+a:42
43
```

Or,

```
        b:1+a:42
        b
43
```

0.3.7 Order of Parsing

The interpreter evaluates the above specification of b by parsing the expression from right-to-left (more on this in **Chapter 3**). If it were verbose,

- The integer 42 is assigned to a variable named a; this value is added to the integer 1, and the result is assigned to a variable named b.

Because the interpreter always parses expressions from right-to-left, programmers can read *q* expressions from left-to-right,

- The variable b gets the value of the integer 1 plus the value assigned to the variable a, which gets the integer 42.

The ability to use the results of assignments in expressions permits a single line of *q* code to perform the work of an entire verbose program. Such an expression may execute more quickly than an equivalent version with the assignments split onto multiple statements, but the tradeoff is a reduction in readability and maintainability. The *q* gods carry terseness to the extreme. This choice of programming style should be avoided by mortals, as it can easily lead to write-only code.

0.4 SAMPLE q PROGRAM

Now that we know how *q* works and how to start it up, let's examine some real code that shows the power of *q*. The following program reads a csv file of time-stamped symbols and prices, places the data into a table and computes the maximum price for each day. It then opens a socket connection to a *q* process on another machine and retrieves a similar daily aggregate. Finally, it merges the two intermediate tables and appends the result to an existing file:

```
sample:{
t:("DSF"; enlist ",") 0: `:c:/q/data/px.csv;
tmpx:select mpx:max Price by Date,Sym from t;
h:hopen `:aerowing:5042;
rtmpx:h "select mpx:max Price by Date,Sym from tpx";
hclose h;
.[`:c:/q/data/tpx.dat; (); ,; rtmpx,tmpx]
}
```

Most people have two immediate reactions upon seeing *q* code for the first time. First, they are amazed at how much can be done with so little code. Second, they wonder if they will ever be able to read it! We promise that by the time you finish this tutorial, this program will be easy, and you'll feel right as rain.

CHAPTER 1
ATOMS

1.0 OVERVIEW

All data is ultimately built from atoms, so we begin with atoms. An *atom* is an irreducible value with a specific data type. The basic data types in *q* correspond to those of SQL with some additional date and time related types that facilitate time series. We summarize the data types in the tables below, giving the corresponding types in SQL, and where appropriate Java and C#. We cover enumerations in §5.3.

q	SQL	Java	C#
boolean	boolean	Boolean	Boolean
byte	byte	Byte	Byte
short	smallint	Short	Int16
int	int	Integer	Int32
long	bigint	Long	Int64
real	real	Float	Single
float	float	Double	Double
char	char(1)	Character	Char
symbol	varchar	(String)	(String)
date	date	Date	
datetime	datetime	Timestamp	DateTime
minute			
second			
time	time	Time	TimeSpan
enumeration			

> **Note**
>
> The words boolean, short, int, etc. are **not** keywords in *q*, so they are not displayed in a special font in this text. They do have special meaning when used as name arguments in some operators. You should avoid using them as names.

The next table collects the important information about the *q* data types. We shall refer to this in subsequent sections.

```
type         size    char    num     notation              null
                     type    type                          value
-------------------------------------------------------------------
boolean      1       b       1       1b                    0b
byte         1       x       4       0x26                  0x00
short        2       h       5       42h                   0Nh
int          4       i       6       42                    0N
long         8       j       7       42j                   0Nj
real         4       e       8       4.2e                  0Ne
float        8       f       9       4.2                   0n
char         1       c       10      "z"                   " "
symbol       *       s       11      `zaphod               `
month        4       m       13      2006.07m              0Nm
date         4       d       14      2006.07.21            0Nd
datetime     4       z       15      2006.07.21T09:13:39.678 0Nz
minute       4       u       17      23:59                 0Nu
second       4       v       18      23:59:59              0Nv
time         4       t       19      09:01:02:042          0Nt

enumeration                  20+     `u$v

table                98              ([] c1:`a`b`c; c2:10 20 30)
dictionary           99              `a`b`c!10 20 30
lambda               100             {x}
null item            101             (::)
```

1.1 INTEGER DATA

The basic integer data type is common to nearly all programming environments.

1.1.1 int

An int is a signed four-byte integer. A numeric value is identified as an int by the fact that it contains only numeric digits, possibly with a leading minus sign, **without** a decimal point. It may also have an optional trailing character i indicating an int. Here is a typical int value,

    42

which can also be written,

    42i

1.1.2 short and long

The other two integer data types are short and long. The short type represents a two byte signed integer and is denoted by a trailing h after optionally signed numeric digits. For example:

```
    b:-123h
    b
-123h
```

Similarly, the long type represents an eight-byte signed long integer denoted by a trailing j after optionally signed numeric digits:

```
    c:1234567890j
    c
1234567890j
```

> **Important**
>
> Type promotion is performed automatically in *q* primitive operations. However, if a specific integer type is required in a list and a narrower type is presented — e.g., an int is expected and a short is presented — the submitted type will **not** be automatically promoted and an error will result. This may be unintuitive for programmers coming from languages of C ancestry, but it will make sense in the context of tables.

1.2 Floating Point Data

Single and double precision floating point data types are supported.

1.2.1 float

The float type represents an IEEE standard eight-byte floating point number, often called **double** in other languages. It is denoted by optionally signed numeric digits containing a decimal point with an optional trailing f. A floating point number can hold at least 15 decimal digits of precision. For example:

```
    pi:3.14159265
    float1:1f
```

1.2.2 real

The real type represents a four-byte floating point number and is denoted by numeric digits containing a decimal point and a trailing e. Keep in mind that this type is called **float** in some languages. A real can hold at least 6 decimal digits of precision, 7 being the norm. Thus,

```
        r:1.4142e

        r
1.4142e
```

is a valid real number.

> **Note**
>
> The *q* console abbreviates the display of float or real values having zeros to the right of the decimal.

```
        2.0
2f

        4.00e
4e
```

The behavior of substituting floating point types of different widths is analogous to the case of integer types.

1.2.3 Scientific Notation

Both float and real values can be specified in IEEE standard scientific notation for floating point values:

```
        f:1.23456789e-10
        r:1.2345678e-10e
```

By default, the *q* console displays only seven decimal digits of accuracy for float and real values by rounding the display in the seventh significant digit:

```
        f
1.234568e-10
```

```
        r
1.234568e-10e
```

You can change this by using the \P command (note upper case) to specify a display width up to 16 digits.

```
        f12:1.23456789012
        f16:1.234567890123456

        \P 12

        f12
1.23456789012
        f16
1.23456789012

        \P 16

        f12
1.23456789012
        f16
1.234567890123456
```

1.3 BINARY DATA

Binary data can be represented as bit or byte values.

1.3.1 boolean

The boolean type uses one byte to store an individual bit and is denoted by the bit value followed by b:

```
        bit:0b

        bit
0b
```

1.3.2 byte

The byte type uses one byte to store 16 bits of data and is denoted by 0x followed by a hexadecimal value:

```
byte:0x2a
```

1.3.3 Binary Data is Numeric

In handling binary data, *q* is more like C than its descendents, in that both binary types are considered to be positive integers that can participate in arithmetic expressions or comparisons with other numeric types. There are no keywords for *true* or *false*, nor are there separate logical operators. With a and pi as above,

```
    a:42
    bit:1b

    a+bit
43
```

is an int and

```
    byte+pi
45.14159
```

is a float. Observe that type promotion has been performed automatically.

1.4 CHARACTER DATA

There are two atomic character types in *q*. They resemble the SQL types CHAR and VARCHAR more than the character types of verbose languages.

1.4.1 char

A char holds an individual ASCII character and is stored in one byte. This corresponds to a SQL CHAR. A char is denoted by a single character enclosed in double quotes:

```
    ch:"q"
    ch
"q"
```

Some keyboard characters, such as the double-quote, cannot be entered directly into a char since they have special meaning in *q*. As in C, these characters are escaped with a preceding back-slash (\). While the console display also includes the escape, these are actually single characters:

```
        ch:"\""      / double-quote
        ch           / console also displays the escape
"\""
        ch:"\\"      / back-slash
        ch:"\n"      / newline
        ch:"\r"      / return
        ch:"\t"      / horizontal tab
```

You can also escape a character with an underlying numeric value expressed as three octal digits:

```
        "\142"
"b"
```

1.4.2 symbol

A symbol holds a sequence of characters as a single unit. A symbol is denoted by a leading back-quote (`` ` ``) also read as **back tick** in *q* circles:

```
        s1:`q
        s2:`zaphod
```

A symbol is irreducible, meaning that the individual characters that comprise it are **not** directly accessible. Symbols are often used in *q* to hold names of other entities.

A symbol is **not** a string. We shall see in **Chapter 2** that there is an analogue of strings in *q*, namely a list of char. While a list of char is a kissing cousin to a symbol, we emphasize that a symbol is **not** made up of char. The symbol `` `a `` and the char a are not the same.

> **Advanced**
>
> You may ask whether a symbol can include embedded blanks and special characters such as back-tick. The answer is yes. You create such a symbol by casting a list of char to a symbol. See §5.1.5 for more on this.

```
        `$"A symbol with `backtick"
`A symbol with `backtick
```

> **Note**
>
> A symbol is somewhat akin a SQL VARCHAR, in that it can hold and arbitrary number of characters. It is different in that it is atomic. The char q and the symbol `` `kdb `` are both atomic entities.

1.5 Temporal Data

A major benefit of *q* is that it can process both time series and relational data in a consistent and efficient manner. *q* extends the basic SQL date and time data types to facilitate temporal arithmetic, which is minimal in SQL and can be clumsy in verbose languages (e.g., Java's date library and its use of time zones). We begin with the equivalents to SQL temporal types. The additional temporal types in *q* deal with constituents of a date or time.

1.5.1 date

A date is stored in four bytes and is denoted by *yyyy.mm.dd*, where *yyyy* represents the year, *mm* the month and *dd* the day. A date value stores the count of days from Jan 1, 2000:

```
d:2006.07.04

d
2006.07.04
```

> **Important**
>
> Months and days begin at 1 (not zero) so January is 01.

Leading zeroes in months and days are required; their omission causes an error:

```
bday:2007.1.1
'2007.1.1
```

> **Advanced**
>
> The underlying day count can be obtained by casting to int.

```
        `int$2000.02.01
31
```

1.5.2 time

A time is stored in four bytes and is denoted by *hh:mm:ss.uuu* where *hh* represents hours on the 24-hour clock, *mm* represents minutes, *ss* represents seconds, and *uuu* represents milliseconds. A time value stores the count of milliseconds from midnight:

```
        t:09:04:59.000

        t
09:04:59.000
```

Again, leading zeroes are required in all constituents of a time.

> **Advanced**
>
> The underlying millisecond count can be obtained by casting to int.

```
        `int$12:34:56.789
45296789
```

1.5.3 datetime

A datetime is the combination of a date and a time, separated by 5 as in the ISO standard format. A datetime value stores the fractional day count from midnight Jan 1, 2000:

```
        dt:2006.07.04T09:04:59.000

        dt
2006.07.04T09:04:59.000
```

> **Advanced**
>
> The underlying fractional day count can be obtained by casting to float.

```
        `float$2000.02.01T12:00:00.000
31.5
```

1.5.4 month

The month type uses four bytes and is denoted by *yyyy.mm* with a trailing m. A month values stores the count of months since the beginning of the year.

```
        mon:2006.07m

        mon
2006.07m
```

> **Advanced**
>
> The underlying month offset can be obtained by casting to int.

```
        `int$2000.04m
3
```

1.5.5 minute

The minute type uses four bytes and is denoted by *hh:mm*. A minute value stores the count of minutes from midnight:

```
        mm:09:04

        mm
09:04
```

> **Note**
>
> We did not use `min` for the variable name because `min` is a reserved name in *q*.

> **Advanced**
>
> The underlying minute offset can be obtained by casting to int.

```
        `int$01:23
83
```

1.5.6 second

The second type uses four bytes and is denoted by *hh:mm:ss*. A second value stores a count of seconds from midnight:

```
sec:09:04:59

        sec
09:04:59
```

The representation of the second type makes it look like an everyday time value. However, a *q* time value is a count of milliseconds from midnight, so the underlying values are different.

> **Advanced**
>
> The underlying values can be obtained by casting to int, which manifests the difference. See below.

```
        `int$12:34:56
45296

        `int$12:34:56.000
45296000
```

However, we do find:

```
    12:34:56=12:34:56.000
1b
```

1.5.7 Constituents and Dot Notation

The constituents of dates, times and datetimes can be extracted using dot notation. The individual field values are all extracted as int. The field values of a date are named **year**, **mm** and **dd**:

```
        d:2006.07.04

        d.year
2006

        d.mm
7

        d.dd
4
```

Similarly, the field values of time are **hh**, **mm**, **ss**.

```
        t:12:45:59.876

        t.hh
12

        t.mm
45

        t.ss
59
```

> **Note**
>
> At the time of this writing, there is no syntax to retrieve the millisecond constituent. Use the construct below.

```
        `int$t mod 1000
00:00:00.876
```

In addition to the individual field values, you can also extract higher-order constituents:

```
        d.month
2006.07m
```

```
        t.minute
12:45

        t.second
12:45:59
```

Of course, this works for a datetime as well:

```
        dt:2006.07.04T12:45:59.876

        dt.date
2006.07.04

        dt.time
12:45:59.876

        dt.month
2006.07m

        dt.mm
7

        dt.minute
12.45
```

> **Advanced**
>
> It is a quirk in *q* that dot notation for accessing temporal constituents does not work on function arguments. An example follows.

```
        fmm:{[x] x.mm}

        fmm 2006.09.15
{[x] x.mm}
'x.mm
```

Instead, cast to the constituent type:

```
        fmm:{[x] `mm$x}

        fmm 2006.09.15
9
```

1.6 Infinities and NaN

In addition to the regular numeric and temporal values, special values represent infinities, whose absolute values are greater than any normal numeric or temporal value.

```
Token      Value
-----      ------
   0w      Positive float infinity
  -0w      Negative float infinity
   0W      Positive int infinity
  -0W      Negative int infinity
  0Wh      Positive short infinity
 -0Wh      Negative short infinity
  0Wj      Positive long infinity
 -0Wj      Negative long infinity
  0Wd      Positive date infinity
 -0Wd      Negative date infinity
  0Wt      Positive time infinity
 -0Wt      Negative time infinity
  0Wt      Positive time infinity
 -0Wt      Negative time infinity
  0Wz      Positive datetime infinity
 -0Wz      Negative datetime infinity
   0n      NaN, or not a number
```

> **Important**
>
> Observe the distinction between lower case w and upper case W.

The result of dividing any positive (or unsigned) non-zero value by any zero value is positive float infinity, denoted 0w. Dividing a negative value by zero results in negative float infinity, denoted by -0w. The way to remember these is that w looks like the infinity symbol ∞.

The integral infinities cannot be produced via an arithmetic division on normal int values, since the result of division in *q* is always a float.

The result of dividing any 0 value by any zero value is undefined, so *q* represents this as the floating point null 0n.

The *q* philosophy is that any valid arithmetic expression will produce a result rather than an error. Therefore, dividing by 0 produces a special float value rather than an exception. You can perform a complex sequence of calculations without worrying about things blowing up in the middle or inserting cumbersome exception trapping. We shall see more about this in **Chapter 3**.

> **Advanced**
>
> While infinities can participate in arithmetic operations, infinite arithmetic is not implemented. Instead, *q* performs the operation on the underlying bit patterns. Math propeller heads (including the author) find the following disconcerting ...

```
     0W-2
2147483645

     2*0W
-2
```

In fact, this can be understood by realizing that each infinity is simply a convenient name for the largest (or smallest) bit pattern of its type. Consequently, ordering is free. Implementing proper infinite arithmetic would entail tests in the arithmetic operators that would slow down normal arithmetic and the cost isn't worth it.

1.7 NULL VALUES

1.7.0 Overview of Nulls

The concept of a null value generally indicates missing data. This is an area in which *q* differs from both verbose programming languages and SQL.

In such languages as C++, Java and C#, the concept of a null value applies to complex entities (i.e., objects) that are accessed indirectly by pointer or by reference. A null value for such an entity corresponds to an un-initialized pointer, meaning that it has not been assigned the address of an allocated block of memory. There is no concept of null for entities that are of simple or value type. For those types that admit null, you test for being null by asking if the value is equal to null.

The NULL value in SQL indicates that the data value is inapplicable or missing. The NULL value is distinct from any value that can actually be contained in a field and does not have = semantics. That is, you cannot test a field for being null with = NULL. Instead, you ask if it IS NULL. Because

NULL is a separate value, Boolean fields actually have three states: 0, 1 and NULL.

In *q*, the situation is more interesting. While most types have distinct null values, some types have no designated way of representing a null value. The following table summarizes the way nulls are handled:

```
type            null
----            ----
boolean         0b
byte            0x00
short           0Nh
int             0N
long            0Nj
real            0Ne
float           0n
char            " "
sym             `
month           0Nm
date            0Nd
datetime        0Nz
minute          0Nu
second          0Nv
time            0Nt
```

1.7.1 Binary Nulls

Let's start with the binary types. As you can see, they have no special null value, which means that null is equivalent to the value zero. Consequently, you cannot distinguish between a missing boolean value and the value that represents false.

In practice, this isn't an issue, since in most applications it isn't a critical distinction. It can be a problem if the default value of a boolean flag in your application is not zero, so you must ensure that this does not occur. A similar precaution applies to byte values.

1.7.2 Numeric and Temporal Nulls

Next, observe that all the numeric and temporal types have their own designated null values. Here the situation is similar to SQL, in that you can distinguish missing data from data whose underlying value is zero. The difference is that there is no universal null value.

The advantage of the *q* approach is that the null values have equals semantics. The tradeoff is that you must use the correct null value in type-checked situations.

1.7.3 Character Nulls

Finally, we consider the character types. Considering a symbol to a variable length character collection justifies why the symbol null value is the empty symbol, designated by a back-tick (`` ` ``).

In contrast, the null value for the char type is the char consisting of the blank character (`" "`). As with binary data, you cannot distinguish between a missing char value and a blank value. Again, this is not seriously limiting in practice, but you should ensure that your application does not rely on this distinction.

> **Note**
>
> The value `" "` is **not** a null char. It is an empty list of char.

CHAPTER 2
LISTS

2.0 OVERVIEW

Data complexity is built up from atoms, which we know, and lists. It is important to achieve a thorough understanding of lists since nearly all *q* programming involves processing lists. The concepts are simple but complexity can build rapidly. Our approach is to introduce the basic notion of a general list in the first section, take a quick detour to cover simple and singleton lists, then return to cover general lists in more detail.

2.1 INTRODUCTION TO LISTS

A list is simply an ordered collection. A collection of what? you ask. More precisely, a *list* is an ordered collection of atoms and other lists. Since this definition is recursive, let's start with the simplest case in which the list comprises only atoms.

2.1.1 List Definition and Assignment

The notation for a general list encloses its items within matching parentheses and separates them with semicolons. For readability, optional whitespace is used after the semicolon separators in the last example:

```
(1;2;3)

("a";"b";"c";"d")

(`Life;`the;`Universe;`and;`Everything)

(-10.0; 3.1415e; 1b; `abc; "z")
```

In the preceding examples, the first three lists are *simple*, meaning that the list comprises atoms of uniform type. The last example is a *general* list, meaning that it is not simple. Otherwise put, a general list contains items that are not atoms of a uniform type. This could be atoms of mixed type, nested lists of uniform type, or atoms and nested lists of mixed type.

> **Important**
>
> The order of the items in the list is positional (i.e., left-to-right) and is part of its definition. The lists (1;2) and (2;1) are different. SQL is based on sets, which are inherently unordered. This distinction leads to some subtle differences between the results of queries on *q* tables versus the result sets from analogous SQL queries.
>
> The inherent ordering of lists makes time series processing natural and fast in *q*, while it is cumbersome and performs poorly in standard SQL.

Lists can be assigned to variables exactly like atoms:

```
L1:(1;2;3)

L2:("z";"a";"p";"h";"o";"d")

L3:(`Life;`the;`Universe;`and;`Everything)

L4:(0b;1b;0b;1b;1b;0b)

L5:(-10.0;3.1415e;1b;`abc;"z")
```

2.1.2 count

The number of items in a list is its *count*. You can obtain the count of a list as follows:

```
        count L1
3
```

This is our first example of a function, which we will learn about in **Chapter 4**. For now, we need only understand that count returns an int value equal to the number of items in the list to its right. Observe that the count of any atom is 1:

```
        count 42
1
        count `abcd
1
```

2.2 SIMPLE LISTS

A simple list — that is, a list of atoms of a uniform type — corresponds to the mathematical notion of a *vector*. Such lists are treated specially in *q*. They have a simplified notation, take less storage and compute faster than general lists. Of course, you can use general list notation for a vector, but *q* converts a general list to a vector whenever feasible.

2.2.1 Simple Integer Lists

A simple list of any numeric type omits the enclosing parentheses and replaces the separating semi-colons with blanks. The following two expressions for a simple list of int are equivalent:

```
(100;200;300)

100 200 300
```

This is confirmed by the console display:

```
    (100;200;300)
100 200 300
```

Similar notation is used for simple lists of short and long with the addition of the type indicator:

```
    H:(1h;2h;255h)
    H
1 2 255h
```

We can conclude that a trailing type indicator in the display applies to the entire list and not just the last item of the list; otherwise, the list would not be simple and would be displayed in general form.

```
    G:(1;2;255h)
    G
1
2
255h
```

2.2.2 Simple Floating Point Lists

Simple lists of float and real are notated similarly. Observe that the *q* console suppresses the decimal point when displaying a float having zero(s) to the right of the decimal, but the value is not an int:

```
F:(123.4567;9876.543;99.0)

F
123.4567 9876.543 99
```

This notational efficiency for float display means that a list of floats having no decimal parts displays with a trailing f:

```
FF:1.0 2.0 3.0

    FF
1 2 3f
```

2.2.3 Simple Binary Lists

The simplified notation for a simple list of binary data juxtaposes the individual data values together with a type indicator. The type indicator for boolean trails the value:

```
bits:(0b;1b;0b;1b;1b)

    bits
01011b
```

The indicator for byte leads:

```
bytes:(0x20;0xa1;0xff)

    bytes
0x20a1ff
```

> **Note**
>
> A simple list of boolean atoms requires the same number of bytes to store as it has atoms. While the simplified notation is suggestive, multiple bits are not compressed to fit inside a single byte. The list bits above holds its values in 5 bytes of storage.

2.2.4 Simple Symbol Lists

The simplified notation for simple lists of symbols juxtaposes the individual atoms with no intervening whitespace:

```
symbols:(`Life;`the;`Universe;`and;`Everything)

symbols
`Life`the`Universe`and`Everything
```

Inserting spaces between the atoms causes an error:

```
        bad:`This `is `wrong
'is
```

2.2.5 Simple char Lists and Strings

The simplified notation for a list of char looks just like a string in most languages, with the juxtaposed sequence of characters enclosed in double quotes:

```
chars:("s";"o";" ";"l";"o";"n";"g")

    chars
"so long"
```

> **Important**
>
> A simple list of char is called a *string*. Don't read too much into this.

2.2.6 Entering Simple Lists

Lists can be defined using simplified notation:

```
L:100 200 300

H:1 2 255h

F:123.4567 9876.543 99.99
```

```
bits:01011b

bytes:0x20a1ff

symbols:`Life`the`Universe`and`Everything

chars:"so long"
```

Finally, we observe that a list entered as intermixed ints and floats is converted to a simple list of floats:

```
    1 2.0 3
1 2 3f
```

2.2.7 Lists of Temporal Data

Specifying a list of mixed temporal types has a different behavior from that of a list of mixed numeric types. In this case, the list takes the type of the first item in the list; other items are widened or narrowed to match:

```
    12:34 01:02:03
12:34 01:02

    01:02:03 12:34
01:02:03 12:34:00
```

To force the type of a mixed list of temporal values, append a type specifier:

```
    01:02:03 12:34 11:59:59.999u
01:02 12:34 11:59
```

2.3 EMPTY AND SINGLETON LISTS

Lists with one or no items merit special consideration.

2.3.1 The General Empty List

It is useful to have lists with no items. A pair of parentheses with nothing between (except possibly whitespace) denotes the empty list, which has no console display:

```
L:( )
L
```

We shall see in **§5.2** that it is possible to define an empty list with a specific type.

2.3.2 Lists with a Single Item

There is a quirk in *q* regarding how it handles a list containing a single item, called a *singleton*. Creation of a singleton presents a notational problem. To see the issue, first realize that a list containing a single atom is distinct from the individual atom. As any UPS driver will readily tell you, an item in a box is not the same as an unboxed item. By now, we recognize the following as atoms:

```
42

1b

0x2a

`beeblebrox

"z"
```

We also recognize the following are all lists with two elements:

```
(42;6)

01b

`zaphod`beeblebrox

"zb"

(40;`two)
```

How to create a list of a single item? Good question. The answer is that there is no syntactic way to do so. You might think that you could simply enclose the item in parentheses, but this doesn't work since the result is an atom:

```
    singleton:(42)

    singleton
42
```

The reason for this is that parentheses are used for multiple purposes in *q*. As we have seen, paired parentheses are used to delimit items in the specification of a general list. Paired parentheses are also used for grouping in expressions — that is, to isolate the result of the expression inside the parentheses. The latter usage forces (42) to be the same as the atom 42 and so precludes the intention in the specification of singleton above.

The way to make a list with a single item is to use the enlist function, which returns a singleton list containing what is to its right:

```
    singleton:enlist 42

    singleton
,42
```

To distinguish between an atom and the equivalent singleton, examine the sign of their types:

```
    signum type 42
-1

    signum type enlist 42
1
```

As a final check before moving on, make sure that you understand that the following also defines a list containing a single item:

```
    singleton:enlist 1 2 3

    count singleton
1
```

2.4 INDEXING

Recall that a list is ordered from left to right by the position of its items. The offset of an item from the beginning of the list is called its *index*. Thus, the first item has index 0, the second item (if there is one) has index 1, etc. A list of count n has index domain 0 to n-1.

2.4.1 Index Notation

Given a list L, the item at index i is accessed by L[i]. Retrieving an item by its index is called *item indexing*. For example:

```
        L:(-10.0;3.1415e;1b;`abc;"z")

        L[0]
-10f

        L[1]
3.1415e

        L[2]
1b

        L[3]
`abc

        L[4]
"z"
```

2.4.2 Indexed Assignment

Items in a list can also be assigned via item indexing. Thus:

```
        L1:1 2 3
        L1[2]:42

        L1
1 2 42
```

> **Important**
>
> Index assignment into a simple list enforces strict type matching with no type promotion. Otherwise put, when you reassign an item in a simple list, the type must match exactly and a narrower type is **not** widened.

```
        L:100 200 300

        L[1]:42h
'type

        f:100.0 200.0 300.0
```

```
        f
100 200 300f

        f[1]:400
'type
```

This may come as a surprise if you are accustomed to numeric values always being promoted to wider types in a verbose language.

2.4.3 Indexing Domain

Providing an invalid data type for the index results in an error:

```
        L:(-10.0;3.1415e;1b;`abc;"z")

        L[`1]
'type
```

If you attempt to index outside of the bounds of the list, the result is **not** an error. Rather, you get a null value. If the list is simple, this is the null for the type of atoms in the list. For general lists, the result is 0n:

```
        L[5]
0n
```

One way to understand this is that the result of asking for a non-existent index is **missing value**. Keep this in mind, since indexing one position past the end of the list is easy to do, especially if you're not used to indexing relative to 0.

2.4.4 Empty Index and Null Item

An empty index returns the entire list:

```
        L[]
-10f
3.1415e
1b
`abc
"z"
```

> **Note**
>
> An empty index is **not** the same as indexing with an empty list. The latter returns an empty list.

```
        L[()]
```

The syntactic form double-colon (::) denotes the null item, which allows explicit notation or programmatic generation of an empty index:

```
        L[::]
-10f
3.1415e
1b
`abc
"z"
```

> **Advanced**
>
> The type of the null item is undefined; in particular, its type does not match that of any normal item in a list. As a consequence, inclusion of the null item in a list forces the list to be general.

```
        L:(1;2;3;::)
        L
1
2
3
::
        type L
0h
```

This can be used to avoid a nasty surprise when *q* is too clever. To see how, consider the general list:

```
        L:(1;2;3;`a)
        type L
0h
```

Now, reassign the last item to an int and note what happens to the list:

```
        L[3]:4
        L
1 2 3 4
        type L
6h
```

The list has been converted to a simple list of int! A subsequent attempt to reassign the last item back to its original value fails with a type error:

```
        L[3]:`a
'type
```

This can be circumvented by placing a null item in the list, forcing it to remain general:

```
        L:(1;2;3;`a;::)
        L[3]:4
        L
1
2
3
4
::
        type L
0h
        L[3]:`a
        L
1
2
3
`a
::
```

2.4.5 Lists from Variables

Lists can be created from variables:

```
        L1:(1;2;100 200)
        L2:(1 2 3;`ab`c)
        L6:(L1;L2)

        L6
(1;2;100 200)
(1 2 3;`ab`c)
```

2.5 JOINING LISTS

We scoop our presentation on operations in the next chapter to describe an important operation on lists. Probably the most common operation on two lists is to join them together to form a larger list. More precisely, the join operator (,) appends its right operand to the end of the left operand and returns the result. It accepts an atom in either argument:

```
        1 2,3 4 5
1 2 3 4 5

        1,2 3 4
1 2 3 4

        1 2 3,4
1 2 3 4
```

Observe that if the arguments are not of uniform type, the result is a general list:

```
        1 2 3,4.4 5.5
1
2
3
4.4
5.5

        1 2 3,"ab"
1
2
3
"a"
"b"
```

41

> **Note**
>
> To accept either a scalar or a list x and produce a uniform shape, use either of the idioms,
>
>   (),x
>
> or
>
>   x,()
>
> which always yields a list with the content of x.

2.6 LISTS AS MAPS

Thus far, we have viewed a list as a static collection of its items. We can also consider a list to be a mapping provided by item indexing. Specifically, a list L of count n represents a monadic mapping over the domain of non-negative integers 0,...,n-1. The list mapping assigns the output value L[i] to the input value i. Succinctly, the I/O association for the list is:

    i -> L[i]

Here are the I/O tables for some basic lists:

```
101 102 103 104     (`a; 123.45; 1b)      (1 2; 3 4)

I  O                I  O                  I  O
-  ---              -  ------             -  ---
0  101              0  `a                 0  1 2
1  102              1  123.45             1  3 4
2  103              2  1b
3  104
```

The first two examples demonstrate ranges of a collection of atoms. The last example has a range comprised of lists. A list not only looks like a map, it **is** a map whose notation is a shortcut for the I/O table assignment. This is a useful way of looking at things. We shall see in **Chapter 3** that a nested list can be viewed as a multivalent map whose range is atoms.

From the prespective of list as map, the fact that indexing outside the bounds of a list returns null means the map is implicitly extended to the domain of all integers with null values outside the list items.

2.7 Nesting

Data complexity is built by using lists as items of lists.

2.7.1 Depth

Now that we're comfortable with simple lists, we return to general lists. We can nest by including lists as items of lists. The number of levels of nesting for a list is called its *depth*. Atoms are considered to have depth 0 and simple lists have depth 1.

The notation of complex lists reflects their nesting. For pedagogical purposes, in this section we shall often use general notation to define even simple lists; however, the console always displays lists in simplified form. In subsequent sections, we shall use only simplified notation for simple lists.

Following is a list of depth two that has three items, the first two being atoms, and the last a list:

```
L1:(1;2;(100;200))

count L1
3
```

Following is the simplified notation for the inner list:

```
L1:(1;2;100 200)

L1
1
2
100 200
```

2.7.2 Pictorial Representation

We present a pictorial representation that may help in visualizing levels of nesting. In the following figure, an atom is represented as a circle containing its value. A list is represented as a box containing its items. A general list is a box containing boxes and atoms:

```
42 "z" 1.4 `ab


( )


enlist 42


(42;"z";1.4;`ab)


1 2 3


((42;"z");(1.4;`ab))


enlist ( )


(1;(42;"z");((42;"z");(1.4;`ab)))
```

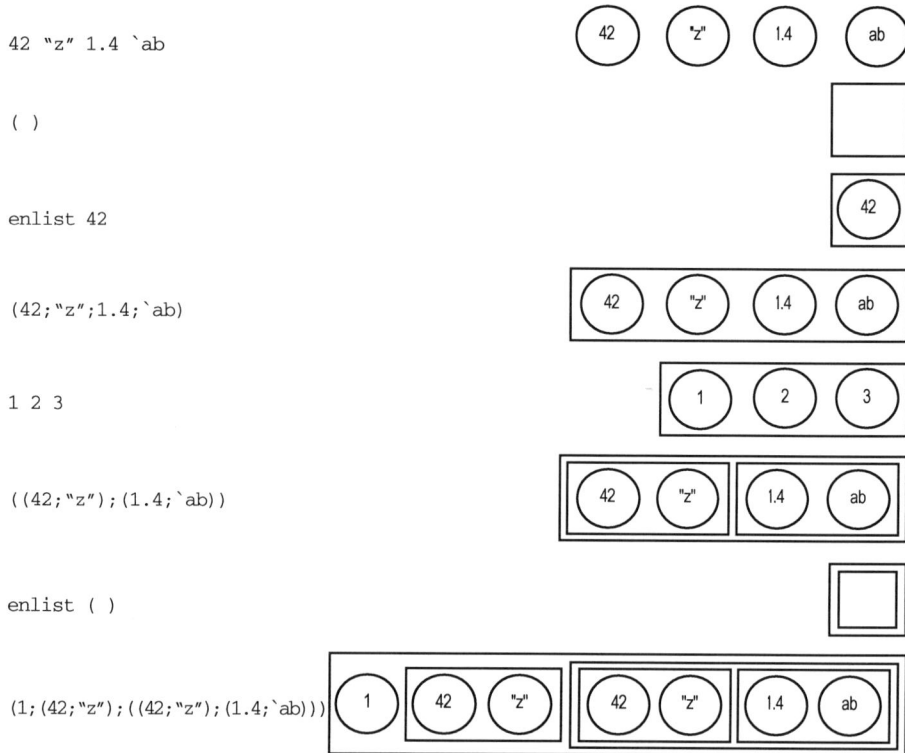

2.7.3 Examples

Following is a list of depth two having two elements, each of which is a simple list:

```
        L2:((1;2;3);(`ab;`c))

        L2
1 2 3
`ab`c

        count L2
2
```

Following is a list of depth two having three elements, each of which is a general list:

```
        L3:((1;2h;3j);("a";`bc);(1.23;4.56e))
```

```
        L3
(1;2h;3j)
("a";`bc)
(1.23;4.56e)

        count L3
3
```

Following is a list of depth two having one item that is a simple list:

```
        L4:enlist 1 2 3 4

        L4
1 2 3 4

        count L4
1

        L4[0]
1 2 3 4
```

Following is list of depth three having two items. The second item is a list of depth two having three items, the last of which is a simple list of four items:

```
        L5:(1;(100;200;(1000;2000;3000;4000)))

        L5
1
(100;200;1000 2000 3000 4000)

        count L5
2

        count L5[1]
3
```

Following is a **rectangular** list that can be thought of as a 3 x 4 matrix:

```
        m:((11;12;13;14);(21;22;23;24);(31;32;33;34))

        m
11 12 13 14
21 22 23 24
31 32 33 34
```

2.8 INDEXING AT DEPTH

It is possible to index directly into the items of a nested list.

2.8.1 Repeated Item Indexing

Retrieving an item via a single index always retrieves an uppermost item from a nested list:

```
        L:(1;(100;200;(1000;2000;3000;4000)))

        L[0]
1

        L[1]
100
200
1000 2000 3000 4000
```

Recalling that *q* evaluates expressions from right-to-left, we interpret the second retrieval above as,

- Retrieve the item at index 1 from L.

Alternatively, reading it functionally as left-of-right,

- Retrieve from L the item at index 1.

Since the result L[1] is itself a list, we can retrieve its elements using a single index:

```
        L[1][2]
1000 2000 3000 4000
```

Read this as,

- Retrieve the item at index 2 from the item at index 1 in L,

or,

- Retrieve the item at index 1 from L, and from it retrieve the item at index 2.

We can repeat single indexing once more to retrieve an item from the innermost nested list:

```
    L[1][2][0]
1000
```

Read this as,

- Retrieve the item from index 0 from the item at index 2 in the item at index 1 in L,

or,

- Retrieve the item at index 1 from L, and from it retrieve the item at index 2, and from it retrieve the item at index 0.

2.8.2 Notation for Indexing at Depth

There is an alternate notation for repeated indexing into the constituents of a nested list. The last retrieval can also be written as:

```
    L[1;2;0]
1000
```

Retrieving inner items for a nested list with this notation is called *indexing at depth*.

> **Important**
>
> The semicolons in indexing at depth are critical.

Assignment via index also works at depth:

```
    L:(1;(100;200;(1000 2000 3000 4000)))
    L[1;2;0]:999

    L
1
(100;200;999 2000 3000 4000)
```

To verify that the notation for indexing at depth is reasonable, we return to our matrix example:

```
    m:((11;12;13;14);(21;22;23;24);(31;32;33;34))

    m[0;2]
13

    m[0][2]
13
```

The indexing at depth notation suggests thinking of m as a multi-dimensional matrix, whereas repeated single indexing suggests thinking of m as an array of arrays. *Chacun à son goût.*

2.9 LIST INDEXING

A list of positions can be used to index a list.

2.9.1 Retrieving Multiple Items

In this section, we begin to see the power of *q* for manipulating lists. We start with:

```
    L1:100 200 300 400
```

We know how to index single items of the list:

```
    L1[0]
100

    L1[2]
300
```

By extension, we can retrieve a list of multiple items via multiple indices:

```
    L1[0 2]
100 300
```

The indices can be in any order, and the corresponding items are retrieved:

```
        L1[3 2 0 1]
400 300 100 200
```

An index can be repeated:

```
        L1[0 2 0]
100 300 100
```

Some more examples:

```
        bits:01101011b

        bits[0 2 4]
011b

        chars:"beeblebrox"

        chars[0 7 8]
"bro"
```

This explains why including the semi-colon separators is essential when indexing at depth. Leaving them out effectively specifies multiple indices, and you will get a corresponding list of values from the top level as a result.

2.9.2 Indexing via a Simple List

You have no doubt noticed that retrieving items via multiple indices looks just like we've substituted a list for the index. Indeed, this is exactly what is happening.

Here are some examples of a simple index list:

```
        I:3 2 0

        L1[I]
400 300 100

        L2:(-10.0; 3.1415e; 1b; `abc; "z")

        L2[I]
`abc
1b
-10f

        L3:(1;(100;200;(1000;2000;3000;4000));5;(600 700))
```

```
        L3
1
(100;200;1000 2000 3000 4000)
5
600 700

        J:2 1 0

        L3[J]
5
(100;200;1000 2000 3000 4000)
1
```

2.9.3 Indexing via a General List

Observe that in every case, the result of indexing a given list via a simple list is a new list whose values are retrieved from the first level of the given list and whose shape is the same as the index list. In particular, the retrieved list has the same shape as the index list. This suggests the behavior with an index that is a non-simple list:

```
        L1:100 200 300 400

        L1[(0 1; 2 3)]
100 200
300 400

        I:(1;(0;(3 2)))

        L1[I]
200
(100;400 300)
```

To figure out the result of indexing by any non-simple list, start with the fact that the result always has the same shape as the index.

> **Advanced**
>
> More precisely, the result of indexing via a list conforms to the index list. The notion of *conformability* of lists is defined recursively. All atoms conform. Two lists conform if they have the same number of items and each of their corresponding items conform. In plain language, two lists conform if they have the same shape.

2.9.4 Assignment with List Indexing

Recall that a list item can be assigned via item indexing:

```
L:100 200 300 400
L[0]:1000

     L
1000 200 300 400
```

Assignment via index extends to indexing via a simple list:

```
L:100 200 300 400
L[1 2 3]:2000 3000 4000

     L
100 2000 3000 4000
```

> **Note**
>
> Assignment via a simple index list is processed in index order — i.e., from left-to-right.

Thus,

```
L[3 2 1]:999 888 777
```

is equivalent to:

```
L[3]:999
L[2]:888
L[1]:777
```

Consequently, in the case of a repeated item in the index list, the right-most assignment prevails:

```
L:100 200 300 400
L[0 1 0 3]:1000 2000 3000 4000

      L
3000 2000 300 4000
```

You can assign a single value to multiple items in a list by indexing on a simple list and using an atom for the assignment value:

```
    L:100 200 300 400
    L[1 3]:999

    L
100 999 300 999
```

2.9.5 Juxtaposition

Now that we're familiar with retrieving and assigning via an index list, we introduce a simplified notation. It is permissible to leave out the brackets and juxtapose the list and index with a separating blank. Some examples follow:

```
        L:100 200 300 400

        L[0]
100

        L 0
100

        L[2 1]
300 200

        L 2 1
300 200

        I:2 1

        L[I]
300 200

        L I
300 200

        L[::]
100 200 300 400

        L ::
100 200 300 400
```

Which notation you use is a matter of personal preference. In this manual, we usually use brackets, since this notation is probably most familiar from verbose programming. Experienced *q* programmers often use juxtaposition since it reduces notational density.

2.9.6 Find (?)

The dyadic primitive find (?) returns the index of the right operand in the left operand list:

```
        1001 1002 1003?1002
1
```

Performing find on a list is the inverse to positional indexing because it maps an item to its position.

If you try to find an item that is not in the list, the result is an int equal to the count of the list:

```
        1001 1002 1003?1004
3
```

The way to think of this result is: the position of an item not in the list, is one past the end of the list, which is where it would be if you were to append it to the list. Of course, find extends to lists of items:

```
        1001 1002 1003?1003 1001
2 0
```

2.10 ELIDED INDICES

2.10.1 Eliding Indices for a Matrix List

We return to the situation of indexing at depth for nested lists. For simplicity, let's start with a list that looks like a matrix.

```
        m:(1 2 3 4; 100 200 300 400; 1000 2000 3000 4000)
```

Analogy with traditional matrix notation suggests that we could retrieve a row or column from m by providing a "partial" index at depth. Indeed, this works:

```
        m[1;]
100 200 300 400

        m[;3]
4 400 4000
```

Observe that eliding the last index reduces to item indexing at the top level:

```
        m[1;]
100 200 300 400

        m[1]
100 200 300 400
```

> **Note**
>
> In the previous example, the two syntactic forms have the same result, but the first more clearly connotes the situation.

The situation of eliding other than the first index is more interesting. The way to read m[;3] above is,

- Retrieve the items in the third position from all items at the top level of m.

2.10.2 Eliding Indices for a General List

Let's tackle another level of nesting:

```
        L:((1 2 3;4 5 6 7);(`a`b`c`d;`z`y`x`;`0`1`2);
          ("now";"is";"the"))

        L
(1 2 3;4 5 6 7)
(`a`b`c`d;`z`y`x`;`0`1`2)
("now";"is";"the")

        L[;1;]
4 5 6 7
`z`y`x`
"is"
```

```
    L[;;2]
3 6
`c`x`2
"w e"
```

Interpret `L[;1;]` as,

- Retrieve all items in the second position of each list at the top level.

Interpret `L[;;2]` as,

- Retrieve the items in the third position for each list at the second level.

Observe that in `L[;;2]` the attempt to retrieve the item at the third position of the string `"is"` resulted in the null value `" "`; hence the blank in `"w e"` of the result.

> **Recommendation**
>
> In general, it will make things more evident if you do not omit trailing semi-colons when eliding indices. For example, with L as above:
>
> ```
>     L[;;]       / instead of L[]
>
>     L[1;;]      / instead of L[1]
>
>     L[;1;]      / instead of L[1;]
> ```

As the final exam for this section, let's combine an elided index with indexing by simple arrays. Let L be as above. Then we can retrieve a cross-section of L using a combination of elided and list indices:

```
    L[0 2;;0 1]
(1 2;4 5)
("no";"is";"th")
```

Interpret this as,

- Retrieve the items from positions 0 and 1 from all columns in rows 0 and 2.

55

2.11 RECTANGULAR LISTS AND MATRICES

2.11.1 Rectangular Lists

In this section, we further investigate the matrix-like lists from the previous section. A *rectangular* list is a list of lists, all having the same count. Understand that this does not mean that a rectangular list is necessarily a traditional matrix, since there can be additional levels of nesting. For example, the following list is rectangular because each of its items has count three, but is not a matrix:

```
        L:(1 2 3; (10 20; 100 200; 1000 2000))

        L
1          2          3
10   20    100 200    1000 2000
```

In a rectangular list, elision of the second index corresponds to generalized row retrieval and elision of the first index corresponds to generalized column retrieval:

```
        r:(`a`b`c;(1 2 3 4;10 20 30 40;100 200 300 400))

        r[0;]
`a`b`c

        r[;1]
`b
10 20 30 40
```

> **Advanced**
>
> A rectangular list can be transposed with `flip` (see **Appendix A**), meaning that that the rows and columns are reflected, effectively reversing the first two indices in indexing at depth. For example, the transpose of L above is:

```
        flip L
1 10 20
2 100 200
3 1000 2000
```

2.11.2 Matrices

Matrices are a special case of rectangular lists and can most easily be defined recursively. A *matrix* of dimension 1 is a simple list. In the context of mathematical operations, the simple list would have numeric type, but this is not a restriction. The count of a one-dimensional matrix is called it *size*. In some contexts, a simple one-dimensional matrix is called a *vector*, its count *length*, and an atom is a *scalar*. Some examples:

```
v1:1 2 3

v2:98.60 99.72 100.34 101.93

v3:`so`long`and`thanks`for`all`the`fish
```

For $n>1$, we define a matrix of dimension n recursively as a list of matrices of dimension $n-1$ all having the same size. Thus, a matrix of dimension 2 is a list of matrices of dimension 1, all having the same size. If all items in a matrix have the same type, we call this the *type* of the matrix.

2.11.3 Two and Three Dimensional Matrices

Two-dimensional matrices are frequently encountered and have special terminology. Let m be a two-dimensional matrix. The items of m are its *rows*. As we have already seen, the ith row of m can be obtained via item indexing as m[i]. Equivalently, we can use an elided index with indexing at depth to obtain the ith row as m[i;].

By laying out the rows of m in tabular form, we realize that the list m[;j] is the jth *column* of m. Note that the expressions m[i][j] and m[i;j] both retrieve the same item — namely, the element in row i and column j. Following is an example of a two dimensional matrix of int, having size 4 x 3:

```
    m:(1 2 3;10 20 30;100 200 300;1000 2000 3000)

    m[0]
1 2 3

    m[0;]
1 2 3

    m[;2]
3 30 300 3000
```

```
m[0][2]
3

m[0;2]
3
```

The specification of m demonstrates that our approach to matrix definition treats m as a collection of rows — i.e., m is in row order. Since each row is a simple list, the elements of a row are in fact stored in contiguous memory. This makes retrieval of an entire row very fast, but retrieval of a column will be slower since its elements are not contiguous. This choice was made so that list indexing would result in the conventional matrix notation.

> **Advanced**
>
> It is equally valid to consider a one-dimensional array as a column and a two dimensional array as a collection of column vectors. This would make column retrieval very fast, but index order would be transposed from conventional notation. As we see in **Chapter 7**, a table is a collection of columns that are notationally transposed for convenience.
>
> The constraints and calculations of q-sql operate on columns, so they are fast, especially when the columns are vectors (i.e., simple lists). In particular, a simple time series can be represented by two parallel ordered columns, one holding the datetimes and the second holding the associated values. Retrieving and manipulating the points stored in time sequence is faster by orders of magnitude than performing the same operations in an RDBMS that stores data by row with undefined row order.

For completeness, here is an example of a three dimensional 2 x 3 x 3 matrix — i.e., each item of mm is a 3 x 3 matrix:

```
mm:((1 2 3;4 5 6;7 8 9);(10 20 30; 40 50 60; 70 80 90))

mm[0]
1 2 3
4 5 6
7 8 9
```

```
    mm[1;2]
70 80 90

    mm[1;;2]
30 60 90
```

2.11.4 Matrix Flexibility

We have seen that matrices in *q* look and act like their mathematical counterparts. However, they have additional features not available in simple mathematical notation or in many verbose languages.

We have seen that a matrix can be viewed and manipulated both as a multi-dimensional array (i.e., indexing at depth) and as an array of arrays (repeated item indexing). In addition, we can extend individual item indexing with indexing via a simple list. With m as above:

```
    m[0 2]
1 2 3
100 200 300
```

CHAPTER 3
PRIMITIVE OPERATIONS

3.0 INTRODUCTION TO FUNCTIONS

3.0.1 Function Notation

Operators and functions are closely related. In fact, operators are just functions used with infix notation. We cover functions in depth in **Chapter 4**, but provide a brief overview here. Function evaluation in *q* uses square brackets to enclose the arguments and semicolons to separate them. Thus the output value of a monadic function f for the input x is written,

    f[x]

Similarly, the value of a dyadic function is written,

    f[x;y]

The simplest functions are those whose domain and range are atomic data types. These functions are called (what else?) *atomic* functions.

3.0.2 Primitives, Verbs and Functional Notation

The normal way of writing addition in mathematics and most programming languages uses an operator with infix notation — that is, a plus symbol between the two operands:

    2+3

In *q*, we can also consider addition to be a dyadic function that takes two numeric arguments and returns a numeric result. You probably wouldn't think twice at seeing,

    sum[a;b]

But you might blink at the following perfectly logical equivalent,

```
+[a;b]
```

A dyadic function that is written with infix notation is called a *verb*. This terminology arises from thinking of the left operand as the subject which acts on the right operand as object.

The *primitive operators* are the built-in atomic verbs, including the basic arithmetic, relation and comparison operators. Some are represented by a single ASCII symbol such as +, - , =, and <. Others use compound symbols, such as <=, >=, and <>. Still others have names such as **not**, and **neg**. The extent of operations is not limited to the primitives, since any monadic or dyadic function can be made into a verb.

Any verb, including all the primitive operators, can also use regular function notation. So, in *q* you can write:

```
    +[2;3]
5
```

It is even possible, and sometimes useful, to write a binary verb using a combination of infix and functional notation for the two operands. This may look very strange at first:

```
    (2+)[3]
5
```

It is also possible to write:

```
    (2+)3
5
```

3.0.3 Item-wise Extension of Atomic Functions

A fundamental feature of an atomic function or operator is that its domain is extended to lists by item-wise application. Thus, a monadic atomic function is applied to a simple list by operating element-wise on the list. A dyadic atomic operator is extended to operate on an atom and a simple list by applying its operation to the atom and the items in each position of the list. Similarly, a dyadic atomic operator is extended to operate on a pair of simple lists by operating pair-wise on elements in corresponding positions.

Symbolically, let *m* be a unary atomic verb, *op* a binary atomic verb, a an atom, L, L1 and L2 simple lists, and i an int index. Then,

i^{th} element of	is
`m[L]`	`m[L[i]]`
`a` *op* `L`	`a` *op* `L[i]`
`L` *op* `a`	`L[i]` *op* `a`
`L1` *op* `L2`	`L1[i]` *op* `L2[i]`

For example, the result of applying `neg` to a simple list is obtained by application to each item of the list:

```
    L:100 200 300 400

    neg L
-100 -200 -300 -400
```

The result of adding an atom to a simple list is obtained by adding the atom to each item of the list:

```
    99+L
199 299 399 499
```

The result of adding two simple lists of the same length is addition of items at corresponding positions:

```
    L1:100 200 300 400
    L2:9 8 7 6

    L1+L2
109 208 307 406
```

3.1 OPERATOR PRECEDENCE

3.1.1 Traditional Operator Precedence

Recall that mathematical notation and verbose programming languages have a concept of operator precedence, which attempts to resolve ambiguities in the evaluation of arithmetic and logical operations in expressions. The arithmetic precedence rules were drummed into you in elementary school: multiplication and division are equal and come before addition and subtraction, etc.

There are similar precedence rules for =, <, >, **and** and **or**.

3.1.2 Left of Right Evaluation

Although the traditional notion of operator precedence has the weight of many years of incumbency, it's time to throw the bum out. As mentioned in **Chapter 1**, *q* has no rules for operator precedence. Instead, it has one simple rule for evaluating any expression:

- Expressions are evaluated left *of* right.

We could also say **right to left** since the interpreter evaluates an expression from right-to-left. However, every action in *q* is essentially a function evaluation, and it is more natural to read **f of x** rather than **x evaluated by f**. Thinking functionally makes **of** a paradigm, not just a preposition.

The adoption of left-of-right expression evaluation frees *q* to treat infix notation simply and uniformly. Which notation is used, infix or functional, depends on what is clearer in the specific context.

Left-of-right expression evaluation also means that there is no ambiguity in any expression. (This is from the compiler's perspective; it is certainly possible to write *q* expressions comprehensible to only the compiler and *q* gods).

Parentheses can still be used to override the default evaluation order but there will be far fewer once you abandon the old (bad) habit of using them to override operator precedence. You should arrange your expressions with a goal of placing parentheses on the endangered species list.

3.1.3 A Gotcha of Left of Right Evaluation

Due to left-of-right evaluation, parentheses **are** needed to isolate the result of an expression that is the left operand of a verb. Omitting such parentheses is a common error for *q* newbies, as this grouping is often unnecessary in verbose languages.

Here is a canonical example, where < and > have their usual meanings. As we shall see shortly, the | operator returns the maximum of its operands; this reduces to **or** for binary types. It is a rite of passage of *q* newbies to write the first expression intending the second:

```
x:100

x<42|x>98
0b

(x<42)|x>98
1b
```

The first expression parses from right to left as:

- x is tested against 98 by greater than, yielding 1b, which is compared for the larger to 42, yielding 42, against which x is tested by less than, yielding 0b.

The second expression parses from right to left as:

- x is tested against 98 by greater than, yielding 1b, which is compared for the larger to 0b (being the result of testing x against 42 by less than), yielding 1b.

Should this seem unnatural, don't worry. By the time you leave this chapter, it'll feel right as rain.

3.1.4 Rationale for No Operator Precedence

Operator precedence is quite feeble in that it requires all the components of an expression to be analyzed (think for a moment about how you do it manually) before it can be evaluated. Ironically, it results in the frequent use of parentheses to override the very rules that are purportedly there to help.

Even more damning is that operator precedence forces semantic content onto infix notation. Suppose a programming language wished to allow dyadic functions to be verbs — i.e., expressed in infix notation — so that,

```
f[x;y]
```

can also be written,

```
x f y
```

This would entail the extension of precedence rules to cover verbs whenever they are mixed with arithmetic operations. Aside from being impractical, this would result in yet more parentheses.

3.2 Match (~)

The non-atomic, binary match operator (~) applies to any two entities, returning a boolean result of 1b if they are identical and 0b otherwise. For two entities to match, they must have the same shape, the same type and the same value(s), but they may occupy separate storage locations. Colloquially, clones are considered identical in *q* because they are indistinguishable.

> **Advanced**
>
> This differs from the notion of identity in some verbose languages, in that distinct *q* entities can be identical. For example, in languages of C ancestry, objects are equal if and only if their underlying pointers address the same memory location. Identical twins are **not** equal. You must write your own equivalence method to determine if one object is a deep copy of another.

There are no restrictions as to the type or shape of the two operands for match. Try to predict each of the following results of match:

```
    42~42
1b

    42~42h
0b

    42f~42.0
1b

    42~`42
0b

    `42~"42"
0b

    4 2~2 4
0b

    42~(4 2;(1 0))
0b

    (4 2)~(4;2*1)
1b

    (1 2;3 4)~(1;2 3 4)
0b
```

While you are learning *q*, applying match can be an effective way to determine if you have entered what you intended, or to discover whether two different ways of expressing something produce the same result. For example, *q* newbies often trip over:

```
        42~(42)
1b
```

This technique can be useful in checking intermediate results when debugging (except for the *q* gods who enter perfect *q* code every time).

3.3 RELATIONAL OPERATORS

The relational operators are atomic verbs that return boolean results. Relational operations on atomic types have requirements regarding the compatibility of the operands.

3.3.1 Equality (=) and Inequality (<>)

We begin with the equality operator (=), which differs from match in that it is atomic, so it tests its operands component-wise instead of in entirety. All atoms of numeric or char type are mutually compatible for equality, but symbols are compatible only with symbols.

Equality is not strict with regard to type, meaning types with the same underlying value are equal. For example, chars are equal to their underlying values:

```
        42h=2*21
1b

        42=42.0
1b

        42=(42)
1b

        42=0x42
0b

        42="*"
1b
```

A symbol and a character are not compatible and an error results from the test:

```
        `a="a"
`type
```

The not-equal primitive is (<>):

```
        42<>0x42
1b
```

> **Note**
>
> The test not equal can also be expressed by applying not to the result of testing with =.

```
        a:42
        b:98.6

        a<>b
1b

        not a=b
1b
```

> **Note**
>
> When comparing floats, *q* uses multiplicative tolerance, which makes arithmetic give rational results.

```
        r:1%3

        r
0.3333333

        2=r+r+r+r+r+r
1b
```

3.3.2 Not Zero (not)

The monadic, atomic relational operator not differs from its equivalent in some verbose languages. It returns a boolean result and has a domain of all numeric and character types; it is not defined for symbols. The not operator generalizes the reversal of true and false values to any entity having an underlying numeric value by testing its argument against an underlying 0. In other words, it answers the Hamletonian question: to be, or not to be, zero.

The test against zero yields the expected results for boolean arguments:

```
        not 0b
1b

        not 1b
0b
```

More generally, the test against zero applies for any numeric type:

```
        not 42
0b

        not 0
1b

        not 0j
1b

        not 0xff
0b

        f:98.6
        not f
0b

        not 0.0
1b
```

For char values, `not` returns false except for the character representing the underlying value of 0:

```
        not "a"
0b

        not " "
0b

        not "\000"
1b
```

For date and datetime values, `not` tests against midnight of Jan 1, 2000, since this is the datetime with underlying value 0:

```
      not 2042.04.02
0b

      not 2000.01.01T00:00:00.000
1b

      not 2000.01.01
1b
```

The last example obtains because omitted temporal constituents default to their underlying numeric 0 values.

For time values, not effectively tests against 00:00:00.000:

```
      not 00:00:00.000
1b

      not 04:02:42.042
0b
```

3.3.3 Ordering: <, <=, >, >=

We consider the binary atomic order operators. Less than (<), greater than (>) less or equal (<=) and greater or equal (>=) are defined for all atoms with the requirement that the operands be of compatible types. Numeric and char types are mutually compatible, but symbols are only compatible with symbols. Comparison for numeric and char types is based on underlying numeric value, independent of type:

```
      4<42
1b

      4h>=0x2a
0b

      -1.59e<=99j
1b
```

For char atoms, the underlying numeric value results in comparison according to ASCII character sequence:

```
      "A"<"Z"
1b

      "a"<="Z"
0b
```

```
        "A"<"0"
0b

        "?"</"
0b
```

A numeric atom and a char are compared according to the underlying numeric value of the char:

```
        42<"z"
1b
```

For symbols, comparison is based on lexicographic order:

```
        `a>=`b
0b

        `ab<`abc
1b
```

Now that we are familiar with relational operations on atoms, let's examine their item-wise extensions to simple lists:

```
        2<1 2 3
001b

        1 2 3h>=-987.65 1.234 567.89
110b

        " "="Life the Universe and Everything"
00001000100000000100010000000000b

        "zaphod"="Arthur"
000100b

        "zaphod">"Arthur"
100000b
```

> **Note**
>
> As of this writing, the primitive > is converted to the equivalent < under the covers by the *q* interpreter.

> That is,
>
>   a>b
>
> is actually evaluated as,
>
>   b<a
>
> This does not matter when a and b are atoms or lists, but it does have consequences when they are dictionaries.

3.4 Basic Arithmetic: +, -, *, %

The arithmetic operators are atomic verbs and come in two flavors: *binary* (in the mathematical sense of having two operands) and *unary* (one operand). We begin with the four operations of elementary arithmetic:

```
Symbol      Name        Example
------      ------      ----------
+           add         42+67
-           minus       42.0-5.3456
*           times       2h*3h
%           divide      42%6
```

On the surface, things look pretty much like other programming languages, except that division is represented by % since / is used to delimit comments. We have:

```
        6*7
42

        a:42
        b:3
        c:a-b
        c
39

        100*a
4200

        c%b
13f
```

> **Note**
>
> The result of division is always a float.

For a programmer not accustomed to left-of-right evaluation, the following may take some getting used to:

```
    2*1+1
4
```

Things can get funky fast for the *q* newbie:

```
    c:1000*b:1+a:42

    c
43000
```

One way to read this is:

- The integer value 42 is assigned to the variable named a, then the assigned value is added to 1, then this result is assigned to the variable named b, whose assigned value is multiplied by 1000 and the result is assigned to the variable named c.

The arithmetic operations are defined for all numeric types, and all numeric types are compatible. The type of the result depends on the operands. Loosely speaking, smaller types are promoted to their wider cousins and division always results in floats. Typing does not get in the way of arithmetic.

When binary types participate in addition, subtraction and multiplication, they are promoted to int. In other words, arithmetic is **not** performed modulo 2 (i.e., in base 2) for binary values, or modulo 256 for byte values:

```
    1b+1b
2

    0x2a+0x11
59

    42+1b
43
```

```
        5*0x2a
210
```

When integer types are used in addition, subtraction and multiplication, the result is an int or the widest type present, whichever is wider:

```
        a:42
        b:123h
        c:1234567890j

        b+b
246

        a+b
165

        a+b+c
12345678055j
```

The result of addition, subtraction and multiplication of integer data types is modulo the width of the result type. That is, overflow is ignored. For example, int arithmetic is modulo 2^{32}:

```
        i:2147483647

        i+3
-2147483646
```

When any numeric types participate in division, they are promoted to float and the result is a float:

```
        1%3
0.3333333

        3%1
3f
```

When floating point data types are mixed, the result is float:

```
        6.0*7.0e
42f
```

> **Note**
>
> The arithmetic operators are **always** dyadic. In particular, while (-) is also used syntactically to denote a negative number, there is no unary function (-) to negate a value. Its attempted use for such generates an error. Use the operator `neg` for this purpose.

```
        a:-4

        a
-4

        -a      / This is an error
`-

        neg a
4
```

According to the discussion in **§3.2**, the arithmetic operators are extended item-wise to lists. Thus:

```
        2+100 200 300
102 202 302

        b:1000.0 2000.0 3000.0 4000.0

        b*2
2000 4000 6000 8000f

        c:2 4 6 8

        b%c
500 500 500 500f
```

In the following example, observe that item-wise atomic application is recursive when all the list components are numeric:

```
        e:(100 200;1000 2000)

        e-2
98   198
998  1998
```

3.5 Maximum (|) and Minimum (&)

The comparison operators are atomic and binary, and return the type of the widest operand. Numeric types and char are mutually compatible; comparison is not defined for symbols.

The maximum operator (|) returns the maximum of its operands based on underlying numeric values; this reduces to logical **or** for binary operands. The minimum operator (&) returns the minimum of its operands based on underlying numeric values; this reduces to logical **and** for binary operands. The same type promotion rules apply as for the arithmetic operators:

```
        0b|1b
1b

        1b&0b
0b

        42|0x2b
43

        4.2e&42j
4.2e

        "a"|"z"
"z"

        "0"&"A"
"0"

        `a|`z       / this is an error
`type
```

Following are examples of comparison extended item-wise to simple lists:

```
        2|0 1 2 3 4
2 2 2 3 4

        11010101b&01100101b
01000101b

        "zaphod"|"arthur"
"zrthur"
```

> **Note**
>
> For the symbolically challenged, the operator | can also be written as `or`. The operator & can be written as `and`.

```
        1 and 3
1
        "a" or "z"
"z"
```

3.6 EXPONENTIAL PRIMITIVES: SQRT, EXP, LOG, XEXP, XLOG

3.6.1 sqrt

The atomic unary `sqrt` has as domain all non-negative numeric values and returns a float representing the square root of its argument:

```
        sqrt 2
1.414214
        sqrt 4
2f
        sqrt 0x42
8.124038
        sqrt -1
0n
```

3.6.2 exp

The atomic unary `exp` has as domain all numeric values and returns a float representing the base e raised to the power of its argument:

```
        exp 1
2.718282
```

```
        exp 4.2
66.68633

        exp -12h
6.144212e-06
```

> **Note**
>
> Do not confuse the e used in the display of scientific notation with the mathematical base of natural logarithms.

3.6.3 log

The atomic unary `log` has as domain all numeric values and returns a float representing the natural logarithm of its argument:

```
        log 1
0f

        log 0x2a
3.73767

        log 0.0001
-9.21034

        log -1
0n
```

3.6.4 xexp

The atomic binary `xexp` has as domain all numeric values in both operands and returns a float representing the left operand raised to the power of the right operand. If the mathematical operation does not make sense, the result is `0n`:

```
        2 xexp 5
32f

        -2 xexp .5
0n
```

3.6.5 xlog

The atomic binary `xlog` has as domain all numeric values in both operands and returns a float representing the logarithm of the right operand with respect to the base of the left operand. If the mathematical operation does not make sense, the result is `0n`:

```
        2 xlog 32
5f

        2 xlog -1
0n
```

3.7 MORE PRIMITIVES: DIV, MOD, SIGNUM, RECIPROCAL, FLOOR, CEILING AND ABS

These functions are useful in calculations.

3.7.1 div and mod (Modulus)

The binary `div` is atomic in its left operand (*dividend*) which is any numeric value. The right operand (*divisor*) is a numeric atom. The result is the integer quotient of dividing the dividend by the divisor. This produces the usual quotient from elementary school for positive integers.

For a positive divisor, the quotient is defined as the integer that yields the largest integral multiple of the divisor not exceeding the absolute value of the dividend. The type of the result is int if the operands are of integer type and float otherwise; it is undefined for negative divisor:

```
        6 div 3
2

        7.3 div 3.5
2f

        4.5 mod 2.3
2.2
```

The binary `mod` is atomic in its left operand (*dividend*) which is any numeric value. The right operand (*divisor*) is a numeric atom. The result is the remainder of dividing the dividend by the divisor. This produces the usual remainder from elementary school for positive integers but is more complicated for general numeric arguments.

For a positive divisor, the remainder is defined as the difference between the dividend and the largest integral multiple of the divisor not exceeding the absolute value of the dividend. The type of the result is int if the operands are of integer type and float otherwise; it is undefined for negative divisor.

```
        7 mod 3
1

        0x2a mod 0x10
10

        4.5 mod 2.3
2.2

        -4.5 mod 2.3
0.1
```

3.7.2 Sign (signum)

The atomic unary `signum` has as domain all integral and floating point types and returns an int representing the sign of its argument. Here 1 represents **positive**, -1 represents **negative** and 0 represents a **zero** argument:

```
        signum 4.2
1

        signum -42
-1

        signum 0
0
```

3.7.3 reciprocal

The atomic unary `reciprocal` has as domain all numeric types and returns a float representing 1.0 divided by the argument:

```
        reciprocal 0.02380952
42.00001
```

q FOR MORTALS | PRIMITIVE OPERATIONS

```
        reciprocal 0
0w
```

3.7.4 floor

The atomic unary `floor` has as domain int and floating point types and returns an int representing the largest integer that is less than or equal to its argument:

```
        floor 4
4

        floor 4.0
4

        floor 4.2
4

        floor -4.0
-4

        floor -4.2
-5
```

The `floor` operator can be used to truncate or round floating point values to a specific number of digits to the right of the decimal:

```
        a:4.242

        0.01*floor 100*a
4.24

        0.1*floor 0.5+10*a
4.2
```

> **Note**
>
> The `floor` function does not apply to boolean, byte, short or long types.

```
        floor 0x2a
'type
```

3.7.5 ceiling

Analogous to `floor`, the atomic unary `ceiling` has as domain int, long and floating point types and returns the smallest int that is greater than or equal to its argument:

```
        ceiling 4
4
        ceiling 4.0
4
        ceiling 4.2
5
        ceiling -4.0
-4
        ceiling -4.2
-4
```

> **Note**
>
> For reasons known only to the *q* gods, `ceiling` does apply to boolean or byte types but not to short or long types.

```
        ceiling 0b
0
        ceiling 42h
'type
```

3.7.6 Absolute Value (abs)

The atomic unary `abs` has as domain all integral and floating point types. It returns its argument if the argument is greater than or equal to zero, or `neg` applied to its argument otherwise. The result of `abs` has the same type as the argument:

```
        abs 4
4
```

```
        abs -4
4

        abs -4.2
4.2

        abs -4.0
4f

        abs -4.2e
4.2

        abs -4j
4j
```

3.8 OPERATIONS ON TEMPORAL VALUES

We have separated temporal types and their operations into this section because they have richer semantics.

3.8.1 Internal Format of Temporal Types

First, we note that a date or datetime is actually stored under the covers as a signed float, with 0.0 corresponding to midnight of January 1, 2000. So:

```
      0.0=2000.01.01T00:00:00.000
1b
```

The integral part of the floating point value corresponds to the number of days after (positive) or before (negative) the start of the millennium. The decimal portion of a datetime is the fractional portion of a 24-hour day represented by its time component. Thus:

```
      33.5=2000.02.03T12:00:00.000
1b
```

Time is stored as the number of milliseconds from the start of day. Thus, a time value is between 0 and 86,400,000 (24*60*60*1000). So:

```
      43200000=12:00:00.000
1b
```

3.8.2 Basic Operations

In contrast to some verbose languages, any expression involving temporal types and numerical types that should make sense, actually does, and it works in the expected fashion. Comparison of dates or datetimes reduces to comparison of the underlying floating point values. Thus:

```
        2006.01.01T00:00:00.000<2005.12.25T12:00:00.000
0b

        2005.12.25=2005.12.25T00:00:00.000
1b

        2005.12.25<2005.12.25T12:00:00.000
1b
```

Time values can be compared with each other and the result is based on the underlying millisecond counts:

```
        12:01:10.987<17:05:42.986
1b
```

A date and a time can be added to give a datetime:

```
        2007.07.04+12:45:59.876
2007.07.04T12:45:59.876
```

> **Note**
>
> A time is implicitly converted to a fractional day when it is added to a date to get a datetime.

3.8.3 Day Counts and Time Counts

A date or datetime can be compared, or tested for equality, with a float:

```
        366.0=2001.01.01
1b
```

A time can be compared with an int:

```
        43200000<12:00:00.001
1b
```

A float representing a fractional day count can be added to or subtracted from a datetime (or date) to give a datetime. In this context, the integral part of the fractional day count represents the number of days and the decimal part represents the fractional part of a 24-hour day. For example, to move forward 33 days and 12 hours:

```
        2000.01.01T00:00:00.000+33.5
2000.02.03T12:00:00.000
```

Or, to move back 2 hours and 30 minutes:

```
        2000.01.01T00:00:00.000-2.5%24
1999.12.31T21:30:00.000
```

An int representing a day count can be added to or subtracted from a date to give a date:

```
        2006.07.04+5
2006.07.09
```

The difference of two datetimes is a float representing the fractional day count between them:

```
        2007.02.03T12:00:00.000-2007.01.01T00:00:00.000
33.5
```

The difference between two dates is an int day count representing the number of days between them:

```
        2006.07.04-2006.04.04
91
```

An int representing a time count of milliseconds can be added to or subtracted from a time to give a time:

```
        12:00:00.000+1000
12:00:01.000
```

In a departure from **2.3**, you can add a timespan that looks like a time but represents elapsed time to a time to get a new time:

```
        12:00:00.000+00:00:01.000
12:00:01.000
```

In another departure from **2.3**, the difference between two times is a timespan representing the elapsed time between the two:

```
        23:59:59.999-00:00:00.000
23:59:59.999
```

Observe that a time does not wrap when it exceeds 24 hours:

```
        23:59:59.999+2
24:00:00.001
```

Advanced

A Brief Note on Time

In the ideal programming world, temporal values fall into two categories: ordinals and cardinals. As the name implies, ordinals have order, meaning that it is possible to ask whether one such is before (or after) another. People waiting in line at a movie theater are ordered by their position. In contrast, cardinals represent magnitudes that have relative size but do not know about before and after. The weights of the folks waiting in line are cardinal values.

Our system of calendars and clocks imposes an order on time, although on closer examination, it isn't quite so orderly. We tell time based on the revolution of the Earth about the sun (years), the revolution of the moon about the earth (months) and the rotation of the Earth on its axis (days). Imposed on this is a sexagesimal system originating in ancient Sumeria in which the numbers 12 and 60 are prominent. There are almost 360 days in a year and almost 28 days in a month and almost 12 hours of daylight and darkness.

This was good enough for farmers and astronomers to predict weather and sky cycles 4000 years ago, but things get complicated when we need more precision.

> For our purposes, we oberve that dates, times and datetimes are ordered by which comes first on the calendar or clock. Thus they are ordinals which can be tested with < and >. The difference between two temporal ordinals represents the time spanned from the first to the second. Such a timespan is a cardinal. A cardinal timespan can be added to (or subtracted from) an ordinal to get another ordinal.
>
> By representing datetimes as fractional day counts since the start of Jan 1, 2000, *q* gets the natural ordering of rational numbers for free. Similarly, representing a date as the integral day count since Jan 1, 2000 and time as elapsed milliseconds since midnight, *q* gets the natural ordering of integers for free.

As of **2.4**, *q* approaches languages such as C# that represent temporal values and arithmetic reasonably. In particular, *q* now considers the difference between two temporal values to be a timespan — that is, elapsed time. The quirk is that timespans have various representations. The difference between two datetimes is a real representing the elapsed fractional days. As a special case, the difference between two dates is an int representing the number of elapsed days. The difference between two times is a timespan that looks just like a time.

In the following summary table, date/time can be a date, a time or a datetime:

```
date/time - date/time      is  timespan
timespan  - timespan       is  timespan
date/time ± timespan       is  date/time
```

3.9 Operations on Infinities and Nulls

As you gain experience with the way *q* handles infinities and nulls, you'll find that it is simpler and more rational than verbose languages. Injection of such an exceptional value into a calculation stream propagates through subsequent steps in a predictable way without the need for special error trapping and handling. While the result will contain some meaningless data, portions that do not depend on the invalid values will still compute correctly.

3.9.1 Producing Infinities

We show how to produce and operate with the infinities we met in **Chapter 1**.

Division of a non-negative numeric value by any 0 results in float infinity, denoted by `0w`:

```
        4.0%0
0w

        3.14%0.0
0w

        0x32%0
0w

        1b%0
0w
```

Similarly, division of a negative numeric value by any 0 results in negative float infinity, denoted by `-0w`:

```
        -4%0.0
-0w

        -3.14%0
-0w
```

The int infinities can not be produced via an arithmetic operation on normal int values, since the result of division in *q* is always of type float:

```
        42%0
0w

        -42%0
-0w
```

3.9.2 Producing NaN

When any numeric zero is divided by zero, the mathematical result is undefined. This is sometimes represented in writing as NaN (Not a Number). It is denoted in *q* by `0n`, which is the float null value:

```
        0%0
0n
```

```
       0.0%0.0
0n

       0.0e%0b
0n

       0j%0x00
0n
```

3.9.3 Basic Arithmetic on Infinities and Nulls

The infinities and nulls act reasonably in numeric expressions and comparisons. Generally, if one member of an expression is infinite or null so is the result. In an arithmetic mix of infinity, null or NaN, the null prevails over infinity and NaN prevails over other nulls. Note that the signs of infinities are carried correctly through arithmetic and meaningless expressions involving infinities result in NaN:

```
       2+0w-3
0w

       0w*-0w
-0w

       -0w+0w
0n

       42+0n
0n

       42+0N
0N

       0w+0n
0n

       0n+0N
0n
```

The exception to the above is that any integral infinity can be added to its negative infinity to yield 0:

```
       -0Wj+0Wj
0j
```

3.9.4 Type Promotion

When nulls occur in expressions of mixed type, the same type promotion rules apply as for finite values:

```
        42+0N
0N

        42j+0N
0Nj

        0N+0Nj
0Nj

        0n+0N
0n
```

3.9.5 Equality

Infinities are distinct from all numeric values and from all nulls as well, since they do not represent missing data. All nulls are equal since they differ only by type:

```
        42=0W    / can compare a numeric value to infinity
0b

        0w=42%0  / can compare float infinity to itself
1b

        0=0N     / 0 is not the same as missing integer
0b

        0=0n     / 0 is not the same as missing float
0b

        0w=0W    / float infinity is not the same as int infinity
0b

        0w=0N    / float infinity is not the same as null integer
0b

        0w=0n    / float infinity is not the same as missing float
0b
```

```
        0Nj=0N   / missing long and missing int are the same
1b

        0N=0n    / missing int and missing float are the same
1b
```

> **Note**
>
> In contrast to some languages, such as C, separate NaNs are equal.

```
        (0%0)=0%0
1b
```

> **Advanced**
>
> The integral infinities, positive and negative, have underlying values whose bit patterns correspond to legitimate base-2 integral values.

```
Value  Bit Representation
-----  --------------------------------------------------
 0Wh   0111111111111111b
-0Wh   1000000000000001b
 0W    01111111111111111111111111111111b
-0W    10000000000000000000000000000001b
 0Wj   0111111111111111111111111111111111111111111111111111111111111111b
-0Wj   1000000000000000000000000000000000000000000000000000000000000001b
```

Consequently, we find:

```
        32767=0Wh
1b

        2147483647j=0W
1b

        -32767=-0Wh
1b

        -2147483647j=-0W
1b
```

3.9.6 Match

Match is a different story because type matters:

```
        42~0w    / can try to match a numeric value to infinity
0b

        0w~42%0  / can match infinity to itself
1b

        0~0N     / 0 does not match an missing integer
0b

        0~0n     / 0 does not match missing float
0b

        0w~0W    / float infinity does not match int infinity
0b

        0w~0N    / infinity does not match missing integer
0b

        0w~0n    / infinity does not match missing float
0b

        0Nj~0N   / missing long and missing int do not match
0b

        0N~0n    / missing int and missing float do not match
0b
```

3.9.7 not

The `not` operator returns `0b` for all infinities and nulls since they all fail the test of equality with `0`:

```
        not 0w
0b

        not 0W
0b

        not 0N
0b

        not 0n
0b
```

3.9.8 neg

The `neg` operator returns -1 times its operand, so it reverses the sign on infinities but does nothing to nulls since sign is meaningless for missing data:

```
         neg 0W
-0W

         neg -0w
0w

         neg 0N
0N

         not " "
0b
```

3.9.9 Comparison

Comparisons apply to infinities and nulls, as summarized in the following diagram:

nulls < -0w = -0we < -0Wj < -0W < -0Wh < *numeric values* < 0Wh < 0W < 0Wj < 0we = 0w

As rules:

- The float and real infinities are equal.

- Positive float infinity is greater than any positive integral infinity.

- Positive integral infinities are ordered by their type, widest largest.

- Nulls and all negative infinities are less than all normal values which are less than all positive infinities.

- Negative float infinity is less than any integral negative infinity.

- Negative integral infinities are ordered by their type, widest least.

- Any null is less than any infinity or numeric value.

> **Note**
>
> These relations characterize the infinities, in the sense that they are larger or smaller than all normal values. The integral infinities have underlying bit patterns corresponding to legitimate base 2 values that yield the above relations. Infinite arithmetic will parse, but the results are not particularly useful. It is recommended that you limit operations on integral infinities to equals, not equals and inequalities.

Some examples:

```
    42<0W
1b

    -0w<42.0
1b

    -0w<1901.01.01
1b

    -0w<0w
1b

    0W<0w
1b

    -0w<0W
1b

    -10000000<0N
0b

    0Nj<42
1b

    0n<-0w
1b
```

The null symbol is less than any other symbol:

```
    `a<`    / the right side is the null symbol
0b
```

3.9.10 Maximum and Minimum

The behavior of | and & with infinities and nulls derives from that of equality and comparison:

```
        42|0w
0w

        -42&0N
0N

        0w|0n
0w

        -0w&0n
0n

        0n|0N
0n

        0n&0n
0n

        0W&0Wj
2147483647j
```

The last result obtains because int infinity is promoted to a long and its bit pattern corresponds to the listed value.

3.10 Alias (Advanced)

An *alias* is a variable that is defined as an expression involving other variables. This differs from ordinary assignment which defines a variable as the **result** of an expression.

3.10.1 Alias and Double assignment

Double assignment (: :) outside a function defines the left operand as an *alias* of the right operand. When the alias is referenced, the underlying expression will be (re)evaluated. For example, the following defines b as an alias for a. Observe that changing the value of a is reflected in b but not in c:

```
a:42
b::a
c:a

b
```
42

```
c
```
42

```
a:98.6
b
```
98.6

```
c
```
42

Aliasing is useful when the underlying expression represents a calculation:

```
u:4
v:3
w::v+sqrt u

w
```
5f

```
u:9
w
```
6f

The result of aliasing can also be achieved with a function. In the previous example, we could define:

```
f:{y+sqrt x}

f[4;3]
```
5f

Aliasing provides convenient variable syntax instead of function semantics, but the dependencies are more evident in the function.

Dependency chains are resolved and loops are detected:

```
a:42
b::a
c::b+1000
```

```
        b
42

        c
1042

        a:98.6
        b
98.6

        c
1098.6

        a::c
'loop
```

> **Important**
>
> Aliasing can be used to provide a view in a database by specifying a query as the right operand. An example follows.

```
        t:([]c1:`a`b`c`a;c2:20 15 10 20;c3:99.5 99.45 99.42 99.4)

        va:select sym:c1,px:c3 from t where c1=`a
        va
sym px
--------
a   99.5
a   99.4
```

3.10.2 Dependencies

Double assignment establishes a dependency of the alias on the entities in its underlying expression. For example:

```
        u:4
        v:3
        w::u+v
```

establishes a dependency of w on u and v. *q* maintains a list of dependencies in the dictionary .z.b:

```
        .z.b
u | w
v | w
```

Each entity in the domain of `.z.b` is mapped to the entities that depend on it. If we add an alias of `u` in our example, we find:

```
        .z.b
u | w z
v | w
```

> **Note**
>
> The table dependencies implicit in views are **not** reflected in `.z.b`.

```
t:([]c1:`a`b`c`a;c2:20 15 10 20;c3:99.5 99.45 99.42 99.4)
s:select c1,c3 from t where c2=20

        .z.b
u | w z
v | w
```

CHAPTER 4
FUNCTIONS

4.0 OVERVIEW

In this chapter, we cover functions in depth. Before starting, you may wish to review the mathematics refresher in **Overview** if it has been a while since your last encounter with mathematical functions.

We describe significant built-in functions in the following chapters. Other times we shall use a built-in function without introduction. Simply look it up in **Appendix A**, which contains specifics and examples of nearly all the *q* built-in functions.

4.1 FUNCTION SPECIFICATION

The notion of a function in *q* corresponds to a (mathematical) map that is specified by an algorithm. A *function* is a sequence of expressions to be evaluated, having optional input parameters and a return value. *Application* of a function is the process of evaluating the expressions in sequence, substituting actual arguments for any formal parameters. If a return value is specified, the function evaluates to its return value.

> **Advanced**
>
> Because a *q* function can access global variables, the corresponding mathematical mapping actually includes the workspace as an implicit parameter. In other words, *q* is not a pure functional language because functions can have side effects.

4.1.1 Function Definition

The distinguishing characteristic of function definition is a matching pair of braces, { and }, enclosing a sequence of expressions separated by semi-colons. In contrast to verbose languages, a function's input parameters and the return value are not typed. In fact, they don't even need to be declared explicitly. Even the function name is optional. Following is a full specification of a function that returns the square of its input:

Observe the added optional whitespace after the parameter, for readability:

```
f:{[x] x*x}
```

You call f by enclosing its actual parameter in square brackets:

```
f[3]
9
```

Here is a compact form of an equivalent function evaluation in which optional aspects are omitted:

```
{x*x}[5]
25
```

4.1.2 Function Notation and Terminology

The notation for function definition is,

```
{[p1;...;pn] e1; ...; en}
```

where the optional $p_1, \ldots, p_n$ are formal parameters and $e_1, \ldots, e_n$ is a sequence of expressions to be evaluated in left-to-right sequence.

For readability, we shall normally insert optional whitespace after the closing square bracket that closes the parameter list, as well as after each semicolon separator. Other styles may differ.

> **Note**
>
> The reason the expressions in a function are evaluated in left-to-right sequence is so that the sequence becomes top-to-bottom when the function definition is split across multiple lines. Specifically, right-to-left expression evaluation would result in the following definition,
>
> ```
> f:{[p1;...;pn]
>      e1;
>      ...;
>      en}
> ```
>
> being evaluated from bottom to top, which would be very unnatural.

The number of formal input parameters, either implicit or explicit, is the function's *valence*. Most common are monadic (valence 1) and dyadic (valence 2). You specify a function with no parameters (*niladic*) with an empty argument list:

```
{[]...}
```

> **Important**
>
> The maximum valence currently permitted is 8, so specifying more than eight arguments will cause an error. You can circumvent this restriction by encapsulating multiple parameters in a list argument.
>
> **Recommendation**
>
> *q* functions should be compact and modular: each function should perform well-defined unit of work. Due to the power of *q* operators and built-in functions, helper functions are often one-liners. When a function exceeds 20 expressions, you should ask yourself if it can be factored.

Variables that are defined within the expression(s) of a function are called *local* variables.

The *return value* of a function is the value carried by the function evaluation. It is determined by the following rules:

- If an empty assignment appears — i.e., a : with no variable name to the left — then its assignment value is returned.

- Otherwise, if any local variables are assigned, the assigned value of the last one is returned.

- Otherwise, the result of the last expression evaluation is result.

For example, the following function specifications result in the same input-output mapping:

```
f1{[x] :x*x}          / explicit return
f2{[x] r:x*x}         / local variable is returned
```

```
f3{[x] x*x}              / last expression is result
```

So does this one, even though it includes useless and unexecuted evaluations:

```
f4:{[x] a:1; :x*x; 3}
```

> **Advanced**
>
> In contrast to **k**, the **q** operators are not overloaded on valence, meaning that an operation does not have different functionality for different numbers of arguments. However, in **q** some operators (and built-in functions) are overloaded on the types of the arguments, or even the sign of the arguments. For example, to understand the exact use of (?), you must carefully examine the operands.

4.1.3 Implicit Parameters

If you omit the formal parameters and their brackets, three implicit positional parameters x, y and z are automatically available in the function's expressions. Thus, the following two specifications are equivalent:

```
f:{[x] x*x}
g:{x*x}
```

And so are:

```
f:{[x;y] x+y}
g:{x+y}
```

When using implicit parameters, x is always the first actual argument, y second and z third. The following function g generates an error unless it is called with three parameters:

```
g:{x+z}          / likely meant x+y; requires 3 parms in call

    g[1;2]       / error... needs three parameters
{z+z}[1;2]

    g[1;2;3]     / OK... 2nd value is required but ignored
```

> **Recommendation**
>
> If you use the names x, y and z in a function, reserve them for the first three parameters, either explicit or implicit. Any other use will almost certainly lead to confusion, if not to trouble.

4.1.4 Anonymous Functions

A function can be defined without being assigned to a variable. Such a function is called *anonymous* since it cannot be evaluated by name:

```
       {x+y}[4;5]
9
```

An anonymous function can be appropriate when it will be evaluated in only one location. A prevalent use is in-line helper functions within other functions:

```
    f{[...] ...; {...}[...]; ...}
```

It is arguably more readable to extract anonymous functions:

```
    g:{...}
    f:{...; g[...]; ....}
```

This is a matter of coding style.

4.1.5 The Identity Function (::)

The identity function : : returns its argument. It is useful for specifying defaults when using functional forms of amend and `select`.

> **Important**
>
> The identity function cannot be used with juxtaposition.

```
       ::[`a]
`a

       ::[1 2 3]
1 2 3
```

```
        :: 42
```

4.1.6 Functions are Nouns

The *q* entities we have met until now have been either nouns or verbs. Atoms and lists are nouns. Operators are verbs. In the following expression,

```
        a:1+L:100 200 300
```

a, L and the literals 100, 200, 300 are nouns, while the assign and plus operators are verbs.

It may come as a surprise that functions are also nouns. We can write:

```
        a:3
        f:{2*x}
        a:f
        a 3
6
```

Operators used as functions are also nouns, so continuing the previous example we can also write:

```
        L:(f;+)

        L
{2*x}
+
```

> **Note**
>
> The display of L illustrates that a function name is resolved to its body at the time of assignment. If the definition of f is subsequently modified, L will **not** change.

4.2 LOCAL AND GLOBAL VARIABLES

4.2.1 Local Variables

A variable that is defined by assignment in an expression in a function is called a *local* variable. For example, `a` is a local variable in the following function:

```
f:{a:42; a+x}
```

> **Important**
>
> As of this writing, the maximum number of local variables permitted in a function is 24.

A local variable exists only from the time it is first assigned until the completion of the enclosing function's evaluation; it has no value until it is actually assigned. Provided there is no variable `a` already assigned in the workspace, evaluation of the function does not create such a variable. Using `f` as above:

```
   f[6]
48

   a
`a
```

4.2.2 Global Variables

Variables that have been assigned outside any function definition are called *global* variables:

```
   b:6
   f:{x*b}
   f[7]
42
```

> **Important**
>
> As of this writing, the maximum number of global variables that can be referenced by name in a function is 32. If this is a problem, store the values in a dictionary (as *q* does). Better yet, redesign your code.

To assign a global variable inside a function, use a double colon (::)

which tells the interpreter not to create a local variable with the same name:

```
    b:6
    f:{b::7; x*b}
    f[6]
42

    b
7
```

4.2.3 Local and Global Collision

When a local variable is defined with the same name as a global variable, the global variable is obscured:

```
    a:42
    f:{a:98; x+a}
    f[6]
104

    a
42
```

> **Important**
>
> When local and global names collide, the global variable is always obscured. Even double colon assignment affects the local variable. An example follows.

```
    a:42
    f:{a:6; a::98; x*a}
    f[6]
588

    a
42
```

You must use `set` to assign an obscured global:

```
    a:42
    g:{a:98.6; `a set x}
```

```
        g[43]
`a

        a
43
```

4.3 AMEND (:)

4.3.1 Amend in C Language

We have already seen the basic form of assignment using amend:

```
    a:42
```

Programmers from languages with C heritage will be familiar with expressions such as

```
    x += 2;    // C expression representing amend
```

which is shorthand for:

```
    x = x + 2; // C expression
```

This is usually read simply **add 2 to x**, but more precisely is **assign to x the result of adding 2 to the current value of x**. This motivates the interpretation of such an operation as **amend**, in which x is re-assigned the value obtained by applying the operation + to the operands x and 2. By implication, a variable can only be amended if it has been previously assigned.

4.3.2 Simple Amend

In *q*, the equivalent to the above C expression uses +: as the operator:

```
    x:42
    x+:2
    x
44
```

There is nothing special about + in the above discussion. Amend is available with any binary verb, as long as the operand types are compatible:

```
        a:42
        a-:1
        a
41
```

We shall see interesting examples of amend with other operators in later chapters.

4.3.3 Amend with Lists

This capability to amend in one step extends to lists and indexing:

```
        L1:100 200 300 400

        L1[1]+:9
        L1
100 209 300 400

        L1[0 2]+:99
        L1
199 209 399 400

        L1:100 200 300 400

        L1[0 1 2]+:1 2 3
        L1
101 202 303 400

        L2:(1 2 3; 10 20 30)

        L2[;2]+:9
        L2
1  2  12
10 20 39

        L2:(1 2 3; 10 20 30)

        L2[0;1]+:100
        L2
1   102  3
10  20   30
```

> **Note**
>
> Amend enforces strict type matching with simple lists, since the result must be placed back into the list.

```
        L1[0]+:42h
`type
```

4.4 Projection

4.4.1 Function Projection

Sometimes a function of valence two or more is evaluated repeatedly while some of its arguments are held constant. For this situation, a multivalent function can have one or more arguments fixed and the result is a function of lower valence called the *projection* of the original function onto the fixed arguments. Notationally, a projection appears as a function call with the fixed arguments in place and nothing in the other positions.

For example, the dyadic function which returns the difference of its arguments,

```
        diff:{[x;y] x-y}
```

can be projected onto the first argument by setting it to 42, written as,

```
    diff[42;]
```

The projected function is the monadic function **subtract from 42**,

```
        diff[42;][6]
36
```

This projection is equivalent to:

```
        g:{[x] 42-x}

        g[6]
36
```

We can also project diff onto its second argument to get **subtract 42**:

```
        diff[;42][6]
-36
```

which is equivalent to:

```
    h:{[x] x-42}
```

When a function is projected onto any argment other than the last, the trailing semi-colons can be omitted. Given `diff` as above:

```
    diff[42][6]
36
```

> **Recommendation**
>
> It will make your intent evident if you do **not** omit trailing semi-colons when projecting. For example, with `diff` as above, a reader will immediately recognize the projection:
>
>   diff[42;][6]   / instead of diff[42][6]

The brackets denoting a function projection are required, but the additional brackets in the projection's evaluation can be omitted with juxtaposition (as for any regular function):

```
    diff[;42] 6
-36
    diff[42] 6
36
```

Which notation to use is a matter of coding style.

4.4.2 Verb Projection

A binary verb can also be projected onto its left argument, although the notation may take some getting used to. For example, the projection of - onto its left argument is:

```
    (42-)6
36
```

A verb cannot be projected onto its right argument, since this would lead to notational ambiguity. For example, `(-42)` is the atom `-42` and not a projection:

```
    (-42)
-42
```

If you really want to project onto the right argument of an operator, you can do so by using the dyadic function form and juxtaposition of the argument:

```
        -[;42] 98
56
```

In fact, whitespace is not necessary in the above example:

```
        -[;42]98
56
```

We warned you about the notation.

4.4.3 Multiple Projections

When the original function has valence greater than two, it is possible to project onto multiple arguments simultaneously. For example, given,

```
        f:{x+y+z}
```

we can project f into its first and third arguments and end up with a monadic function:

```
        f[1;;3][5]
9
```

We arrive at the same result by taking the projection f[1;;] — now a dyadic function — and projecting onto its second argument to arrive at f[1;;][;3]:

```
        f[1;;][;3][5]
9
```

This is equivalent to projecting in the reverse order:

```
        f[;;3][1;][5]
9
```

> **Note**
> If g is defined as a projection of f and the definition of f is changed, g remains the projection of the original f.

```
        f:{[x;y] x-y}
        g:f[42;]

        g
{[x;y] x-y}[42;]

        g[6]
36

        f:{[x;y] x+y}

        g[6]
36
```

This can be seen by displaying g on the console:

```
        g
{[x;y] x-y}[42;]
```

4.5 LISTS AND FUNCTIONS AS MAPS

This section explores the deeper relationship between lists and functions. While it can be skipped on first reading by the mathematically faint of heart, that would be like not eating your vegetables when you were a kid.

4.5.1 Similarity of Notation

You have no doubt noticed that the notation for list indexing is identical to that for function evaluation. That is:

```
        L:(0 1 4 9 16 25 36)
        f:{[x] x*x}

        L[2]
4

        f[2]
4

        L 5
25

        f 5
25
```

```
        L 3 6
9 16

        f 3 6
9 16
```

This is not an accident. In §2.5 we saw that a list is a map defined by means of the implicit input-output correspondence given by item indexing. A function is a map defined by a sequence of expressions representing the algorithm used to obtain an output value from the input parameters. For consistency, the two different mechanisms for implementing a map do have the same notation. It may take a little time to get accustomed to the rationality of *q*.

4.5.2 Item-wise Extension of Atomic Functions

With the interpretation of lists and functions as maps, we can motivate the behavior of list indexing and function application when a simple index or atomic parameter is replaced by a simple list of the same. Specifically, we are referring to,

```
        L[2 5]
4 25

        f[2 5]
4 25
```

in the previous examples. The expression enclosed in brackets is a simple list; call it I. Viewing the list I as a map, the two expressions are the composition of L and I, and the composition of f and I:

```
    L[2 5]    is    (L[2]; L[5])

    f[2 5]    is    (f[2]; f[5])
```

For a general list L, function f and item index list I, the compositions are:

```
    L·I(j) = L(ij)

    f·I(j) = f(ij)
```

4.5.3 Indexing at Depth and Ragged Arrays

Next, we show the deeper correspondence between list indexing and multivalent function evaluation. Notationally, a nested list is a list of lists, but it can also be viewed functionally as a compact form of the input-output relationship for a multivariate map. This mapping transforms tuples of integers onto the constituent atoms of the list and has valence equal to one plus the level of nesting of the list. For example, a list with no nesting is a monadic map of integers to its atoms via item indexing:

```
L1:(1;2h;`three;"4")

L1[3]
"4"
```

A list with one level of nesting can be viewed as an irregular (or ragged) array by laying its rows out one above another. For example, the list L2 specified as,

```
L2:((1b;2j;3.0);(4.0e;`five);("6";7;0x08;2000.01.10))
```

can be thought of as a ragged array. The console display does just this:

```
L2
(1b;2j;3f)
(4e;`five)
("6";7;0x08;2000.01.10)
```

This representation of a ragged array is a generalization of the I/O table for monadic maps. From this perspective, indexing at depth is a function whose output value is obtained by indexing into the ragged array via position. In other words, the output value L2[i;j] is the jth element of the ith row:

```
L2[1;0]
4e
```

This motivates the interpretation of L2 as dyadic map over a sub-domain of the two-dimensional Cartesian product of non-negative integers and with range equal to the atoms of L2. The duple *i,j* is mapped positionally, analogous to simple item indexing.

> **Advanced**
>
> It is possible create a ragged array of a given number of rows or columns using 0N as the number of rows using 0N with the reshape operator (#). See example following.

```
        2 0N#til 10
0 1 2 3 4
5 6 7 8 9

        0N 3#til 10
0 1 2
3 4 5
6 7 8
,9
```

4.5.4 Projection and Index Elision

You may have noticed that the notations of function projection and elided indices in a list are identical. Revisiting the example of elided indices we used in **§2.6,**

```
L :((1 2 3;4 5 6 7);(`a`b`c`d;`z`y`x`;`0`1`2);("now";"is";"the"))
```

define the list L1 by eliding the first and last index as:

```
        L1:L[;1;]
        L1
4 5 6 7
`z`y`x`
"is"
```

Viewing L as a map of valence three whose output value is obtained by indexing at depth, this makes L1 the projection of L onto its second argument. From this perspective, L1 is a dyadic map that retrieves values from a sub-list:

```
        L1[1;2]
`x
```

4.5.5 Out of Bounds Index

The previous discussion also motivates the explanation for the behavior of item indexing in case an **out of bounds** index is presented. In verbose languages, this would either result in some sort of error — the infamous indexing off the end of an array in C — or an exception in Java and C#.

By viewing a list as a function defined on a sub-domain of integers, it is reasonable to extend the domain of the function to all integers by assigning a null output value to any input not in the original domain. In this context, null should be thought of as **missing value.** This is exactly what happens.

In the following examples, observe that the type of null returned matches the item type for simple lists and is 0N for a general list:

```
    L1:1 2 3
    L1[-1]
0N

    Lf2:100.1 200.2 300.3 400.4
    Lf2[100]
0n

    L3:"abcde"
    L3[-1]
" "

    L4:1001101b
    L4[7]
0b

    L5:(1;`two;3.0e)
    L5[5]
0N
```

4.6 CREATING STRINGS FROM DATA

As mentioned earlier, *q* strings are simple lists of char, which play a role similar to strings in verbose languages. It is possible to convert data into strings, akin to the toString() method in O-O languages.

The function string can be applied to any *q* entity to produce a textual representation suitable for display or use in external contexts such as text editors, Excel, etc. In particular, the string result does not contain any *q* formatting information. Also, note that the result of string is always a list of char. Following are some examples:

```
    string 42
"42"

    string 6*7
"42"

    string 42422424242j
"42422424242"

    string `Zaphod
"Zaphod"
```

See **Appendix A** for more details on `string`.

4.7 Adverbs

Syntactically *q* has nouns, verbs and adverbs. Data entities such as atoms, lists, dictionaries and tables are nouns. Functions are also nouns. Primitive symbol operators and operations expressed in infix notation are verbs. For example, in the expression,

```
c:a+b
```

`a`, `b` and `c` are nouns, while `:` and `+` are verbs. On the other hand, in

```
c:+[a;b]
```

`a`, `b`, `c` and `+` are nouns, while `:` is a verb.

An *adverb* is an entity that modifies a verb or function to produce a new verb or function with behavior derived from the original. The following adverbs are available in *q*:

```
Symbol      Name
--------    ------
'           each both
each        each monadic
/:          each right
\:          each left
/           over
\           scan
':          each previous
```

> **Note**
> The character that represents each is the single quote (') that is distinct from the back-tick (`) used with symbols.

4.7.1 each-both (')

Loosely speaking, the adverb each-both (') modifies a verb or function by applying its behavior item-wise to corresponding list elements. This concept is similar to the manner in which an atomic verb or function is extended to lists.

> **Important**
>
> There cannot be any whitespace between ' and the verb it modifies.

Perhaps the most common example of each is join-each (, ') which concatenates two lists item-wise. In its base form, join takes two lists and returns the result of the second appended to the first:

```
        L1:1 2 3 4
        L2: 5 6

        L1,L2
1 2 3 4 5 6
```

Two lists of the same count can be joined item-wise to form pairs:

```
        L3:100 200 300 400

        L1,'L3
1 100
2 200
3 300
4 400
```

As in the case of item-wise extension of atomic functions, the two arguments must be of the same length, or either can be an atom:

```
        L1,'1000
1 1000
2 1000
3 1000
4 1000

        `One,'L1
`One 1
`One 2
`One 3
`One 4

        "a" ,' "z"
"az"
```

When both arguments of a derived function are atoms, the adverb has no effect:

```
        3,'4
3 4
```

> **Advanced**
>
> A useful example of join-each arises when both arguments are tables. Since a table is a list of records, it is possible to apply join-each to tables with the same count. The item-wise join of records results in a sideways join of the tables.

```
        t1:([] c1:1 2 3)
        t2:([] c2:`a`b`c)
        t1
c1
--
1
2
3
        t2
c2
--
a
b
c
        t1,'t2
c1 c2
-----
1  a
2  b
3  c
```

4.7.2 Monadic each

There is a form of each that applies to monadic functions and unary operators. It applies a (non-atomic) function to each element of a list. Monadic each can be notated in two equivalent ways for a monadic function f,

```
f each
```

```
each[f]
```

The latter form underscores the fact that `each` transforms a function into a new function:

```
        reverse each (1 2;`a`b`c;"xyz")
2 1
`c`b`a
"zyx"

        each[reverse] (1 2;`a`b`c;"xyz")
2 1
`c`b`a
"zyx"
```

The transform is arguably more readable when the base operation is a projection:

```
        (1#) each 1001 1002 1004 1003
1001
1002
1004
1003

        each[1#] 1001 1002 1004 1003
1001
1002
1004
1003
```

Observe that the result of the last example can also be obtained with `enlist`:

```
        enlist each 1001 1002 1004 1003
1001
1002
1004
1003

        flip enlist 1001 1002 1004 1003
1001
1002
1004
1003
```

The last expression executes fastest for long lists.

4.7.3 each-left (\:)

The each-left adverb \: modifies the base function so that it applies the entire second argument to each item of the first argument.

> **Important**
>
> There cannot be any whitespace between \: and the verb it modifies.

To append a given string to every string in a list:

```
        ("Now";"is";"the";"time") ,\: ", "
"Now, "
"is, "
"the, "
"time, "
```

4.7.4 each-right (/:)

The each-right adverb /: modifies the base function so that it applies the entire first argument to each item of the second argument.

> **Important**
>
> There cannot be any whitespace between /: and the verb it modifies.

To prepend a given string to every string in a list:

```
        " ," ,/: ("Now";"is";"the";"time")
" ,Now"
" ,is"
" ,the"
" ,time"
```

4.7.5 Cartesian Product (,/:\:)

To achieve a Cartesian (cross) product of two lists, begin with join-right ,/: and modify it with each-left. The net effect is to join every item of the first argument with every element of the second argument:

```
    L1:1 2
    L2:`a`b`c

    L1,/:\:L2
1 `a 1 `b 1 `c
2 `a 2 `b 2 `c
```

There is an extra level of nesting that can be eliminated with `raze`:

```
    raze L1,/:\:L2
1 `a
1 `b
1 `c
2 `a
2 `b
2 `c
```

You can also begin with join-left `,\:` and modify it with each-right:

```
    raze L1,\:/:L2
1 `a
2 `a
1 `b
2 `b
1 `c
2 `c
```

Observe that the orders of the resulting items for `,/:\:` and for `,\:/:` are transposed.

> **Note**
>
> Cartesian product is also encapsulated in the function `cross`.

```
    L1 cross L2
1 `a
1 `b
1 `c
2 `a
2 `b
2 `c
```

121

4.7.6 Over (/)

The over adverb / modifies a base dyadic function so that the items of the second argument are applied iteratively to the first argument.

> **Important**
>
> There cannot be any whitespace between / and the function it modifies.

To add multiple items to another entity:

```
        L:100 200 300

        ((L+1)+2)+3
106 206 306

        L+/1 2 3
106 206 306

        0+/10 20 30         / easy way to add a list
60
```

To raze a list:

```
        L1:(1; 2 3; (4 5; 6))
        (),/L1
1
2
3
4 5
6
```

To use your own function:

```
        f:{2*x+y}
        100 f/ 1 2 3
822
```

> **Advanced**
>
> To delete multiple items from a dictionary, see below.

```
        d:1 2 3!`a`b`c
        d _/1 3
2| b
```

4.7.7 Scan (\)

The scan adverb \ modifies a base dyadic function so that the items of the right operand are applied cumulatively to the left operand.

> **Important**
>
> There cannot be any whitespace between \ and the function it modifies.

To find running sums:

```
        100+\1 2 3
101 103 106

        0+\10 20 30     / easy way to find running sums of list
10 30 60
```

To use your own function:

```
        f:{2*x+y}

        100 f\ 1 2 3
202 408 822
```

4.7.8 each-previous (':)

The each-previous adverb ': modifies a base dyadic function so that each item of the right operand is applied to its predecessor. The left operand of the adverb is taken as the predecessor for the initial item.

> **Important**
>
> There cannot be any whitespace between ': and the function it modifies.

To find the running 2-item sum with 0 before the initial item:

```
    0+':1 2 3 4 5
1 3 5 7 9
```

More interesting is to determine the positions where items decrease in value:

```
    0w>':8 9 7 8 6 7
010101b

    -0w>':8 9 7 8 6 7
110101b
```

The left operand controls the initial result. The first expression results in initial `0b` for all numeric lists, while the second results in initial `1b`. Why?

4.7.9 Pay No Attention to the *k* behind the Adverbs

We have previously seen that `/`, `\` and `':` are used to iterate a function over a list. In these usages, the result of applying an adverb to a dyadic function is a related dyadic function whose left argument is the initial value and whose right argument is the list of values to iterate over the function.

There is an alternate form in which applying the adverb to a dyadic function results in a related monadic function that takes the initial item in the list as its initial value and then iterates over the remaining items of the list with the original function. While the dyadic form is more general and it can always obtain the same results, in some situations the monadic form is simpler or more intuitive.

> **Important**
>
> The rub is that the monadic versions are not present in *q*; instead they are part of *k*, the underlying implementation language of *q*. Because the monadic forms are actually in *k*, you must convince the *q* parser to accept them. One way to do this is to enclose the modified function in parentheses, which allows the parser to interpret it as *k*.

A few simple examples should clarify things:

```
    0+/1 2 3 4                     / q dyadic version
10
```

```
        (+/)1 2 3 4              / k monadic version
10
        0+\1 2 3 4               / q dyadic version
1 3 6 10
        (+\)1 2 3 4              / k monadic version
1 3 6 10
        0-':1 2 3 4              / q dyadic version
1 1 1 1
        (-':)1 2 3 4             / k monadic version
1 1 1 1
```

Of course, you can use your own dyadic function:

```
        f:{x+2*y}
        (f/)1 2 3 4
19
        (f\)1 2 3 4
1 5 11 19
```

It is also possible to force the *q* parser to accept the monadic forms by enclosing the arguments in [and]. In other words, don't use juxtaposition:

```
        +/[1 2 3]
6
        +\[1 2 3]
1 3 6
```

> **Note**
>
> Many of the built-in aggregate and uniform functions are simply covers for the monadic version of adverbs applied to common operators.
>
> ```
>         sum 1 2 3 4             / q aggregate
> 10
>         (+/)1 2 3 4             / k over
> 10
> ```

```
    sums 1 2 3 4         / q uniform
1 3 6 10
    (+\)1 2 3 4          / k scan
1 3 6 10
    prd 1 2 3 4          / q aggregate
24
    (*/)1 2 3 4          / k over
24
    prds 1 2 3 4         / q uniform
1 2 6 24
    (*\)1 2 3 4          / k scan
1 2 6 24
    deltas 1 2 3 4       / q uniform
1 1 1 1
    (-':)1 2 3 4         / k scan
1 1 1 1
```

4.8 Verb Forms of Indexing and Evaluation

We are familiar with the syntactic forms of indexing and function application using either square brackets or juxtaposition:

```
    L:(1 2;3 4 5; 6)
    L[0]
1 2
    L[0 2]
1 2
6
    L 0 2
1 2
6
    L[1;2]
5
```

```
        f:{x*x}
        f[0]
0
        f[0 2]
0 4
        f 0 2
0 4
        g:{x+y}
        g[1;2]
3
```

There are equivalent verb forms for indexing and function application. The verb forms are read **index** or **apply** depending on the context.

4.8.1 Verb @

The verb @ takes a list or a unary function as its left operand and a list of indices or a list of arguments as its right operand. For a list operand, @ returns the items specified by the right operand — i.e., indexing at the top level. For a function operand, @ returns the result of applying the function to the arguments item-wise.

With L and f as above:

```
        L@0
1 2
        L@0 2
1 2
6
        f@0
0
        f@0 4
0 16
```

Evaluating a niladic function with @ requires an arbitrary scalar operand:

```
        fn:{6*7}
        fn[]
42
```

```
    fn@0N
42
```

> **Advanced**
>
> The verb @ also applies to dictionaries, tables and keyed tables. For dictionaries and keyed tables it performs lookup. Since a table is a list of records, it indexes records.

```
    d:`a`b`c!10 20 30
    d@`b
20
    t:([]c1:1 2 3; c2:`a`b`c)
    L@1
c1| 2
c2| `b
    kt:([k:`a`b`c]f:1.1 2.2 3.3)
    kt@`c
f| 3.3
```

4.8.2 Verb Dot (.)

The verb . takes a list or a multivalent function as its left operand and a list of indices or a list of arguments as its right operand. For a list left operand, verb . returns the result of indexing the list at depth as specified by the right operand. For a function left operand, verb . returns the result of applying the function to the arguments.

> **Important**
>
> Verb . must be separated from its operands by whitespace if they are names or literal constants.

With L and g as above:

```
        L . 1 2
5

        g . 1 2
3
```

The verb . evaluates functions of any valence. This is useful when the function or arguments are supplied programmatically and the valence cannot be known beforehand.

> **Note**
>
> The right argument of . must be a list.

```
        f . 4
'type

        f . enlist 4
16
```

Use the null item : : to elide an index when using verb . to index at depth:

```
        m:(1 2 3;4 5 6)

        m[;1]
2 5

        m . (::;1)
2 5
```

Evaluating a niladic function with . requires a singleton operand, which is arbitrary:

```
        fn:{6*7}

        fn[]
42

        fn . enlist 0N
42
```

> **Advanced**
>
> Verb . provides a generalization of indexing at depth for complex entities comprised of general lists, dictionaries, tables and keyed tables. Perhaps the easiest way to understand its action is to view all such entities as composite mappings. Verb . evaluates the composite map by iteratively applying indexing/lookup on each item of the right operand to the result of the previous step.

The use of verb . in the first following complex is list indexing in all positions; in the second, the middle item is a lookup:

```
L1:(1;2 3;(4; 5 6))

L1 . 2 1 1
6

L2:(1;2 3;`a`b!(4;5 6))

L2 . (2;`b;1)
6
```

In the following complex dictionary, the first use of verb . yields lookup followed by indexing, whereas the second use is two lookups:

```
dd:`a`b`c!(1 2;1.1 2.2 3.3;`aa`bb!10 20)

dd . (`a;1)
2

dd . (`c`bb)
20
```

Because a table is a list of records, verb . indexes a record on the first item and then performs a field lookup on the second:

```
t:([]c1:1 2 3;c2:`a`b`c)

t . (1;`c2)
`b
```

Because a keyed table is a dictionary mapping between two tables, verb . performs key lookup on the first item and then a field lookup on the second:

```
    kt:([k:`a`b`c]f:1.1 2.2 3.3)
    kt . `b`f
2.2
```

4.9 FUNCTIONAL FORMS OF AMEND

The functions @ and . can be used with valence three or four to apply any function to an indexed sublist and an optional second argument. The fact that the list can be a table that may be stored on disk makes this very powerful.

4.9.1 Apply (@) for Dyadic Functions

The form of functional @ for a dyadic function is,

```
@[L;I;f;y]
```

While the notation is suggestive of lists, in fact L can be any mapping with explicit domain such as a list, dictionary, table, keyed table or handle to a table on disk. Then I is a list of items in the domain of the map, f is a dyadic function and y is an atom or list conforming to I. When L is a list, the result is the item-wise application to the items of L, **indexed at the top level** by I, of f and the parameter y. Over the subdomain I, the map output becomes:

```
    L[I] f y        / written as binary verb

    f[L[I];y]       / written as dyadic function
```

Or, using verb @ for indexing,

```
    (L@I) f y       / written as binary verb

    f[L@I;y]        / written as dyadic function
```

For example, to add 42 to certain items in a list:

```
    L:100 200 300 400
    I:1 2

    @[L;I;+;42 43]
100 242 342 400
```

To replace these items:

```
        @[L;I;:;42 43]
100 42 43 400
```

Observe that the argument L is unchanged:

```
        L
100 200 300 400
```

In order to change L, it must be referenced by name:

```
        @[`L;I;:;42 43]        / update L
`L

        L
100 42 43 400
```

> **Note**
>
> The result of functional amend with a reference by name is a symbol containing the name of the entity affected, and should not be confused with an error message.
>
> **Advanced**
>
> As mentioned previously, L can be a dictionary, a table, or even a handle to a table on disk. In the general case, the result f[L@I;y] is applied along the subdomain.

```
        d:`a`b`c!10 20 30

        @[d;`a`c;+;9]
a| 19
b| 20
c| 39

        t:([] c1:`a`b`c; c2:10 20 30)

        @[t;0;:;(`aa;100)]
```

```
c1 c2
------
aa 100
b  20
c  30
```

4.9.2 Apply (@) for Monadic Functions

The form of functional @ for a monadic function on a list is:

```
@[L;I;f]
```

Again the notation is suggestive of lists, but L is any map with explicit domain, I is a list of items in the domain of L, and f is a monadic function. When L is a list, the result is the item-wise application of f to the items of L **indexed at the top level** by I. Over the subdomain I, the map output becomes:

```
f L[I]   / written as unary verb

f[L[I]] / written as monadic function
```

Or, using the verb form of @,

```
f[L@I]
```

For example:

```
    L:101 102 103
    I:0 2

    @[L;I;neg]
-101 102 -103
```

> **Advanced**
>
> In the general case, the result f[L@I] is applied along the subdomain.

```
    d:`a`b`c!10 20 30
```

```
        @[d;`a`c;neg]
a| -10
b| 20
c| -30
```

4.9.3 Dot (.) for Dyadic Functions

The form of functional . for a dyadic function is:

```
.[L;I;f;y]
```

Again the notation is suggestive of lists, but L is a mapping with explicit domain, I is a list in the domain of L, f is a dyadic function and y is an atom or list of the proper shape. For a list, the result is the item-wise application to the items of L **indexed at depth** by I, of f and the parameter y. Over the subdomain I, the map output becomes:

```
(L . I) f y      / binary operator

f[L . I;y]       / dyadic function
```

For example, to add along a sublist:

```
        L:(100 200;300 400 500)
        I1:1 2
        I2:(1;0 2)

        .[L;I1;+;42]
100 200
300 400 542

        .[L;I2;+;42 43]
100 200
342 400 543
```

To replace the same items:

```
        .[L;I2;:;42 43]
100 200
42 400 43
```

Observe that the argument L is not modified:

```
        L
100 200
300 400 500
```

In order to change `L`, it must be referenced by name:

```
    L:(100 200 300;300 400 500)

    .[`L;I;:;42]            / update L
`L

    L
100 200 300
300 400 42
```

> **Note**
>
> The result of functional amend with a reference by name is the name of the entity affected, not an error message.
>
> **Advanced**
>
> In the general case, the result `f[L . I;y]` is applied along the subdomain.

```
    d:`a`b`c!(100 200;300 400 500;600)

    .[d;(`b;1);+;42]
a| 100 200
b| 300 442 500
c| 600
```

4.9.4 Dot (.) for Monadic Functions

The form of functional `.` for a monadic function on a list is:

```
    .[L;I;f]
```

Again the notation is suggestive of lists, but `L` is any map with explicit domain, `I` is a list in the domain of `L`, and `f` is a monadic function. For a list, the result is the item-wise application of `f` to the items of `L` **indexed at the depth** level by `I`. Over the subdomain `I`, the map output becomes:

```
f[L . I]
```

For example:

```
        L:(100 200;300 400 500)
        I:1 2

        .[L;I;neg]
100 200
300 400 -500
```

> **Advanced**
>
> In the general case, the result `f[L . I]` is applied along the subdomain.

```
        d:`a`b`c!(100 200;300 400 500;600)

        .[d;(`b;1 2);neg]
a| 100 200
b| 300 -400 -500
c| 600
```

CHAPTER 5
CASTING AND ENUMERATIONS

5.1 TYPES AND CAST

Casting manifests the malleability of data. In some cases, such as changing a symbol to a string, this is obvious and straightforward. Converting a char to its underlying ASCII code or converting a datetime to a float require a little more consideration. Enumerations also fit into the cast pattern.

5.1.1 Basic Types

Every atom has associated char, numeric and symbolic data types. For convenience, we repeat the data types table from **Chapter 1**:

type	type symbol	type char	type num
boolean	`boolean	b	1h
byte	`byte	x	4h
short	`short	h	5h
int	`int	i	6h
long	`long	j	7h
real	`real	e	8h
float	`float	f	9h
char	`char	c	10h
symbol	`	s	11h
month	`month	m	13h
date	`date	d	14h
datetime	`datetime	z	15h
minute	`minute	u	17h
second	`second	v	18h
time	`time	t	19h

5.1.2 type

The monadic function `type` can be applied to any entity in *q* to find its (numeric) short data type. It is a quirk of *q* that the data type of an atom is a short with the **negative** of the value in the fourth column above.

```
-6h       type 42

-1h       type 1b

-9h       type 4.2

-5h       type 4h

-11h      type `42

-10h      type "4"

-14h      type 2007.04.02
```

Observe that infinities also have type:

```
-6h       type 0W

-9h       type -0w
```

The type of a simple list is a short containing the **positive** value of the type of its constituent atoms:

```
6h        type 1 2 3

10h       type "abc"

9h        type 1 2 3f
```

The type of any general list is 0:

```
0h        type (1;2h;3j)
```

```
        type (1;2;(3 4))
0h

        type (`1;"2";3)
0h
```

5.1.3 Type of a Variable

How *q* handles the type of a variable may be confusing to those coming from verbose languages. In many typed languages, the variable's type must be specified before the variable is assigned a value — that is, when it is declared. In *q*, a variable is assigned without declaration. The variable can subsequently be reassigned a new value of a different type:

```
        a:42
        type a
-6h

        a:98.6
        type a
-9h
```

This can be understood by considering that *q* considers a variable to be a name (symbol) associated with a value. The association is made upon assignment. A variable has the type of the value associated with its name.

In the example at hand, a variable with name a is created when the initial assignment is made. Since this is the first time that the name a is assigned, the *q* interpreter creates an entry for a in its dictionary of variable names and associates it with the int value 42. On the second assignment, there is already an entry for a in the dictionary, so this name is simply re-associated with the float value 98.6.

When you ask *q* for the type of a variable, it returns the type of the value associated with the variable's name. Thus, after you reassign the variable, the type of the variable reflects the type of its new value.

5.1.4 Cast ($)

As in verbose languages, it is possible to cast an entity from one type to another, provided the underlying values are compatible. Such a cast informs the compiler that you want it to consider the variable to be of the specified type for subsequent operations. Such a cast may result in a compile-time or run-time error if it can not be performed.

The *q* cast operator, denoted $, is a binary verb that is atomic in its right operand *source* value, and whose left operand is the *target* type. The *target* can be represented in any of three type designators in the table of **§5.1.1**:

- The type's (positive) numeric short value.
- A char type value.
- A type name symbol.

First, examples using the numeric type:

```
        5h$42
42h

        6h$4.2
4
```

This form is useful when the target type is obtained programmatically using the `type` function. It is arguably more readable to use the type char in a cast:

```
        "i"$4.2
4

        "x"$42
0x2a

        "d"$2004.04.02T04:02:24.042
2004.04.02
```

The most readable (but longest) form uses the symbolic type name:

```
        `int$4.2
4

        `short$42
42h

        `date$2004.04.02T04:02:24.042
2004.04.02
```

The result of casting between superficially distinct types can be derived by considering the underlying numeric values. Chars correspond to their underlying ASCII sequence; dates to their offset from Jan 1, 2000; and times to their count of milliseconds.

```
        "c"$0x42
"B"
```

```
        `date$42
2000.02.12
```

Because cast is atomic in its right operand, it is extended item-wise to a list:

```
        "x"$(10 20 30;255)
0x0a141e
0xff
```

Cast is also atomic in its left operand:

```
        5 6 7h$42
42h
42
42j
```

> **Advanced**
>
> When integral infinities are cast to integers of wider type, they are considered to be their underlying bit patterns. Since these bit patterns are legitimate values for the wider type, the cast results in a finite value.

```
        "i"$0Wh
32767

        "i"$-0Wh
-32767

        "j"$-0W
-2147483647j

        "j"$0W
2147483647j
```

5.1.5 Creating Symbols from Strings

Casting from a string (i.e., a list of char) to a symbol is a convenient way to create symbols. It is the preferred way to create symbols with embedded blanks or other special characters. To cast a char or a string to a symbol, use the empty symbol (`` ` ``) as the target domain:

```
        `$"z"
`z

        `$"Zaphod Beeblebrox"
`Zaphod Beeblebrox

        `$"Zaphod \"Z\""
`Zaphod "Z"

        `$("Life";"the";"Universe";"and";"Everything")
`Life`the`Universe`and`Everything
```

Cast is atomic in both operands.
    A string is trimmed as part of the cast:

```
        `$"   abc   "
`abc

        string `$"   abc   "
"abc"
```

5.1.6 Parsing Strings to Data

Cast can also be used to parse data from a string by using an upper case type char in the left argument:

```
        "I"$"4267"
4267

        "T"$"23:59:59.999"
23.59.59.999
```

Date string parsing is flexible with respect to the format of the date:

```
        "D"$"2007-04-24"
2007.04.24

        "D"$"12/25/2006"
2006.12.25

        "D"$"07/04/06"
2006.07.04
```

5.1.7 Coercing Types

Casting can be used to coerce type-safe assignment. Recall that assignment into a simple list must strictly match the type:

```
        c:10 20 30 40

        c[1]:42h
`type
```

This situation can arise when the list and the assignment value are created dynamically. You can coerce the type by casting it to that of the target:

```
        c[1]:(type c)$42h
        c
10 42 30 40

        c[0 1 3]:(type c)$(1.1; 42j; 0x2a)
        c
1 42 30 42
```

5.2 CREATING TYPED EMPTY LISTS

We met the empty list in **Chapter 2**. Observe that it has type 0h, meaning that is a general list whose elements have no specific type:

```
        type ()
0h
```

This empty list can be considered as the degenerate case of a general list, so we call it the *general empty list*. In situations where type enforcement is desired, it is necessary to have an empty list with a specific type. Casting the general empty list using a symbolic type name makes this clear:

```
        L1:`int$()
        type L1
6h

        L2:`float$()
        type L2
9h
```

```
        L3:`$()
        type L3
-11h
```

A typed empty list is the degenerate case of a simple list of the specified type. This is useful because type matching is enforced when you append items:

```
        L1,:4.2
'type
        L1,:42
        L1
,42
```

5.3 ENUMERATIONS

We have seen that the dyadic cast operator ($) transforms its right operand into a conforming entity of type specified by the left operand. In the basic operation, the left operand can be a char type abbreviation, a type short, or a symbol type name. In this section, casting is extended to user-defined target domains, providing a functional version of enumerated types.

5.3.1 Traditional Enumerations

To begin, recall that in verbose languages, an enumerated type is a way of associating a series of names with a corresponding set of integral values. Often the sequence of numbers is consecutive and begins with 0. The specific set of names/values is called the domain of the enumerated type and its name identifies the enumeration.

A traditional enumerated type serves multiple purposes:

- It allows a descriptive name to be used instead of an arbitrary number — e.g., 'blue' instead of 3.

- It permits strong type checking to ensure that only permissible values are supplied — i.e., choosing a named color from a list instead of remembering its number is less prone to error.

- It can provide name spaces, meaning the same name can be reused in different domains without fear of confusion — e.g., color.blue and note.blue.

There is also a subtler, more powerful use of enumerations: normalizing data.

5.3.2 Data Normalization

Broadly speaking, data normalization seeks to eliminate duplicates and retain the minimum amount of data. Suppose you know that you will have a list — in either the colloquial or *q* sense — of text entries taken from a fixed and reasonably short set of values. Storing a long list of such strings verbatim presents two problems:

- Values of variable length complicate storage management.

- There is potentially much duplication of data arising from repeated values.

An enumeration solves both problems.

To see how, we start with the case of a *q* list v containing arbitrary symbols. Let u be the unique values in v. This is achieved with the `distinct` function (see **Appendix A** for a description):

```
u:distinct v
```

Let's try a simple example:

```
    v:`c`b`a`c`c`b`a`b`a`a`a`c
    u:distinct v

    u
`c`b`a
```

Observe that order of the items in u is the order of their first appearance in v.

Now consider a new list k that represents the positions in u of each of the items in v. This is achieved with the find (?) operator (See **§2.8.6**):

```
    k:u?v

    k
0 1 2 0 0 1 2 1 2 2 2 0
```

Then we have:

```
    u[k]
`c`b`a`c`c`b`a`b`a`a`a`c
```

```
        v~u[k]
1b
```

We observe that `u` and `k` indeed normalize the data of `v`. In general, `v` will have many repetitions of each of the underlying values, but `u` stores each value once. Changing an underlying value requires only one operation in the normalized version but potentially many updates to the non-unique list.

Extra credit for recognizing that `v` is simply the composite map $u \cdot k$. Effectively, we have factored the map of the non-unique list `v` through the unique list `u` via the index map `k`:

$$v = u \cdot k$$

Why would we want to do this? Easy: compactness and speed.

> **Advanced**
>
> Let's say that the count of `u` is a and the maximum width (in the colloquial sense) of the symbols in `u` is b. For a list `v` of variable count x, the amount of storage required is potentially
>
> $b*x$
>
> For the factored form, the storage is known to be,
>
> $a*b+4*x$
>
> which represents the fixed amount of storage for `u` plus the variable amount of storage for the simple integer list `k`. If a is small and b is even moderately large, the factorization is significantly smaller.
>
> This can be seen by comparing the sizes of `v`, `u` and `k` in a slightly modified version of our example, below.

```
        v:`ccccccc`bbbbbbb`aaaaaaa`ccccccc`ccccccc`bbbbbbb
        u:distinct v

        u
`ccccccc`bbbbbbb`aaaaaaa

        k:u?v

        k
0 1 2 0 0 1
```

Now imagine v and k to be much longer. Reading and writing the factored index list from/to disk is a block operation that will be very fast.

Assuming that items of v are symbols stored in a hash-table, item indexing in the un-factored list requires looking up each symbol. Indexing into the factored list can be done directly via position since it is a uniform list of integers. This will be faster.

5.3.3 Enumerations

Enumeration encapsulates the above factorization of an arbitrary list of symbols through a list of unique values. An enumeration uses the binary cast operator ($) and is a generalization of the basic cast between types. The general form of an enumerated value is,

```
`u$v
```

where u is a simple list of unique symbol values and v is either an atom in u or a list of such. The projection `u$ is the *enumeration*, u is the *domain* of the enumeration and `u$v represents the *enumerated value(s)*.

Under the covers, applying the enumeration `u$ to a vector v actually factors v through u as in the previous section. The resulting index list k is stored internally and the lookup is performed automatically.

5.3.4 Working with an Enumeration

We recast our factorization example as an enumeration:

```
u:`c`b`a
v:`c`b`a`c`c`b`a`b`a`a`a`c
ev:`u$v

ev
`u$`c`b`a`c`c`b`a`b`a`a`a`c
```

While the display of the enumeration ev shows the values of v within the domain u, only the implicit int index list is actually stored. The enumeration ev acts just like the original v:

```
    v[3]
`c

    ev[3]
`u$`c
```

```
        v[3]:`b
    v
`c`b`a`b`c`b`a`b`a`a`a`c

        ev[3]:`b
    ev
`u$`c`b`a`b`c`b`a`b`a`a`a`c

        v=`a
001000101110b

        ev=`a
001000101110b

        v in `a`b
011101111110b

        ev in `a`b
011101111110b
```

> **Note**
>
> While the enumeration is item-wise equal to — and can be freely substituted for — the original, they are **not** identical.

```
        v=ev
111111111111b

        v~ev
0b
```

The find operator (?) can be used with an enumeration to locate the first position of specific values:

```
        v?`a
2

        ev?`a
2
```

The function where can be used to find all occurrences of a specific value:

```
      where v=`a
2 6 8 9 10

      where ev=`a
2 6 8 9 10
```

5.3.5 Updating an Enumeration

The normalization provided by an enumeration reduces updating all occurrences of a value to a single operation. This can have significant performance implications for large lists with many repetitions.

With u, v and e as above:

```
      u[1]:`x

      ev
`u$`c`x`a`c`c`x`a`x`a`a`a`c

      v
`c`b`a`c`c`b`a`b`a`a`a`c
```

To make the equivalent update to v, it is necessary to change **every** occurrence:

```
      v[where v=`b]:`x

      v
`c`x`a`c`c`x`a`x`a`a`a`c
```

5.3.6 Appending to an Enumeration

One situation in which an enumeration is more complicated than working with the denormalized data is when you want to add a new value. Continuing with the example above, appending a new item to v is a single operation but this is not the case for the corresponding enumeration ev:

```
      u:`c`b`a
      v:`c`b`a`c`c`b`a`b`a`a`a`c
      ev:`u$v

      v,:`d

      v
`c`b`a`c`c`b`a`b`a`a`a`c`d
```

```
        ev,:`d
'cast
```

What went wrong? The new value must first be added to the unique list:

```
        u,:`d
        ev,:`d

        ev
`u$`c`b`a`c`c`b`a`b`a`a`a`c`d
```

You may have recognized that this presents a complication in practice. Because you may not know whether the value to be appended to v is already in u, in order to maintain uniqueness in u you must test this before appending.

Fortunately, *q* has anticipated this situation. When dyadic ? is used with the **name** of a (simple) list of symbols as its left argument and a symbol as its right argument, it appends the symbol to the list if and only if it is not an item in the list:

```
        u
`c`b`a`d

        `u?`a
`u$`a

        u
`c`b`a`d

        `u?`e
`u$`e

        u
`c`b`a`d`e
```

If you wish to append items to an enumerated value programmatically, simply add to the unique list using ? before appending to the enumerated value.

```
        u:`c`b`a
        v:`c`b`a`c`c`b`a`b`a`a`a`c
        ev:`u$v

        `u?`e
`u$`e
```

150

```
    ev,:`e
    u
`c`b`a`e

    ev
`u$`c`b`a`c`c`b`a`b`a`a`a`c`e
```

5.3.7 Resolving an Enumeration

If you are given an enumerated value, you can recover the original value by applying `value`. In our example:

```
    ev
`u$`c`b`a`c`c`b`a`b`a`a`a`c`e

    value ev
`c`b`a`c`c`b`a`b`a`a`a`c`e
```

5.3.8 Type of an Enumeration

Each enumeration is assigned a new numeric data type, beginning with 20h. If you start a new *q* session and load no script files, you will observe the following:

```
    u1:`c`b`a
    u2:`2`4`6`8
    u3:`a`b`c
    u4:`c`b`a

    type `u1$`c`a`c`b`b`a
20h

    type `u1$`a`a`b`b`c`c
20h

    type `u2$`8`8`4`2`6`4
21h

    type `u3$`c`a`c`b`b`a
22h

    type `u4$`c`a`c`b`b`a
23h
```

> **Note**
>
> Enumerations with distinct domains are distinct, even when the domains match.

```
        u1~u4
1b

        v:`c`a`c`b`b`a

        (`u1$v)~`u4$v
0b
```

CHAPTER 6
DICTIONARIES

6.0 OVERVIEW

Dictionaries are generalizations of lists and provide the foundation for tables. A dictionary is a (mathematical) mapping defined by an explicit I/O association between a domain list and range list. The two lists must have the same count and the domain list should be a unique collection. While general lists can be used to create a dictionary, many useful dictionaries involve lists of special forms. The domain is frequently a collection of symbols representing names. As we shall see, a dictionary whose domain is a unique list of symbols and whose range is rectangular corresponds to a table.

6.1 DICTIONARY BASICS

A dictionary is an ordered collection of key-value pairs — that is, a hashtable in verbose languages.

6.1.1 Definition

A *dictionary*, also called an *association*, is a mapping defined by an explicit I/O association between a domain list and a range list via positional correspondence. Creation of a dictionary uses the xkey primitive (!),

$$L_{domain} ! L_{range}$$

Recall from §0.2 the view of a map's I/O table as a pair of input and output columns. Dictionary notation is simply the map's I/O table turned on its side for ease of entry and compactness of display.

> **Note**
>
> All dictionaries have type 99h.

The domain list comprises the *keys* of the dictionary and the range list its *values*. The keys of a dictionary are retrieved by the unary primitive `key` and the values by the unary primitive `value`. The *count* of the dictionary is the (common) count of its keys or values.

> **Note**
>
> Although *q* does not enforce the requirement that the key items are unique, a dictionary does provide a unique output value for each input value, thus guaranteeing a well-defined mathematical map. See below for details.

The most basic dictionary maps a simple list to a simple list. The following I/O table represents a mapping of three symbols containing names to the corresponding individual's intelligence quotient:

```
I                O
---              ---
`Dent            98
`Beeblebrox      42
`Prefect         126
```

This mapping is defined compactly as a dictionary:

```
        d:`Dent`Beeblebrox`Prefect!98 42 126

        count d
3

        key d
`Dent`Beeblebrox`Prefect

        value d
98 42 126
```

The console displays a dictionary I/O table in columnar form:

```
            d
Dent       | 98
Beeblebrox | 42
Prefect    | 1263
```

The function `cols` also returns the domain:

```
        cols d
`Dent`Beeblebrox`Prefect
```

> **Note**
>
> The order of the items in the domain and range lists is significant, just as positional order is significant for lists. Although the I/O assignments and the associated mappings are equivalent regardless of order, differently ordered dictionaries are **not** identical.

```
        d1:`Prefect`Beeblebrox`Dent!126 42 98

        d~d1
0b
```

6.1.2 Lookup

Finding the dictionary output value corresponding to an input value is called *looking up* the input. This actually is achieved via a hash-table lookup under the covers. Similar to functions and lists, the notations `d[x]` and `d x` lookup the output value for x:

```
        d[`Beeblebrox]
42

        d `Beeblebrox
42
```

As with item indexing, lookup of a key not in the domain of a dictionary results in an appropriately typed null value, **not** an error:

```
        d[`Slartibartfast]
0N
```

As with lists and functions, key lookup in a dictionary is extended item-wise to a simple list of keys:

```
        d[`Dent`Prefect]
98 126
```

> **Advanced**
>
> We can interpret key list lookup as the composition of the key lookup map with the item indexing map. Symbolically, let d be a dictionary and K a key list in the domain of d. Then for $0 \leq j <$ count K:
>
> ```
> d[K][j] = d[K[j]]
> ```

Using one of our examples:

```
    d:`Dent`Beeblebrox`Prefect! 98 42 126
    K:`Dent`Prefect

    d[K][1]
126

    d[K[1]]
126
```

Or, using the entire index list:

```
    d K
98 126

    d[K]
98 126
```

6.1.3 Dictionary vs. List

A dictionary is a generalization of a list in which item indexing has been extended to a non-integral domain. In particular, a dictionary cannot be indexed implicitly via position. Attempting this on any dictionary generates an error:

```
    d:"abcde"!1.1 2.2 3.3 4.4 6.5

    d["c"]
3.3

    d[0]
`type
```

We can define a dictionary whose lookup emulates the mapping of list item indexing:

```
        L3:`one`two`three

        L3[1]
`two

        d3:0 1 2!`one`two`three

        d3[1]
`two
```

When we ask *q* to compare the two entities for equality, it obliges by considering both as mappings with integral domain. It then tests the assignments item-wise:

```
        L3=d3
0| 1
1| 1
2| 1
```

However, the dictionary so specified is **not** the same as the list:

```
        L3~d3
0b
```

Although retrieving items from a list-like dictionary is notationally identical to item indexing, it is not the same. Item indexing is a positional offset, whereas dictionary retrieval is a lookup. They are implemented differently under the covers.

6.1.4 Lookup with Verb @

Recall that indexing into a list can be achieved with verb @ as:

```
        L:100 200 300

        L[1]
200

        L@1
200
```

The same syntax works for dictionary lookup:

```
        d:`a`b`c!10 20 30
```

```
        d[`b]
20

        d@`b
20
```

6.1.5 Uniqueness of Keys

We noted earlier that *q* does not enforce uniqueness in a dictionary domain list. In the event of a repeated domain item, only the output value associated with the first occurrence in left-to-right order is accessible via lookup. This guarantees that a dictionary provides a unique output for each input value and is thus a well-defined mathematical map. For example:

```
        ddup:8 4 8 2 3 1!`one`two`three`four`five`six

        ddup[8]
`one
```

> **Advanced**
>
> Reverse lookup works properly for a non-unique domain.

```
        ddup?`three
8
```

6.1.6 Non-simple Domain or Range

The range values of a dictionary are not required to be atoms. The range can be a general list that contains nested lists:

```
        dgv:(1;2h;3.3;"4")!(`one;2 3;"456";(7;8 9))

        dgv["4"]
7
8 9
```

Nor are keys required to be atoms:

```
        dgk:(0 1; 2 3)!`first`second
```

```
        dgk[0 1]
`first

        dgk[2 3]
`second
```

> **Advanced**
>
> If the keys are not a list of items of uniform shape, lookup does not work in a useful way.

```
        dweird:(0 1; 2; 3)!`first`second`third

        dweird[0 1]
`first

        dweird[2]
`

        dweird[3]
`
```

The observed behavior is that key lookup fails at the first key of different shape.

6.1.7 Extracting a Sub-Dictionary by Key

Dictionary lookup on a key or a list of keys returns the associated values. It is also possible to extract the key-value associations using the take operator (#). The left operand is a **list** of keys, the right operand is the *source* dictionary and the result is a new dictionary whose mapping is that of *source* restricted to the specified keys:

```
        (enlist `c)#d
c| 30

        `a`c#d
a| 10
c| 30
```

This works when the keys are not simple:

```
        dns:(1 2; 3 4; 5 6)!("onetwo"; "threefour"; "fivesix")
```

```
        (1 2; 5 6)#dns
1 2| "onetwo"
5 6| "fivesix"
```

6.2 OPERATIONS ON DICTIONARIES

6.2.1 Amend and Upsert

As with lists, the items of a dictionary can be modified via indexed assignment:

```
        d:10 20 30!"abc"

        d[30]:"x"
        d
10| a
20| b
30| x
```

> **Important**
>
> In contrast to lists, dictionaries **can** be extended via index assignment.

For example:

```
        d[40]:"y"

        d
10| a
20| b
30| x
40| y

        L:"abc"

        L[3]:"x"
'length
```

Let's examine this capability to modify or extend a dictionary via index assignment more closely. Let d be a dictionary, c be an atom whose type matches the domain of d, and x an item whose type is compatible with the range of d. The assignment,

```
d[c]:x
```

updates the existing range value if c is in the domain of d, but inserts a new entry at the end of the dictionary if c is not in the domain of d.

This insert/update behavior is called *upsert* semantics. Because tables are essentially dictionaries, upsert semantics carry through to tables.

6.2.2 Reverse Lookup with Find (?)

Recall that the dyadic primitive find (?) returns the index of the right operand in a list:

```
      1001 1002 1003?1002
1
```

Extending this concept to dictionaries means reversing the domain-to-range mapping. We expect ? to perform reverse lookup by mapping a range element to its domain element:

```
      d:`a`b`c!1001 1002 1003

      d?1002
`b
```

The result of find on an entity not in the range is a null whose type matches the domain list. For simple domain lists, the null matches the type of the list; for general domain lists, the null is 0N:

```
      d?1004          / the result is the null symbol `
`

      dg:(1;`a;"z")!10 20 30

      dg?50
0N
```

> **Note**
> For a non-unique range element, find returns the *first* item mapping to it.

```
      d:`a`b`c`d!1001 1002 1003 1002
```

161

6.2.3 Removing Entries

The binary operation delete (_) returns the result of removing an entry from a dictionary by key value. The left operand of delete is the dictionary (*target*) and the right operand is a key value whose type matches that of *target*.

> **Note**
>
> Whitespace is required to the left of _ if the first operand is a variable.

For example:

```
        d:1 2 3!`a`b`c

        d _ 2
1| a
3| c
```

Observe that attempting to remove a key that does not exist has no effect:

```
        d _ 42
1| a
2| b
3| c
```

The binary delete, also denoted by an underscore (_), returns the result of removing multiple entries from a dictionary. The left operand of delete is a list of key values whose type matches that of the dictionary and the right operand is the dictionary (*target*). The result is a dictionary obtained by removing the specified key-value pairs from *target*.

> **Note**
>
> Whitespace is also required to the left of _ if the first operand is a variable. Note also, since the left operand is required to be a list, a single key value must be enlisted.

For example:

```
        d:1 2 3!`a`b`c

        (enlist 2)_d
1| a
3| c

        1 3_d
2| b

        (enlist 42)_d
1| a
2| b
3| c
```

Attempting to remove a key that does not exist has no effect:

```
        4 5_d
1| a
2| b
3| c
```

Observe that removing all the entries in a dictionary leaves a dictionary with empty domain and range lists of the appropriate types:

```
        1 2 3_d
_
```

The binary operator `cut` is the same as (_) on a dictionary:

```
        (enlist 2) cut d
1| a
3| c
```

6.2.4 Primitive Operations

Because dictionaries are maps, it is possible to compose their mappings with function mappings to perform operations on dictionaries. Of course, this assumes that the range of each dictionary is in the domain of the indicated operation, so that the operation makes sense. The application of a unary operator is straightforward:

```
      d1:`a`b`c!1 2 3

      neg d1
a| -1
b| -2
c| -3

      2*d1
a| 2
b| 4
c| 6

      d1=2
a| 0
b| 1
c| 0
```

When the domains of two dictionaries are identical, performing binary operations is also straightforward. For example, to add two dictionaries with a common domain, add their corresponding range elements:

```
      d2:`a`b`c!10 20 30

      d1+d2
a| 11
b| 22
c| 33
```

How do we operate on two dictionaries whose domains are not identical? First, the domain of the resulting dictionary is the union of the domains of its operands. For items in the intersection of the domain lists, clearly we should simply apply the indicated operation on the corresponding range items.

The real question is, what to do on non-common domain items? The answer: do what makes sense for the operation. We start with joining two dictionaries.

6.2.5 Join

In the simple case of joining two disjoint dictionaries, the result should be the merge:

```
      d3:`e`f`g!100 200 300

      d1,d3
```

```
a| 1
b| 2
c| 3
e| 100
f| 200
g| 300
```

```
     d3,d1
e| 100
f| 200
g| 300
a| 1
b| 2
c| 3
```

Observe that although the mappings arising from opposite-order joins have equivalent input-output assignments, the dictionaries are not identical because order is significant.

We examine another simple example of joining dictionaries with a special form. The particular dictionaries map symbols to lists of simple lists. When the two are disjoint, the result should be the merge. For example:

```
dc1:`a`b!(1 2 3; 10 20 40)
dc2:(enlist `c)!enlist 10 20 30
```

```
   dc1,dc2
a| 1  2  3
b| 10 20 40
c| 10 20 30
```

As in the previous eample, join simply appends the domains and ranges in the obvious way. We shall refer to this case later.

Now we tackle the case of merging non-disjoint dictionaries. The issue is how to merge items that are common to both dictionary domains, since these elements each have two I/O assignments.

> **Important**
>
> In a join of dictionaries, the right operand's I/O assignment prevails for common domain elements.

This is another illustration of upsert semantics. Each I/O assignment of the right operand is applied as an update if the domain element is assigned in the left operand, or as an insert if the domain element is not already assigned. With d1 as above:

```
      d3:`c`d!33 44

      d1,d3
a|  1
b|  2
c|  33
d|  44
```

Observe that upsert is not commutative, even over a common domain. Join order matters:

```
      d4:`a`b`c!300 400 500

      d1,d4
a|  300
b|  400
c|  500

      d4,d1
a|  1
b|  2
c|  3
```

6.2.6 Arithmetic Operations

Now that we understand how to join two dictionaries, we examine other operations. When arithmetic and comparison operations are performed on dictionaries, the indicated operation is performed on the common domain elements and the dictionaries are merged elsewhere:

```
      d5:`c`x`y!1000 2000 3000

      d1+d5
a|  1
b|  2
c|  1003
x|  2000
y|  3000

      d1*d5
```

```
a| 1
b| 2
c| 3000
x| 2000
y| 3000


    d1|d5
a| 1
b| 2
c| 1000
x| 2000
y| 3000
```

When a relational operation is performed on two dictionaries, the indicated operation is performed over the entire union domain. Effectively, each dictionary is extended to the union domain with (type-matched) nulls. Otherwise put, for non-common domain items, the operation is performed on a pair of items in which a type-matched null is substituted for the missing range item.

In the following examples, observe that operations on d1 and d6 are equivalent to the corresponding operations on d11 and d66:

```
    d1:`a`b`c!1 2 3
    d6:`b`c`d`e!22 3 44 55

    d1=d6
a| 0
b| 0
c| 1
d| 0
e| 0

    d1<d6
a| 0
b| 1
c| 0
d| 1
e| 1

    d6<d1
b| 0
c| 0
d| 0
e| 0
a| 1
```

```
        d1>d6
b| 0
c| 0
d| 0
e| 0
a| 1


        d11:`a`b`c`d`e!1 2 3 0N 0N
        d66:`a`b`c`d`e!0N 22 3 44 55

        d11=d66
a| 0
b| 0
c| 1
d| 0
e| 0

        d11<d66
a| 0
b| 1
c| 0
d| 1
e| 1

        d66<d11
a| 1
b| 0
c| 0
d| 0
e| 0

        d11>d66
a| 1
b| 0
c| 0
d| 0
e| 0
```

> **Note**
>
> The > operation is evidently converted to the equivalent < operation with reversed operands.

6.3 COLUMN DICTIONARIES

Column dictionaries are the foundation for tables.

6.3.1 Definition and Terminology

A very useful type of dictionary is one that maps a simple list of symbols to a rectangular list of lists. Such a dictionary has the form,

$c_1 \ldots c_n ! (v_1; \ldots; v_n)$

where each c_i is a symbol and the v_i are lists with common count. Such a dictionary associates the symbol c_i with the list of values v_i.

Interpreting each symbol as a column name and the corresponding list as a vector of column values, we call such a list a *column dictionary*. The *type* of the column named by c_i is the type of the list v_i. For many column dictionaries, the v_i are all simple lists, meaning that each column is a vector of atoms of uniform type. We call this a *simple column dictionary*.

6.3.2 Simple Example

Let's reorganize a previous example as a simple column dictionary:

```
scores:`name`iq!(`Dent`Beeblebrox`Prefect;42 98 126)
```

In this dictionary, the values for the *name* column are:

```
scores[`name]
`Dent`Beeblebrox`Prefect
```

It's possible to retrieve the values for a column in a column dictionary using dot notation:

```
scores.name
`Dent`Beeblebrox`Prefect
```

The value in row 1 of the *name* column is:

```
scores[`name][1]
`Beeblebrox
```

Similarly, the value in row 2 of the *iq* column is:

```
scores[`iq][2]
126
```

The dictionary console shows the mapping clearly:

```
        scores
name| Dent Beeblebrox Prefect
iq  | 98   42        126
```

6.3.3 Accessing Values

For a general column dictionary defined as,

$$d_{cols}: c_1 \ldots c_n ! (v_1; \ldots; v_n)$$

the ith element of column c_j is retrieved by,

$$d_{cols}[c_j][i]$$

What should we make of the following notation?

$$d_{cols}[c_j; i]$$

We can interpret it in three ways:

- Indexing at depth in the dictionary.

- A generalization of a two dimensional matrix in which item indexing in the first dimension has become lookup into the list of column names.

- A dyadic mapping.

All interpretations are equivalent and give the same result,

$$d_{cols}[c_j][i]$$

In our example:

```
        scores[`iq][2]
126
```

```
        scores[`iq; 2]
126
```

6.3.4 Rows and Columns

Viewing the dictionary as a dyadic function, we can project onto its first argument by fixing it to obtain a monadic function — i.e., $d_{cols}[c_j;]$. This projected form yields item indexing into the column list.

In simple terms, projecting onto a first argument name retrieves the corresponding vector of column values from a column dictionary:

```
        scores[`iq;]
42 98 126
```

Analogously, we would expect projection onto the second argument to retrieve a "row" corresponding to the values in the ith position of each column vector. What form does such a row take?

Observe that projection of the dyadic function onto its second argument by fixing the item index,

```
    d_cols[;i]
```

is a monadic function corresponding to generalized indexing by column name — i.e., dictionary lookup. Thus, we expect the ith row to be a dictionary that maps each column name to the value in that column's i^{th} row. This is exactly what we find:

```
        scores[;2]
name|  `Prefect
iq  |  126
```

Notational differences aside, this resembles the result of retrieving a record from a table using a SQL query: we get the column names and the associated row values.

A column dictionary seems to be the right structure to serve as the basis for a table: a generalized matrix with indexed rows and named columns. But you no doubt notice the fly in the ointment: the indices are in the wrong order. It is unnatural to retrieve a column in the first index and a row in the second.

6.3.5 Column Dictionary with a Single Column

The domain of a column dictionary must be a **list** of symbols and the range must be a **list** of column vectors. Consequently, when there is only one column you must enlist the domain and range. The following **is** a valid column dictionary (the parentheses are necessary):

```
    ds:(enlist `c)!enlist 1 2 3
```

The following dictionary that maps a symbol to a list is **not** a valid column dictionary:

```
dnot:`c!1 2 3
```

6.4 Flipping a Dictionary

6.4.1 Transpose of a Column Dictionary

A column dictionary can be viewed as a generalized rectangular matrix. Let d be a column dictionary defined as,

$$d: c_1 \ldots c_n!\, (v_1;\ldots;v_n)$$

where c_i is a symbol and the v_i have common count, say m. We can index at depth into d for each c_i and each j,

$$d[c_i;j] \text{ is } v_i[j]$$

Since all the v_i have count m, in analogy with matrices, it makes sense to define the transpose t of d by,

$$t[j;c_i] \text{ is } d[c_i;j]$$

Exactly what is t that is so defined? The answer comes from realizing that indexing at depth into t should be the same as repeated indexing:

$$t[j;c_i] \text{ is } t[j][c_i]$$

The right hand side of this equality makes explicit that t is a list of n items t[j], for $0 \le j < n$.

What is each item in the list t? Combining the three previous equalities, we see that,

$$t[j][c_i] = v_i[j]$$

Now fix j in this equation. We see that t[j] is a dictionary with the same domain as d, meaning the list of c_i. This dictionary assigns to each item c_i the output value $v_i[j]$. Thus, the range of the dictionary is the collection of values:

$v_1[1], \ldots, v_n[j]$.

We summarize our findings:

- The transpose of a column dictionary is a list of dictionaries.

- The dictionaries in the transpose have as common domain the column names of the original dictionary.

- The dictionary in the jth item of the transpose maps the column names to the jth row of values across the column vectors.

6.4.2 Flip of a Column Dictionary

As in the case of lists, the transpose of a dictionary is obtained by applying the unary `flip` operator,

```
flip d
```

When `flip` is applied to a column dictionary, no data is actually rearranged. The console display confirms the transposition of rows and columns:

```
      d:`name`iq!(`Dent`Beeblebrox`Prefect;98 42 126)

      flip d
name         iq
--------------
Dent         98
Beeblebrox   42
Prefect      126
```

The net effect of flipping a column dictionary is simply reversing the order of the indices. This is logically equivalent to transposing rows and columns.

6.4.3 Flip of a Flipped Column Dictionary

If you transpose a dictionary twice, you should obtain the original dictionary, and you do:

```
      d~flip flip d        / true for any column dictionary d
1b
```

q FOR MORTALS | DICTIONARIES

Consequently, if you are given `t` as the transpose of a column dictionary and you flip it, you obtain a column dictionary:

```
t:flip d         / pretend you didn't see this step

     flip t
name| Dent Beeblebrox Prefect
iq  | 98   42        126
```

> **Advanced**
>
> As of this writing, `flip` has been implemented in *q* for dictionaries of columns, although the operation makes sense for any rectangular dictionary. In the event that `flip` is implemented for a general rectangular dictionary (i.e., any dictionary in which the range is a list of lists all having the same count) we would find the following:
>
> - The transpose of a rectangular dictionary is a list of dictionaries. The dictionaries in the transpose have a common domain that is the domain of the original dictionary. The jth dictionary of the transpose maps the original domain to the jth row of values across the range list.
>
> In this case, data likely will be rearranged.

CHAPTER 7
TABLES

7.0 OVERVIEW

Tables form the basis for kdb+. A table is basically a collection of named columns implemented as a dictionary. Consequently, *q* tables are column-oriented, in contrast to the row-oriented tables in relational databases. Moreover, a column's values in *q* comprise an **ordered** list; this contrasts to SQL, in which the order of rows is undefined. The fact that *q* tables comprise ordered column lists makes kdb+ very efficient at storing, retrieving and manipulating sequenced data. One important example is data that arrives in time sequence.

Kdb+ handles relational and time series data in the unified environment of *q* tables. There is no separate data definition language, no separate stored procedure language and no need to map internal representations to a separate form for persistence. Just *q* tables, expressions and functions.

Tables are built from dictionaries, so it behooves the cursory reader to review **Chapter 6** before proceeding.

7.1 TABLE DEFINITION

7.1.1 Table is the flip of Column Dictionary

You undoubtedly realized at the end of **Chapter 6** that a table is implemented as a column dictionary that has been flipped (i.e., transposed). The **only** effect of flipping the column dictionary is to reverse the order of its indices; no data is rearranged under the covers.

> **Note**
> All tables have type 98h.

For example:

```
d:`name`iq!(`Dent`Beeblebrox`Prefect;98 42 126)
```

```
        d[`iq;]
98 42 126

        d[;2]
name| `Prefect
iq  | 126

        d[`iq; 2]
126

        t: flip `name`iq!(`Dent`Beeblebrox`Prefect;98 42 126)

        t[;`iq]
98 42 126

        t[2;]
name| `Prefect
iq  | 126

        t[2;`iq]
126
```

To access items in a table t created by flipping a column dictionary d, simply reverse the order of the arguments in the projections of d. We also reverse the roles of *i* and *j* compared to **Chapter 6** to make things more natural from the table perspective:

```
t[i;]   / row i is dictionary mapping column names to values

t[i]    / i^th element of list t...same as previous

t[;cj]  / vector of column values for column cj
```

This validates the implementation of a table as a flipped column dictionary. Retrieving rows and columns conforms to conventional matrix notation in which the first index denotes the row and the second index the column.

7.1.2 Table Display

Observe that rows and columns of a table display are indeed the transpose of the dictionary display, even though the internal data layout is the same:

```
        d
name| Dent Beeblebrox Prefect
iq  | 98   42         126
```

```
t
name        iq
-----------------
Dent        98
Beeblebrox  42
Prefect     126
```

7.1.3 Table Definition Syntax

Table definition can also be accomplished using a syntax that manifests the columns,

$$([\,]\ c_1:L_1;\ \ldots;\ c_n:L_n)$$

Here c_i is a symbol containing a column name and L_i is the corresponding list of column values. The L_i are lists of equal count, but in some circumstances can be atoms. The purpose of the square brackets is to specify a primary key and will be explained in **§7.3**.

> **Note**
>
> For readability, we shall normally include optional whitespace after the closing square bracket and to the right of semicolon separators.

In our example, we can define t as:

```
        t:([] name:`Dent`Beeblebrox`Prefect; iq:98 42 126)

        t[;`iq]
98 42 126

        t[2;]
name|  `Prefect
iq  |  126

        t[2;`iq]
126
```

Defining t syntactically yields the same result as creating the column dictionary and flipping it. It is arguably simpler and clearer.

The value columns can be stored in variables, which is useful for programmatic table definition.

```
        c1:`Dent`Beeblebrox`Prefect
        c2:98 42 126
        t:([] c1; c2)

           t
c1         c2
--------------
Dent       98
Beeblebrox 42
Prefect    126
```

> **Note**
>
> When **all** L_i are singleton lists — that is, you are defining a table with a single row — they must be enlisted.

```
        tt:([] c1:`a; c2:100)
'type

        tt:([] c1:enlist `a; c2:enlist 100)
```

> **Note**
>
> When **at least one** column is a list and one or more columns are atoms, each atom column is extended into a list whose count matches the other columns. This appears to assign a default value, but is only valid during definition.

```
        tdef:([] c1:`a`b`c; c2:42; c3:1.1 2.2 3.3)

        tdef
c1 c2 c3
--------
a  42 1.1
b  42 2.2
c  42 3.3
```

> **Advanced**
>
> If you create a table as the flip of a column dictionary, item-wise extension of an atom column is not performed on the dictionary definition but **is** performed when the column dictionary is flipped into a table.

```
        ddef:`c1`c2`c3!(`a`b`c;42;1.1 2.2 3.3)

        ddef
c1| `a`b`c
c2| 42
c3| 1.1 2.2 3.3

        flip ddef
c1 c2 c3
---------
a  42 1.1
b  42 2.2
c  42 3.3
```

7.1.4 Table Metadata

The column names of a table can be retrieved by using the unary `cols`:

```
        t:([] name:`Dent`Beeblebrox`Prefect; iq:98 42 126)

        cols t
`name`iq
```

Recall that it is possible to retrieve the column values in a column dictionary using dot notation. This is also true after it is flipped to a table. For a table `t` and a column `c`, the expression `t.c` retrieves the value list for column `c`. In our example,

```
        t.name
`Dent`Beeblebrox`Prefect

        t.iq
98 42 126
```

the dot effectively disassociates a column's values from its name.

The function `meta` can be applied to a table `t` to retrieve its metadata. The result is a keyed table with one record for each column in `t`. The key column `c` of the result contains the column names. The column `t` contains a symbol denoting the (lower case) type char of the column. The column `f` contains the domains of any foreign keys. The column `a` contains any attributes associated with the column:

```
        meta t
```

```
c   | t f a
----| -----
name| s
iq  | i
```

> **Advanced**
>
> If the result of meta displays an **upper** case type char for a column, this indicates that column is a **non-simple** list in which each item is a list of the corresponding type. Such tables arise, for example, when you group without aggregating in a select.

```
        t:([] sc:1 2 3; nsc:(1 2; 3 4; 5 6 7))

        t
sc nsc
-------
1  1 2
2  3 4
3  5 6 7

        meta t
c   | t f a
----| -----
sc  | i
nsc | I
```

> **Advanced**
>
> The function tables takes a symbol representing a context (see **Chapter 11**) and returns a sorted list of symbol names of the tables in that context. For example:
>
> tables `.
> `s#`t`tt
>
> lists all the tables in the default context. Alternatively, the command \a provides the same result. If no parameter is provided, it returns the result for the current context.

7.1.5 Records

We observe that `count` returns the number of rows in the table because each row is an item in the list. In our example:

```
t:([] name:`Dent`Beeblebrox`Prefect; iq:98 42 126)

count t
```
3

Now let's inspect the sequence of dictionaries that comprise the rows:

```
     t[0]
name| `Dent
iq  | 98

     t[1]
name| `Beeblebrox
iq  | 42
```

The dictionary in each row maps the common domain list of column names to the column values of the row. This motivates calling each row dictionary a *record* in the table.

> **Important**
>
> A table is a sequentially ordered list of records. Each record is an association of column names with one row's values.

Sometimes it is useful to separate a record's values from its column names. In this context, we shall refer to the *row value list*. The row value list for the ith row of a table is obtained by retrieving the ith item of each of the column vectors. This is simply the range of the record dictionary:

```
     value t[1]
`Beeblebrox
42
```

7.1.6 Flipped Column Dictionary vs. List of Records

Is a table a flipped column dictionary or a list of records? Logically it is both, but physically it is stored as a column dictionary with a flipped indicator.

To verify this, we create a list of records, each of which is a dictionary that maps (common) column names to a row's values:

```
lrows:(`name`iq!(`Dent;98); `name`iq!(`Beeblebrox;42))
```

While this list is apparently different from the equivalent column dictionary, observe the curious result when you display the list of rows:

```
           lrows
name        iq
-------------
Dent        98
Beeblebrox  42
```

The *q* interpreter has recognized that this list conforms to the requirements for a list of records of a table — i.e., the domain lists of all the dictionaries are the same, the range lists have common count, and the types of the range lists are consistent by position. It has converted the list of dictionaries to a flipped column dictionary by reorganizing the values that we specified record-by-record into column vectors.

Now that we understand that a table is logically both a list of dictionary records and a flipped column dictionary, let's investigate a simple case the trips up *q* newbies. We start with a simple dictionary and enlist it to create a singleton list containing the dictionary:

```
d:`a`b!1 2
L:enlist d
```

What is the value of type L?

```
        type L
98h
```

If you answered 0 as the type of a general list, join the club. Why does L have the type of a table? Displaying L provides the clue:

```
        L
a b
---
1 2
```

So, *q* says L is a table. Why? The answer is that d has the form of a very simple column dictionary. Indeed, it is the same as extracting the first record from the following table:

```
        t:([] a:1 20; b:2 20)

        t[0]
a| 1
b| 2

        t[0]~d
1b
```

With this understanding, we now realize why the enlist of d is a table: it is a list of one record, otherwise known as a one-row table:

```
        ([] a:enlist 1; b:enlist 2)~enlist d
1b
```

> **Advanced**
>
> In general, column retrieval and manipulation on a simple column dictionary will be significantly faster than operations on rows. The values in a simple column are stored contiguously, whereas the values in each row must be retrieved by indexing into all columns.

Be mindful that deletion of a row is an expensive operation because all the column lists must be compressed to close the resulting gap. This can result in large amounts of data being moved in a table with many rows.

7.2 Empty Tables and Schema

We saw in the previous section that a table can be defined and populated in one step using table syntax:

```
        t:([] name:`Dent`Beeblebrox`Prefect; iq:98 42 126)
```

In practice, this is infrequently done with individual values other than for small tests. The values are often deferred to run-time or the lists may be prohibitively long to type at the keyboard. In these circumstances, it is useful to create an empty table initially and then populate it later. The empty parentheses here signify the empty list:

```
        t:([] name:(); iq:())
```

The table could then be populated, for example, by reading the values from a file.

When an empty table is created as above, the columns are lists of general type, so data of any type can initially be loaded. The type of each column is determined by the type of the first item placed in it. Thereafter, type checking is enforced for all inserts and updates, with **no** type promotion performed.

It is possible to fix the type of any column in an empty table definition by specifying a null list of the appropriate type:

```
t:([] name:`symbol$(); iq:`int$())
```

Shorter, and arguably less obvious:

```
t:([] name:0#`; iq:0#0N)
```

> **Note**
> Either of the previous two forms of empty table definition is the *q* version of the table's schema.

7.3 BASIC SELECT AND UPDATE

We shall use the following definition in this section:

```
t:([] name:`Dent`Beeblebrox`Prefect; iq:98 42 126)
```

7.3.1 Syntax of select

We shall cover `select` in depth in **Chapter 8**, but we provide an introduction here in order to extract and display data in our examples. The basic `select` expression takes the form,

```
select cols from table
```

where *table* is either a table or a keyed table and *cols* is a comma-separated list of columns from *table*. This expression results in a list of all records for the specified columns in *table*. The simplest form of select is,

```
select from table
```

which corresponds to the SQL statement,

```
SELECT * FROM table
```

In *q* you do not write the wildcard character when you want all columns in the table.

> **Note**
>
> The basic select expression may look familiar from SQL, but it should seem odd to the *q* newbie who is finally accustomed to parsing expressions right-to-left. Neither `select` nor `from` represents a function that can stand alone. Instead, they are part of a template and must always appear together.

q has a host of extensions to the basic select template whose elements appear between the `select` and `from` or after the `table` element. As we shall see in **Chapter 8**, it is possible to convert any select template to a purely functional form, although this form isn't particularly friendly to the *q* newbie.

7.3.2 Displaying the Result

Since the result of `select` is a list of records, it too is a table:

```
         select from t
name          iq
-----------------
Dent          42
Beeblebrox    98
Prefect       126
```

We shall use this method of display in what follows unless we need to see the structure of the underlying column dictionary.

7.3.3 Selecting Columns

To select specific columns, list them in the desired order, comma-separated, between `select` and `from`:

```
         select name from t
```

```
name
----------
Dent
Beeblebrox
Prefect

        select iq,name from t
i q   name
--------------
98    Dent
42    Beeblebrox
126   Prefect
```

7.3.4 Basic update

The syntax of basic `update` is similar to `select`, but named columns represent replacement by the specified values. In our example:

```
        update iq:iq%100 from t
name         iq
-----------------
Dent         0.98
Beeblebrox   0.42
Prefect      1.26
```

7.4 PRIMARY KEYS AND KEYED TABLES

7.4.1 Keyed Table

In SQL, it is possible to declare column(s) of a table as a primary key. Amongst other things, this means that the values in the column(s) are unique, making it possible to retrieve a row via its key value. These two features motivate how *q* implements a primary key.

We begin with a simple key — i.e., the key is a single column of simple type. The idea is to place the key column in a separate table parallel to a table containing the remaining columns. How to associate each key with its corresponding value record? Simple: set up a dictionary mapping between the key records and the associated value records.

A *keyed table* is a dictionary that maps each row in a table of unique keys to a corresponding row in a table of values.

7.4.2 Simple Example

Let's see how this works for our previous example. Viewing the data table as a flipped dictionary of rows will make things explicit:

```
values:flip `name`iq!(`Dent`Beeblebrox`Prefect;98 42 126)
```

Now say we want to add a key column named *eid* containing employee identifiers. We place the identifiers in a separate table. Recall from §6.3.5 that we must enlist both the column name and the value list for a column dictionary having a single column:

```
k:flip (enlist `eid)!enlist 1001 1002 1003
```

Now we establish the mapping between the two tables:

```
kt:k!values
```

Voilà! A keyed table. The console display of a keyed table lists the key column(s) on the left, separated by a vertical bar from the value columns on the right:

```
      kt
eid | name       iq
----|---------------
1001| Dent       98
1002| Beeblebrox 42
1003| Prefect    126
```

> **Note**
>
> The key mapping assumes that the key rows and value records are in corresponding order since the dictionary associates a key with the data row in the same position.
>
> **Note**
>
> The keys should normally be unique. As we have already noted, dictionary creation does not enforce uniqueness, but a value row associated with a repeat key is not be accessible via key lookup. It can be retrieved via a select on the key column.

7.4.3 Keyed Table Specification

The console display of a keyed table demonstrates how to define it in one step as a dictionary of flipped dictionaries:

```
kt:(flip (enlist `eid)!enlist 1001 1002 1003)!
    flip `name`iq!(`Dent`Beeblebrox`Prefect;98 42 126)
```

Unless you are constructing the keyed table from its constituents, it is usually simpler to use table syntax. The key column goes between the square brackets and the value columns to the right as in a normal table definition:

```
kt:([eid:1001 1002 1003]
    name:`Dent`Beeblebrox`Prefect; iq:98 42 126)
```

To define an empty keyed table, use empty key and value columns:

```
ktempty:([eid:()] name:(); iq:())
```

The empty columns can be typed with either of the following constructs:

```
ktempty:([eid:`int$()] `symbol$name:(); iq:`int$())

ktempty:([eid:0#0] name:0#`; iq:0#0)
```

7.4.4 Accessing Records of a Keyed Table

Since a keyed table is a dictionary mapping, it provides access to records in the value table via key lookup. Remember that the records in the key table and value table are dictionary mappings for their rows:

```
      kt[`eid!1002]
name| `Beeblebrox
iq  | 42
```

You can abbreviate the full dictionary specification of a key record to its key value. Our example reduces to:

```
      kt[1002]
name| `Beeblebrox
iq  | 42
```

An individual column in the value record can be accessed via repeated indexing or indexing at depth:

```
        kt[1002][`iq]
42

        kt[1002;`iq]
42
```

> **Important**
>
> The net effect of placing a key on a table is to convert item indexing of the rows to generalized indexing via key value. Otherwise put, the first index is converted from positional retrieval to key lookup.

7.4.5 Retrieving Multiple Records

Given that it is possible to lookup a single record in a keyed table by the key value,

```
    kt[1001]
```

you might think it is possible to retrieve multiple records from a keyed table via a simple list of keys. You would be wrong:

```
        kt[1001 1002]
`length
```

To lookup multiple key values in a keyed table, you must use a list of enlisted keys:

```
        kt[(enlist 1001;enlist 1002)]
name        iq
-------------
Dent        98
Beeblebrox  42
```

A fast way to do this is:

```
        kt[flip enlist 1001 1002]
name        iq
-------------
Dent        98
Beeblebrox  42
```

Another convenient way to lookup multiple keys is to index using a table having a single column with the name of the primary key and value list of the desired keys. In our example,

```
        kt[([] eid:1001 1002)]
name       iq
-----------------
Dent       98
Beeblebrox 42
```

this works because the records of the inner table are in the domain of the keyed table dictionary. See **§6.1.2** for details.

If you want to retrieve the full entries of the keyed table instead of just the value records, use the # operator:

```
     ([] eid:1001 1002)#kt
eid | name       iq
----|----------------
1001| Dent       98
1002| Beeblebrox 42
```

7.4.6 Reverse Lookup

Because a keyed table is a dictionary, it is possible to perform reverse lookup from a value to a key. In a simple example:

```
     kts:([eid:1001 1002 1003] name:`Dent`Beeblebrox`Prefect)
     kts
eid | name
----|----------
1001| Dent
1002| Beeblebrox
1003| Prefect

     kts?`Prefect
eid| 1003
```

As in the case of key lookup, you can perform reverse lookup on multiple values by encapsulating them in a single column table whose column name matches the value column in the keyed table:

```
     kts?([] name:`Prefect`Dent)
eid
----
1003
1001
```

7.4.7 Components of a Keyed Table

Since a keyed table is a dictionary mapping between the table of keys and the table of values, the functions `key` and `value` provide a convenient way to retrieve the two constituent tables:

```
        key kt
eid
----
1001
1002
1003

        value kt
name        iq
--------------
Dent        98
Beeblebrox  42
Prefect     126
```

A list containing the names of the key column(s) can be retrieved with the function `keys`:

```
        keys kt
,`eid
```

Observe that `cols` retrieves both the key and value column names for a keyed table:

```
        cols kt
`eid`name`iq
```

7.4.8 Tables vs. Keyed Tables

It is sometimes convenient to convert between a regular table having a column of (presumably) unique values and the corresponding keyed table.

The dyadic primitive `xkey` converts a table to a keyed table. The right argument of `xkey` is the table and the left operand is a symbol (or list of symbols) with the name of the column(s) to be used as the key(s):

```
t:([] eid:1001 1002 1003;
    name:`Dent`Beeblebrox`Prefect; iq:98 42 126)

t
```

```
eid  name        iq
-------------------
1001 Dent        98
1002 Beeblebrox  42
1003 Prefect     126


       `eid xkey t
eid | name         iq
----|----------------
1001| Dent         98
1002| Beeblebrox   42
1003| Prefect      126
```

Conversely, to convert a keyed table to a regular table, use `xkey` with an empty list as the left operand:

```
     kt:([eid:1001 1002 1003]
         name:`Dent`Beeblebrox`Prefect; iq:98 42 126)


       kt
eid | name         iq
----|----------------
1001| Dent         98
1002| Beeblebrox   42
1003| Prefect      126


      () xkey kt
eid  name        iq
-------------------
1001 Dent        98
1002 Beeblebrox  42
1003 Prefect     126
```

> **Note**
>
> The conversion expressions above do not affect the original table. You must refer to the table by name to modify the original.

```
       `eid xkey `t
`t

    t
```

```
eid | name       iq
----|  --------------
1001| Dent        98
1002| Beeblebrox  42
1003| Prefect    126

        () xkey `kt
`kt

        kt
eid name       iq
------------------
1001 Dent       98
1002 Beeblebrox 42
1003 Prefect   126
```

> **Advanced**
>
> It is possible to apply xkey against a column that does not contain unique values. The result is a keyed table that does not have a primary key.

```
        t:([] eid:1001 1002 1003 1001;
           name:`Dent`Beeblebrox`Prefect`Dup )

        t
eid  name
---------------
1001 Dent
1002 Beeblebrox
1003 Prefect
1001 Dup

        ktdup:`eid xkey t

        ktdup
eid | name
----|----------
1001| Dent
1002| Beeblebrox
1003| Prefect
1001| Dup
```

Duplicate key values are not accessible via key lookup,

```
            ktdup 1001
name|  Dent
```

but they are accessible via `select`:

```
        select from ktdup where eid=1001
eid  |  name
-----|  ----
1001 |  Dent
1001 |  Dup
```

7.4.9 Compound Primary Key

We understand that the *q* implementation of a SQL table with a simple key is actually a dictionary mapping between a pair of tables in which the first table has a single key column. This has a straightforward extension to a compound key.

Recall that a compound key in SQL is a collection of two or more columns that together provide a unique value for each row. To implement a compound key in *q*, we generalize the key table from a single column to multiple columns by requiring that each record in the key table has a unique combination of column values.

Here is our example redone to replace the employee id with a compound key comprising the last and first names:

```
ktc:([lname:`Dent`Beeblebrox`Prefect;
    fname:`Arthur`Zaphod`Ford];
    iq:98 42 126)
```

Observe that the console displays a compound keyed table with the key columns on the left separated by a vertical bar (|) from the value columns on the right:

```
            ktc
lname       fname  | iq
-------------------| ---
Dent        Arthur | 98
Beeblebrox  Zaphod | 42
Prefect     Ford   | 126
```

As in the case of a simple primary key, for retrieval we can abbreviate the full key record to the key value:

```
        ktc[`Dent`Arthur]
iq| 98
```

Here is how to initialize our example as an empty table:

```
ktc:([lname:();fname:()] iq:())
```

The empty keyed table can be typed with either of the following:

```
ktc:([lname:`symbol$();fname:`symbol$()] iq:`int$())
ktc:([lname:0#`;fname:0#`] iq:0#0)
```

We shall see in **Chapter 8** how to fill both key columns and data tables in a keyed table simultaneously.

For the fundamentalist, here is the same compound keyed table built from its constituent pair of tables:

```
ktc:(flip `lname`fname!
        (`Dent`Beeblebrox`Prefect;`Arthur`Zaphod`Ford))!
     flip (enlist `iq)!enlist 98 42 126
```

And here is retrieval by full key record:

```
     ktc[`lname`fname!`Beeblebrox`Zaphod]
iq| 42
```

Most will agree that the table definition syntax and abbreviated key value retrieval is simpler.

7.4.10 Retrieving Records with a Compound Primary Key

Retrieval of multiple records via a compound primary key is actually easier than with a simple key, since each compound key value is already a list:

```
    ktc (`Dent`Arthur;`Prefect`Ford)
iq
---
98
126
```

As was the case with a keyed table having a simple key, retrieval can be performed via a table whose columns and values match the key columns:

```
    K:([] lname:`Dent`Prefect; fname:`Arthur`Ford)
```

```
        ktc[K]
iq
---
98
126

        ktc K               /use juxtaposition
iq
---
98
126
```

As in the case of a simple key, you can use # to retrieve the full entities of the keyed table instead of just the value records:

```
        K#ktc
lname    fname | iq
---------------|----
Dent     Arthur| 98
Prefect  Ford  | 126
```

7.4.11 Key Lookup with txf

Looking up keys in a keyed table is complicated by the different formats for simple and compound keys. The triadic function txf provides a uniform way to perform such key lookup. The first argument is a keyed table (*target*). The second argument is a list of key values, either simple or compound. The third argument is a list of symbol column names in the value table of *target*. The result is a list comprising the matching row values from the specified columns of the value table of *target*.

In the following example using a simple key, observe the column order of the result:

```
        kts:([k:101 102 103] c1:`a`b`c; c2:1.1 2.2 3.3)

        txf[kts;101 103;`c2`c1]
1.1 `a
3.3 `c
```

With a compound key, the values to be looked up must be listed in columns:

```
        ktc:([k1:`a`b`a; k2:`x`y`z] c1:100 200 300; c2:1.1 2.2 3.3)

        txf[ktc;(`a`b;`z`y);`c1`c2]
300 3.3
200 2.2
```

7.5 FOREIGN KEYS AND VIRTUAL COLUMNS

A foreign key in SQL is a column in one table whose values are members of a primary key column in another table. Foreign keys are the mechanism for establishing relations between tables.

One of the important features of a foreign key is that the RDBMS enforces referential integrity, meaning that the value in a foreign key column is **required** to be in the referenced primary key column. To insert a foreign key value that is not in the primary key column, it must first be inserted into the primary key column.

7.5.1 Definition of Foreign Key

q has the notion of a foreign key that also provides referential integrity. Extra credit to the reader who has guessed that a foreign key is implemented using an enumeration. In our introduction to enumerations, we saw that an enumeration domain can be any list with unique items. A keyed table meets the criterion of a unique domain, since the key records in the dictionary domain are unique.

A *foreign key* is a table column defined as an enumerated value over a keyed table. As an enumeration, a foreign key indeed provides referential integrity by restricting values in the foreign key column to be in the list of primary key values.

7.5.2 Example of Simple Foreign Key

An enumeration over a keyed table domain acts just like our simple enumeration examples. Let's return to a previous keyed table example:

```
kt:([eid:1001 1002 1003]
    name:`Dent`Beeblebrox`Prefect; iq:98 42 126)
```

To enumerate over the primary key of kt, use a symbol containing the keyed table name as the domain in the enumeration,

```
`kt$
```

The primary key table records provide the unique set of values for enumerating records:

```
    `kt$`eid!1001
`kt$1001
```

As usual, *q* saves us the trouble of being so explicit and allows the enumeration to be applied to items in the value list for the primary key dictionary — that is, the primary key values:

```
e1:`kt$1002 1001 1001 1003 1002 1003

     e1 = 1003
000101b
```

As with any enumeration, attempting to enumerate a key value that is not in the domain causes an error:

```
        `kt$1004
`cast
```

We can use table definition syntax to define a table with a foreign key over `kt`:

```
tdetails:([] eid:`kt$1003 1001 1002 1001 1002 1001;
          sc:126 36 92 39 98 42)
```

The foreign key column has simply been defined as an enumeration over the keyed table. We see the foreign key table in the f column when we invoke `meta` on the table:

```
     meta tdetails
c   | t f  a
--- | ------
eid | i kt
sc  | i
```

As of release **2.4**, the built-in function `fkeys` returns a dictionary in which each foreign key column name is mapped to its key domain — its primary key table name:

```
treport:([] eid:`kt$1001 1002 1003; mgrid:`kt$1002 ON 1002)

      fkeys treport
eid   | kt
mgrid | kt
```

7.5.3 Resolving a Foreign Key

There are occasions when you wish to resolve a foreign key, by which we mean substitute the actual values in place of the enumerated values. As with an ordinary enumeration, this is done by applying the `value` function to the foreign key column:

```
        update eid:value eid from tdetails
eid  sc
--------
1003 126
1001 36
1002 92
1001 39
1002 98
1001 42
```

7.5.4 Foreign Keys and Relations

In SQL, an inner join is used to splice back together data that has been normalized via relations. The splice is usually done along a foreign key, which establishes a relation to the keyed table via the primary key. In the join, columns from both tables are available using dot notation. In *q* the same effect is achieved using foreign keys without explicitly creating the joined table. The notation is similar, but different enough to warrant close attention.

Let tf be a table having a foreign key f whose enumeration domain is the keyed table kt. All columns in kt are available via dot notation in any select expression whose from domain is tf. A column c in kt that is accessed in this way is called a *virtual column* and is specified with dot notation f.c in the select expression.

For example, given t as above, we create a details table that contains individual test results for each person. We name the foreign key in the details table the same as the primary key it refers to, but this is not required:

```
tdetails:([] eid:`kt$1003 1002 1001 1002 1001 1002;
          sc:126 36 92 39 98 42)
```

Now we can access columns in t via a select on tdetails:

```
        select eid.name, sc from tdetails
name         sc
--------------
Prefect      126
Beeblebrox   36
Dent         92
Beeblebrox   39
Dent         98
Beeblebrox   42
```

The case in which the enumeration domain of a foreign key has a compound primary key is slightly more complicated. We cover this in **§7.7.2**.

7.6 Working with Tables and Keyed Tables

In this section, we use the following examples:

```
t:([] name:`Dent`Beeblebrox`Prefect; iq:98 42 126)

kt:([eid:1001 1002 1003] name:`Dent`Beeblebrox`Prefect;
    iq:98 42 126)
```

7.6.1 First and Last Records

Because a table is a list of records, the functions `first` and `last` retrieve the first and last records, respectively:

```
     first t
name | `Dent
iq   | 98

     last t
name | `Prefect
iq   | 126

     first kt
name | `Dent
iq   | 98

     last kt
name | `Prefect
iq   | 126
```

These functions are useful in `select` expressions, especially with grouping and aggregation.

> **Note**
>
> Every table in kdb+ has a first and last record since it is an ordered list of records. Moreover, the result of a `select` template is a table and so is also ordered. Contrast this with SQL, in which tables and result sets are unordered and you must use ORDER BY to impose an order.
>
> You can retrieve the first or last *n* records of a table or keyed table using the take operator (#).

```
        2#t
name            iq
-----------------
Dent            98
Beeblebrox      42


        -3#kt
eid | name          iq
----| ----------------
1001| Dent          98
1002| Beeblebrox    42
1003| Prefect      126
```

See **Appendix A** for more on using take. Also see **Chapter 8** for another way to achieve this result using `select[n]`.

7.6.2 Find

The find operator (?) used with a table performs a reverse lookup of a record and returns the corresponding row number. With t as above:

```
        t?`name`iq!(`Dent;98)
0
```

As usual, the record can be abbreviated to a list of row values:

```
        t?(`Dent;98)
0
```

You can reverse-lookup a list of multiple row values:

```
        t?((`Dent;98);(`Prefect;126))
0 2
```

Since a keyed table is a dictionary, find performs a reverse lookup of a value record and returns the key record:

```
        kt?`name`iq!(`Dent;98)
eid| 1001

        kt?(`Dent;98)
eid| 1001
```

In the case of find on a table with a single column, each list of row values must be a singleton list:

```
        t1:([] eid:1001 1002 1003)

        t1?(enlist 1001;enlist 1002)
0 1
```

The list of singletons can be created by the following expressions, although the first executes faster, especially for long lists:

```
        flip enlist 1001 1002
1001
1002

        enlist each 1001 1002
1001
1002
```

7.6.3 Primitive Join (,)

The join operator (,) is defined for tables and keyed tables. You can use join to append a record to a table:

```
        t:([] c1:`a`b; c2:10 20)

        t,`c1`c2!(`c;30)
c1 c2
-----
a  10
b  20
c  30
```

This join is one situation in which you cannot use a list of row values:

```
        t,(`a;30)
'type
```

You can, however, use a list of row values to amend the original table:

```
        t,:(`a;30)

        t
c1 c2
-----
a  10
b  20
a  30
```

Only tables having exactly the same list of column names and compatible column types can be joined. Since a table is a list of records, the result is obtained by appending the rows of the right operand to those of the left operand:

```
        t1:([] a:1 2 3; b:100 200 300)
        t2:([] a:3 4 5; b:300 400 500)

        t1,t2
a b
-----
1 100
2 200
3 300
3 300
4 400
5 500
```

Note that common rows are duplicated in the result.

Two tables with the same columns in different order cannot be joined with , because the order of columns in records is significant in *q*:

```
        t3:([] b:1001 2001 3001; a:101 201 301)

        t1,t3
'mismatch
```

Two keyed tables with the same key and value columns can be joined. Because a keyed table is a dictionary, the result has upsert semantics, as we saw in **Chapter 6**. Keys in the right operand that are not in the left operand are treated as inserts, whereas the right operand acts as an update on common key values:

```
        kt1:([k:1 2 3] c:10 20 30)
        kt2:([k:3 4 5] c:300 400 500)

        kt1,kt2
k| c
-| ---
1| 10
2| 20
3| 300
4| 400
5| 500
```

7.6.4 Coalesce (^)

The coalesce operator (^) is defined for keyed tables and differs from primitive join (,) in its treatment of null column items in the value tables.

When two keyed tables have the same key and value columns and the column values of both keyed tables are non-null atoms, ^ behaves the same as primitive join (,):

```
kt1:([k:1 2 3] c1:10 20 30; c2:`a`b`c)
kt2:([k:3 4 5] c1:300 400 500; c2:`cc`dd`ee)

      kt1,kt2
k| c1   c2
-| ------
1| 10   a
2| 20   b
3| 300  cc
4| 400  dd
5| 500  ee

      kt1^kt2
k| c1   c2
-| ------
1| 10   a
2| 20   b
3| 300  cc
4| 400  dd
5| 500  ee
```

When the right operand has null column values, the column values of the left operand are updated only with non-null values of the right operand:

```
kt3:([k:2 3] c1:0N 3000; c2:`bbb`)

      kt3
k| c1    c2
-| --------
2|       bbb
3| 3000

      kt1,kt3
k| c1    c2
-| --------
1| 10    a
2|       bbb
3| 3000
```

204

```
      kt1^kt3
k| c1   c2
-| --------
1| 10   a
2| 20   bbb
3| 3000 c
```

> **Note**
>
> The performance of ^ is slower than that of , since each column item of the right operand must be checked for null.

7.6.5 Column Join

Two tables with the same number of rows can be combined with join-each (, ') to form a sideways, or column, join in which the columns are aligned in parallel:

```
      t1:([] a:1 2 3)
      t2:([] b:100 200 300)

      t1,'t2
a b
-----
1 100
2 200
3 300
```

When the column lists of the tables are not disjoint, the operation on the common columns has upsert semantics because each record is a dictionary:

```
      t3:([] a:10 20 30; b:100 200 300)

      t1,'t3
a  b
------
10 100
20 200
30 300
```

Because keyed tables are dictionaries, they can only be sideways joined if they have identical key columns. We can deduce the behavior in this situation by recalling from §6.2 that any operation on a dictionary is applied on the common elements of the merged domains and is extended to the non-common domain elements with appropriate nulls.

Thus, a sideways join on keyed tables with identical key columns has simple upsert semantics for common data columns. More interesting are the non-common data columns, where the result becomes a column join spliced along common key values:

```
        t4:([a:1 2 3] x:100 200 300)

        t4
a| x
-| ---
1| 100
2| 200
3| 300

        t5:([a:3 4 5] y:1000 2000 3000)

        t5
a| y
-| ----
3| 1000
4| 2000
5| 3000

        t4,'t5
a| x   y
-| --------
1| 100
2| 200
3| 300 1000
4|     2000
5|     3000
```

7.7 COMPLEX COLUMN DATA

7.7.1 Simple Example

Recall from the definition of a column dictionary in §6.3 that there is no restriction that the column vectors must be lists of simple type. We have heretofore worked with examples having homogenous atomic values in each column because they correspond to familiar SQL tables, but there is no need to limit ourselves to simple columns.

Suppose we want to keep track of a pair of daily observations, say a low temperature and a high temperature. We can do this by storing the low and high values in separate columns:

```
        t1:([] d:2006.01.01 2006.01.02; l:67.9 72.8; h:82.1 88.4)

        t1
d          l    h
------------------
2006.01.01 67.9 82.1
2006.01.02 72.8 88.4

        t1[0]
d| 2006.01.01
l| 67.9
h| 82.1

        t1.l
67.9 72.8

        t1.h
82.1 88.4
```

We can also store pairs in a single column:

```
        t2:([] d:2006.01.01 2006.01.02; lh:(67.9 82.10; 72.8 88.4))

        t2
d          lh
------------------
2006.01.01 67.9 82.1
2006.01.02 72.8 88.4

        t2[0]
d  | 2006.01.01
lh | 67.9 82.1

        t2.lh
67.9 82.1
72.8 88.4

        t2.lh[;0]
67.9 72.8

        t2.lh[;1]
82.1 88.4
```

The first form is arguably more natural if you intend to manipulate the low and high values separately. This example can easily be generalized to the situation of *n*-tuples. In this case, storing multiple values in a single column has a definite advantage since defining and populating *n* columns is unwieldy when n is not known in advance. Storing and retrieving *n*-tuples to/from a single column is a simple operation in *q*. A useful example in finance is storing daily values for a yield curve.

7.7.2 Operations on Compound Column Data

We generalize the above example to the case of storing a set of repeated observations in which the number of observations is not fixed — i.e., varies with each occurrence. Say we want to perform a statistical analysis on the weekly gross revenues for movies and we don't care about the specific titles. Since there will be a different number of movies in release each week, the number of observations will not be constant. An oversimplified version of this might look something like:

```
t3:([] wk:2006.01.01 2006.01.08;
    gr:( 38.92 67.34; 16.99 5.14 128.23 31.69))

       t3
wk           gr
---------------------------------
2006.01.01 38.92 67.34
2006.01.08 16.99 5.14 128.23 31.69
```

Handling the situation in which the number of column values is not known in advance, or is variable, is cumbersome in SQL. You normalize the data into a master-detail pair of tables, but you cannot re-assemble the details into separate columns via a join. Instead, for each master record you get a collection of records that must be iterated over via some sort of cursor/loop. In verbose programming, this results in many lines of code that are slow and prone to error on edge cases.

By storing complex values in a single column in a *q* table, sophisticated operations can be performed in a single expression that executes fast. In the following q-sql examples, don't worry about the details of the syntax, and remember to read individual expressions from right to left. Observe that because there are no stinking loops, we never need to know the number of detail records.

Using our movie data, we can produce the sorted gross, the average and high gross for each week in one expression:

```
select wk, srt:desc each gr, avgr:avg each gr,
    hi:max each gr from t3
```

```
wk              srt                        avgr     hi
-----------------------------------------------------------
2006.01.01      67.34 38.92                53.13    67.34
2006.01.08      128.23 31.69 16.99 5.14    45.5125  128.23
```

While sorts and aggregates such as Max and Avg are standard SQL, think of how you'd produce the sorted sublist and the aggregates together. In your favorite verbose programming environment, you'll soon discover that you have a sordid list of rows requiring a loop to unravel into a single output line.

Now think about what you'd do to compute the percentage drops between successive gross numbers within each week. Because the sorted detail items are rows in SQL, this requires another loop. In *q*:

```
        select wk, drp:neg 1_'deltas each desc each gr,
            avgr:avg each gr, hi:max each gr from t3
wk          drp               avgr     hi
-----------------------------------------------
2006.01.01 ,28.42             53.13    67.34
2006.01.08 96.54 14.7 11.85   45.5125  128.23
```

7.7.3 Compound Foreign Key

Storing multiple values in a column is how to make a foreign key on a compound primary key. We return to the example using last name and first name as the primary key:

```
    ktc:([lname:`Dent`Beeblebrox`Prefect;
         fname:`Arthur`Zaphod`Ford]; iq:98 42 126)
```

We create a details table with a foreign key enumeration over `ktc` by placing the names in the foreign key column:

```
        tdetails:([] name:`ktc$(`Beeblebrox`Zaphod;
            `Prefect`Ford;`Beeblebrox`Zaphod); sc:36 126 42)
```

The columns of `ktc` are available as virtual columns from `tdetails`:

```
        select name.lname, name.iq, sc from tdetails
lname          iq   sc
----------------------
Beeblebrox     42   36
Prefect        126  126
Beeblebrox     42   42
```

When defining the schema of a table with a compound key column, specify the foreign key as a cast of nulls of the appropriate type:

```
tfc:([] name:`ktc$``;sc:`int$())
tfc,:(`ktc$`Dent`Arthur;sc:100)
```

When the foreign key comprises multiple types, use the corresponding nulls in the prototype. Note the similar cast in the following record append:

```
ktc:([k1:1 2 3; k2:2001.01.01 2001.01.02 2001.01.03] v: 1. 2. 3.)

      ktc
k1 k2         | v
--------------| -
1  2001.01.01 | 1
2  2001.01.02 | 2
3  2001.01.03 | 3

tfc:([] fk:`ktc$(0N;0Nd); s:`symbol$())
tfc,:(`ktc$(1;2001.01.01);`a)
tfc,:(`ktc$(2;2001.01.20);`a)
'cast
```

The failure of the cast in the second append is due to referential integrity.

7.8 Attributes

Attributes are metadata applied to lists of special form. They are used on a dictionary domain or a table column to reduce storage requirements and speed retrieval. When it sees an attribute, the *q* interpreter can make certain optimizations based on the structure of the list.

> **Important**
>
> Attributes are descriptive rather than prescriptive. Consequently, applying an attribute (other than `g#) to a list will not make it so.
>
> Moreover, a modification that respects the form specified by the attribute leaves the attribute intact (other than `p#), while a modification that breaks the form is permitted but the attribute is lost on the result.

The syntax for applying an attribute looks like the verb # with a left operand containing the symbol for the attribute and the list as the right operand. However, this use of # is syntactic rather than functional.

> **Note**
>
> You will not see significant benefit from an attribute for less than a million items. This is why attributes are not automatically applied in mundane situations such as the result of til or distinct. You should test your particular situation to see whether applying an attribute actually provides performance benefit.

7.8.1 Sorted (`s#)

Applying the sorted attribute (`s#) to a list indicates that the items of the list are sorted in ascending order.

> **Note**
>
> As of this writing, there is no way to indicate a descending sort.

When a list has the sorted attribute, the default linear search used in lookups is replaced with binary search. Sorted also makes certain operations much faster — for example min and max. The following fragments show situations in which this applies:

```
x?v
... where x = v, ...
... where x in v, ...
... where x within v, ...
```

The sorted attribute can be applied to a simple list,

```
    L:`s#1 2 2 4 8
    L
`s#1 2 2 4 8
```

```
        L,:16                   / respects sort

        L
`s#1 2 2 4 8 16

        L,:0                    / does not, so attribute lost

        L
1 2 2 4 8 16 0
```

or a column of a table:

```
    t:([] `s#t:04:02:42.001 04:02:42.003; v:101.05 100.95)
```

The sorted attribute can be applied to a dictionary, which makes the dictionary into a step function:

```
        ds:`s#1 2 3 4 5!`a`b`c`d`e

        ds
1| a
2| b
3| c
4| d
5| e
```

Applying the sorted attribute to a table implies binary search on the table and also that the first column is sorted:

```
        ts:`s#([] t:04:02:42.001 04:02:42.003; v:101.05 100.95)

        ts
t            v
------------------
04:02:42.001 101.05
04:02:42.003 100.95
```

Applying the sorted attribute to a keyed table means that the dictionary, its key table and its key column(s) are all sorted:

```
        kt:`s#([k:1 2 3 4] v:`d`c`b`a)

        kt
```

```
k| v
-| -
1| d
2| c
3| b
4| a
```

7.8.2 Unique (`u#)

Applying the unique attribute (`u#) to a list indicates that the items of the list are distinct. Knowing that the elements of a list are unique dramatically speeds up `distinct` and allows *q* to exit some comparisons early.

Operations on the list must preserve uniqueness or the attribute is lost:

```
      LU:`u#4 2 6 18 1

      LU
`u#4 2 6 18 1

      LU,:0                       / uniqueness preserved

      LU
`u#4 2 6 18 1 0

      LU,:2                       / attribute lost

      LU
4 2 6 18 1 0 2
```

The unique attribute can be applied to the domain of a dictionary, a column of a table, or the key column of a keyed table. It cannot be applied to a dictionary, a table or a keyed table directly.

7.8.3 Parted (`p#)

The parted attribute (#p) indicates that the list represents a step function in which all occurrences of a particular output value are adjacent. The range is an int or temporal type that has an underlying int value, such as years, months, days, etc. You can also partition over a symbol provided it is enumerated.

> **Advanced**
>
> Applying the parted attribute causes the creation of an index dictionary that maps each unique output value to the position of its first occurrence.

When a list is parted, lookup is much faster since linear search is replaced by hashtable lookup.

Sorting in ascending or descending order is one way to produce the partitioned structure, but the list need not be in sorted order. For example:

```
L:`p#2 2 2 1 1 4 4 4 4 3 3
```

The parted attribute is not preserved under an operation on the list, even if the operation preserves the partitioning:

```
L,:3

       L
2 2 2 1 1 4 4 4 4 3 3 3
```

Saving a parted table to disk requires a physical segmentation by directory across the range values.

> **Note**
>
> The parted attribute should be considered when the number of entities reaches a billion and most of the partitions are of substantial size — i.e., there is significant repetition.

7.8.4 Grouped (`g#)

The grouped attribute (`g#) differs from other attributes in that it imposes additional structure on the list by causing *q* to create and maintain an index. Grouping can be applied to a list when no other assumptions about its structure can be made.

Applying the grouped attribute to a table column roughly corresponds to placing a SQL index on a column. For example, if you wish to query a table via a symbol column sym, applying the grouped attribute to the column drastically speeds up queries such as:

```
select[-100] ... where sym=`xyz
```

Here we are retrieving the last 100 records matching a `sym` value.

> **Advanced**
>
> The index is a dictionary that maps each unique output value to a list of the positions of all its occurrences. This speeds lookups and some operations (e.g., `distinct`). The tradeoff is significant storage overhead.

For example:

```
L:`g#1 2 3 2 3 4 3 4 5 2 3 4 5 4 3 5 6
      L
`g#1 2 3 2 3 4 3 4 5 2 3 4 5 4 3 5 6
```

> **Note**
>
> The grouped attribute is preserved for both inserts and upserts.

Applying the grouped attribute to a table column:

```
t:([]`g#c1:1 2 3 2 3 4 3 4; c2:`a`b`a`c`a`d`b`c)
```

In view of the storage requirement, you should consider grouping when the table is large (a million rows) and there is significant repetition.

> **Note**
>
> As of this writing, the maximum number of `` `g# `` attributes that can be placed on a single table is 99.

CHAPTER 8
QUERIES: q-sql

8.0 OVERVIEW

q has a collection of functions for manipulating tables that are similar to their counterparts in SQL. This collection, which we call q-sql, includes the usual suspects such as insert, select, update, etc., as well as functionality that is not available in traditional SQL. While q-sql provides a superset of SQL functionality, there are some significant differences in the syntax and behavior.

The first important difference is that a *q* table has well-defined record and column orders. This is particularly useful in dealing with the situation in which records are inserted in a canonical order. Subsequent actions against the table will then retrieve records in this order. For example, a time series can be created by inserting (in time order) pairs consisting of a time (or date, or datetime) value and data value(s). The result of any `select` will then be in time order, without requiring a sort.

A second difference is that a *q* table is stored physically as a collection of column vectors. This means that operations on column data are easy and fast since atomic, aggregate or uniform functions applied to columns are optimized vector operations.

A third difference is that q-sql provides upsert semantics. This means that one dataset can be applied to another without the need to separate inserts from updates. Upsert can simplify operations in practice.

In this chapter, we cover the important features of q-sql, including all the basic operations in kdb+. We demonstrate each feature with a simple example. Gradually, more complex examples are introduced.

Many examples are based on the `sp.q` distribution script. The schemas for the tables in the script are:

```
s:([s:()] name:(); status:(); city:())

p:([p:()] name:(); color:(); weight:(); city:())

sp:([] s:`s$(); p:`p$(); qty:())
```

The contents of the tables are:

```
s
```

```
s | name  status city
--|-------------------
s1| smith 20     london
s2| jones 10     paris
s3| blake 30     paris
s4| clark 20     london
s5| adams 30     athens


      p
p | name  color weight city
--|------------------------
p1| nut   red   12     london
p2| bolt  green 17     paris
p3| screw blue  17     rome
p4| screw red   14     london
p5| cam   blue  12     paris
p6| cog   red   19     london


       sp
s  p  q ty
----------
s1 p1 300
s1 p2 200
s1 p3 400
s1 p4 200
s4 p5 100
s1 p6 100
s2 p1 300
s2 p2 400
s3 p2 200
s4 p2 200
s4 p4 300
s1 p5 400
```

8.1 INSERT

Insert appends records to a table or keyed table.

8.1.1 Basic Insert

To append records to a table, use the dyadic function `insert`,

```
insert[s_t; L]
```

where s_t is a symbol containing the name of a table (*target*) and L is a list whose items correspond to records of *target*. The result of `insert` is a list of int representing the position(s) of the new record(s).

> **Note**
>
> Since the items in L are appended to the column vectors of s_t, each value must type-match the corresponding column vector. If the columns of *target* are not typed, they take the types of the first record inserted.

For a regular (i.e., non-keyed) table, the effect of insert is to append a new record holding the specified values. Let's use our simple example:

```
t:([] name:`Dent`Beeblebrox`Prefect; iq:42 98 126)
```

Insert a list into t as follows:

```
         insert[`t;(`Slartibartfast;156)]
,3

         t
name            iq
-----------------
Dent            42
Beeblebrox      98
Prefect         126
Slartibartfast  156
```

> **Note**
>
> It is possible to insert records into a table that is not defined. The effect is to create the table with columns matching those of the first record inserted. For example, assume that z does not exist in the workspace. Then the following creates it.

```
         z
'z
         insert[`z;flip `c1`c2!(10 20;`a`b)]
0 1
         z
```

```
c1 c2
-----
10 a
20 b
```

8.1.2 Alternate Forms

Since the dyadic `insert` is also a verb, it can take various notational forms. For example, the previous insert can be written as a binary operator:

```
`t insert (`Slartibartfast;156)
```

It can also be expressed as a projection onto the first argument with juxtaposition of the second argument:

```
insert[`t] (`Slartibartfast;156)
```

You may find one of these more readable. We shall use them interchangeably. You can also insert a record, as opposed to a list of row values:

```
`t insert `name`iq!(`Slartibartfast;156)
```

This is useful when you wish to insert a table that is the result of a `select`.

8.1.3 Repeated Inserts

For a (non-keyed) table, repeatedly inserting the same data is permissible and it results in duplicate records:

```
        t:([] name:`Dent`Beeblebrox`Prefect; iq:98 42 126)

        `t insert (`Slartibartfast;156)      / one form
,3
        insert[`t] (`Slartibartfast;156)     / equivalent form
,4
        t
name                iq
---------------------
Dent                98
Beeblebrox          42
Prefect             126
Slartibartfast      156
Slartibartfast      156
```

8.1.4 Columnar Bulk Insert

In the preceding, we have considered the case when the list in an insert represents a set of values for a single row. Each item is an atom destined for the corresponding column in the table. It is also possible to bulk insert multiple entries.

Recall that a table is a dictionary of columns. So in the example,

```
t:([] name:`Dent`Beeblebrox; iq:98 42)
`t insert (`Prefect;126)
,2
```

the right operand looks like a row, but is in fact a list of column values. With this perspective, a bulk insert can be achieved with a compound list, each of whose items is a list of column values destined for the corresponding column in the table:

```
t:([] name:`Dent`Beeblebrox; iq:98 42)
`t insert (`Prefect`Mickey;126 1024)
2 3
```

8.1.5 Table Insert

It is also possible to bulk insert records (i.e., rows). A table can be viewed as a list of records (and vice versa), so it is reasonable to insert one table into another provided the columns are compatible:

```
t:([] name:`Dent`Beeblebrox`Prefect; iq:98 42 126)
tnew:([] name:`Slartibartfast`Mickey; iq:158 1042)

`t insert tnew
3 4

t
name             iq
--------------------
Dent             98
Beeblebrox       42
Prefect          126
Slartibartfast   158
Mickey           1042
```

8.1.6 Insert into Keyed Tables

Inserting data into a keyed table works just like inserting data into a regular table, with the additional requirement that the key must not already exist in the table. Using our previous example of a keyed table:

```
        t:([eid:1001 1002] name:`Dent`Beeblebrox; iq:98 42)
        t
eid | name         iq
----| --------------
1001| Dent         98
1002| Beeblebrox   42

        `t insert (1004;`Slartibartfast;158)
,2
        t
eid | name              iq
----| --------------------
1001| Dent              98
1002| Beeblebrox        42
1004| Slartibartfast    158
```

The following insert now fails because the key 1004 already exists in t:

```
        `t insert (1004;`Slartibartfast;158)
'insert
```

> **Note**
> The records in a keyed table are stored in insert order, not key order.

```
        `t insert (1003;`Prefect;126)
,3
        t
eid | name              iq
----| --------------------
1001| Dent              98
1002| Beeblebrox        42
1004| Slartibartfast    158
1003| Prefect           126
```

8.1.7 Insert into Empty Tables

For an empty table with no column types specified, the column types are inferred from the first insert:

```
        t:([] name:(); iq:())

        type t.name
0h

        type t.iq
0h

        `t insert (`Dent;98)
,0

        type t.name
11h

        type t.iq
6h
```

If you define an empty table without types, be especially careful to get the first insert correct:

```
        `t insert (98;`Dent)
            .
            .
            .
        `t insert (`Beelbebrox;42)
`type
```

It is advantageous to define an empty table with types. In our example:

```
        t:([] name:`symbol$(); iq:`int$())
        t:([] name:0#`; iq:0#0)              / an equivalent way

        type t.name
11h

        type t.iq
6h
```

8.1.8 Insert and Foreign Keys

When inserting data into a table that has a foreign key, everything works like a regular table, except that a value destined for a foreign key column must already exist as a key in the corresponding primary key table.

> **Note**
>
> This last requirement is how *q* implements referential integrity.

Returning to our example of the previous section:

```
kt:([eid:1001 1002 1003]
    name:`Dent`Beeblebrox`Prefect; iq:98 42 126)

tdetails:([] eid:`kt$1003 1002 1001 1002 1001;
    sc:126 36 92 39 98)

      kt
eid | name        iq
----|--------------
1001| Dent        98
1002| Beeblebrox  42
1003| Prefect     126

      tdetails
eid  sc
--------
1003 126
1002 36
1001 92
1002 39
1001 98

      `tdetails insert (1002;42)
,5

      tdetails
eid  sc
--------
1003 126
1002 36
1001 92
1002 39
1001 98
1002 42
```

The following insert fails because the key 1004 does not exist in `kt`:

```
      `tdetails insert (1004;158)
'cast
```

8.2 THE SELECT AND EXEC TEMPLATES

In this section, we investigate the general form of `select`, which we met briefly in §7.3. We present `select` as a template having required and optional elements. The template elements, in turn, contain phrases whose expressions involve column values. The *q* interpreter applies the template against the specified table to produce a result table. While the syntax and results resemble those of the analogous SQL statement, the underlying mechanics are quite different.

We shall examine each of the constituents of the `select` template in detail. Our approach is to introduce the concepts with illustrative examples using trivial tables and then to proceed with more meaningful examples using time series. Here are our sample table definitions:

```
kt:([eid:1001 1002 1003]
    name:`Dent`Beeblebrox`Prefect;
    iq:98 42 126)

tdetails:([] eid:`kt$1003 1002 1001 1002 1001 1002;
    sc:126 36 92 39 98 42)
```

8.2.1 Syntax

The `select` template has the following form, where elements enclosed in matching angle brackets (<...>) are optional:

```
select <ps> <by pb> from texp <where pw>
```

The `select` and `from` keywords are required, as is t_{exp}, which is a *q* expression whose result is a table or keyed table. The elements p_s, p_b and p_w are the *select*, the *by* and the *where* phrases, respectively. The result of `select` is a list of records or, equivalently, a table.

> **Note**
>
> If `where` is present and t_{exp} is itself the result of a `select`, the expression that produces t_{exp} must be enclosed in parentheses.

Some simple examples follow:

```
        select from kt
eid | name       iq
----|--------------
1001| Dent       98
1002| Beeblebrox 42
1003| Prefect    126

        select eid, name from kt where name=`Dent
eid  name
---------
1001 Dent

        select cnt:count sc by eid.name from tdetails
name       | cnt
-----------|---
Beeblebrox | 3
Dent       | 2
Prefect    | 1

        select topsc:max sc, cnt:count sc by eid.name
            from tdetails where eid.name<>`Prefect

name       | topsc cnt
-----------|---------
Beeblebrox | 42    2
Dent       | 98    2
```

The order of execution for `select` is:

- from expression t_{exp}
- where phrase p_w
- by phrase p_b
- select phrase p_s

In particular, the from expression is always evaluated first and the select phrase last.

> **Note**
>
> If p_s is absent, all columns are returned. There is no need for the * wildcard of SQL.

Each phrase in the `select` template is a comma-separated list of subphrases. A *subphrase* is an expression involving columns of t_{exp} or virtual columns, which may be in a table related to t_{exp} via foreign key. The subphrases within a phrase are evaluated left-to-right, but each expression comprising a subphrase is parsed right-to-left, like any *q* expression.

> **Important**
>
> The commas separating the subphrases are separators, meaning that it is not necessary to enclose a subphrase in parentheses. However, any expression containing the join operator (,) must be enclosed in parentheses to distinguish it from the separator.

8.2.2 The where Phrase

The where phrase controls which records appear in the result. The action of this phrase is a generalization of the built-in `where` function on lists (See **Appendix A**).

Each subphrase is a criterion on columns that produces a boolean result vector corresponding to records passing or failing the criterion. The effect of a where subphrase is to select only the records that pass its criteria.

The individual where subphrases are applied from left-to-right. Each step produces a result whose rows are a subset of the previous one. The net effect is a series of progressively narrowed interim results:

```
      select from kt where iq <100
eid   name        iq
-----------------------
1001  Dent        98
1002  Beeblebrox  42

      select from tdetails where eid=1002
eid   sc
-------
1002  36
1002  39
1002  42

      select from tdetails where eid=1002, sc<eid.iq
eid   sc
-------
1002  36
1002  39
```

```
      select from tdetails where (eid=1002)&sc<eid.iq
eid   sc
-------
1002  36
1002  39
```

We point out that the last two queries return the same result but execute differently; we shall see more about this later. Also observe that the parentheses in the last query are necessary due to right-to-left evaluation of expressions.

8.2.3 The select Phrase

The select phrase controls which columns appear in the result. Each select subphrase produces a column. The name of the result column from each subphrase is taken from the last underlying column referenced in the subphrase evaluation unless the result is renamed by assignment:

```
        select LastName:name, iq from kt
LastName    iq
--------------
Dent        98
Beeblebrox  42
Prefect     126
```

If a column is repeated in the select phrase, it appears more than once in the result. This behaves like SQL SELECT:

```
       select iq, iq   from kt
iq   iq
-------
98   98
42   42
126  126
```

> **Important**
>
> A virtual column i holding the position of each record is implicitly available in the `select` phrase. This is useful, for example, in aggregation if you want a column with record counts without reference to a specific column name.

```
      select cnt:count i by eid from tdetails
```

```
eid  | cnt
-----|----
1001 | 2
1002 | 3
1003 | 1
```

In this situation, `i` plays a role somewhat similar to * in SQL, but is more useful since it can be used to select specific records. For example, criteria on `i` can be used to fill only one page of results when you do not wish to transmit an entire result set. Here is the second page of detail records for a page size of 3, noting that the `within` function includes both its endpoints (see **Appendix A**):

```
     select from tdetails where i within (3;5)
eid  sc
-------
1002 39
1001 98
1002 42
```

This is difficult to do in SQL and vendors have added proprietary extensions to handle it.

8.2.4 The by Phrase

The by phrase controls how rows with common column values are grouped in the result. The action of this phrase is a generalization of the built-in `group` function on lists (See **Appendix A**).

Each by subphrase is an expression involving a column, which produces a grouping criterion for that column. The columns specified in the by phrase become the primary keys of the `select` result. Multiple subphrases in the by phrase result in a compound primary key in the result.

> **Note**
>
> If the by phrase is present, the `result` of select is a keyed table; if it is omitted, the result is a table.
>
> **Important**
>
> Every column included in the by phrase is automatically included in the result and should not be included separately in the select phrase.

It is possible to group without aggregation. The result is a table with non-simple lists for columns — that is, non-atomic column values (see §7.7 for more on tables with non-simple column lists):

```
         select sc by eid from tdetails
eid  |   sc
-----|---------
1001 |   92 98
1002 |   36 39 42
1003 |   ,126
```

This cannot be achieved easily with GROUP BY in SQL.

The function `ungroup` can be used to normalize a grouped result back into a flat table.

```
         seid:select sc by eid from tdetails

         seid
id   |   sc
-----|---------
1001 |   92 98
1002 |   36 39 42
1003 |   ,126

         ungroup seid
eid  sc
--------
1001 92
1001 98
1002 36
1002 39
1002 42
1003 126
```

8.2.5 The exec Template

The syntax of the `exec` template is identical to `select`:

   exec <p_s> <by p_b> from t_{exp} <where p_w>

The difference from `select` is that the result is not a table.

If only one column is produced by the select phrase, the result of `exec` is a list containing the column values produced. This contrasts with `select`, which produces a table with a single column in this situation.

With `kt` as above:

```
        kt
eid  | name       iq
-----| --------------
1001 | Dent       42
1002 | Beeblebrox 98
1003 | Prefect    126

        select name from kt
name
----------
Dent
Beeblebrox
Prefect

        exec name from kt
`Dent`Beeblebrox`Prefect
```

Using `exec` to extract a single column of a table (as opposed to a keyed table) is more powerful than other mechanisms to extract the column because you can apply constraints on other columns:

```
        tdetails.sc
126 36 92 39 98 42

        tdetails[`sc]
126 36 92 39 98 42

        exec sc from tdetails
126 36 92 39 98 42

        exec sc from tdetails where eid in 1001 1002
36 92 39 98 42
```

If more than one column is produced by the select phrase, the result of `exec` is a dictionary mapping the column names to the values produced. This contrasts with `select`, which produces a table with the specified columns:

```
        select eid, name from kt
eid  name
---------------
1001 Dent
1002 Beeblebrox
1003 Prefect

        exec eid,name from kt
eid  | 1001 1002       1003
name | Dent Beeblebrox Prefect
```

8.2.6 Using distinct with select and exec

The built-in `distinct` function (see **Appendix A**) applied to a source table returns a table containing the unique records in the source:

```
        tdup:([] c1:10 20 10 30 10 20 40 30; c2:`a`b`a`c`z`b`d`c)
        tdup
c1 c2
-----
10 a
20 b
10 a
30 c
10 z
20 b
40 d
30 c

        distinct tdup
c1 c2
-----
10 a
20 b
30 c
10 z
40 d
```

By including `distinct` in the select phrase of a `select` or exec query, you can similarly suppress duplicates from the result:

```
        select distinct c1 from tdup
c1
--
10
20
30
40

        exec distinct c2 from tdup
`a`b`c`z`d
```

> **Note**
>
> When `distinct` is used in `select`, it appears immediately after

> "select" and is applied across all the specified columns, meaning that it returns rows with distinct values in those columns.
>
> By contrast, in exec, distinct can apply to any column and the result will be a non-rectangular in general.

```
        select distinct c2, c1 from tdup
c2 c1
-----
a  10
b  20
c  30
z  10
d  40

        exec distinct c2, c1 from tdup
c2| `a`b`c`z`d
c1| 10 20 10 30 10 20 40 30

        exec distinct c2, distinct c1 from tdup
c2| `a`b`c`z`d
c1| 10 20 30 40
```

One way to understand this behavior is as follows: the result of `select` is a table, which is rectangular; hence `distinct` must produce full rows. The result of `exec` is a dictionary, so each column name (i.e., result key) can have a different number of values.

8.2.7 Using each in where

If a function or operator used in a where criterion is not atomic or uniform in its argument, you must use an each adverb. This is because the criterion is applied across the column vector(s):

```
        ts:([] f:1.1 2.2 3.3; s:("abc";"d";"ef"))

        select from ts where s~"abc"
f s
---

        select from ts where ("abc"~) each s
```

```
f   s
-------
1.1 "abc"
```

The first `select` does not achieve the desired result because it asks if the entire column matches the specified string. The second `select` works correctly because it is the projection of the binary match operator applied to each item of the column.

8.2.8 Nested where

As was mentioned in **§8.2.2**, the criteria in the subphrases of a where phrase are applied to the records of the table sequentially from left to right. Consequently, the final list of records is obtained via a succession of intermediate results, each of which is narrowed by the following subphrase criterion. Otherwise put, the where subphrases constitute a nested set of criteria.

The order of the subphrases in a nested where can have significant performance implications for queries against large tables. Whenever possible, list the subphrases in order of decreasing restrictiveness. That is, choose the subphrase at each position to be the one that results in the greatest narrowing. Each intermediate table will be smallest and consequently less memory and processing will be required.

> **Note**
>
> If there is one where subphrase that will always result in a significantly smaller result set, it should be placed first in the sequence. In the case of a partitioned table, place any constraint on the partition column first.

A typical example is a series of measurements for entities with an identifier. This could be real-time stock prices, daily bond yields, yearly batting averages, test scores, etc. Say there are many different identifier values and you want to select certain records for a given identifier: it is better to filter on the identifier first since this will immediately restrict the result set to a small subset of the original. This can lead an order of magnitude improvement.

Let's take our trivial example of iq test scores and imagine that the table contains the result of SAT scores for all high school seniors in the United States. In this case, there will be several million students with only a few records per student. Clearly, if you want to perform an analysis on the scores of an individual, it is best to limit the result by student first, since the initial and subsequent intermediate tables will be tiny.

Imagine the following table containing millions of student social security numbers and scores:

```
tscores:(ssn:0#`;sc:0#int)
`tscores insert (`$"111-11-1111"; 999)
`tscores insert (`$"222-22-2222"; 1242)
`tscores insert (`$"333-33-3333"; 735)
`tscores insert (`$"444-44-4444"; 1600)
`tscores insert (`$"555-55-5555"; 1178)
`tscores insert (`$"111-11-1111"; 1021)
`tscores insert (`$"666-66-6666"; 882)
.
.
.
```

Since each student takes the test only a few times, the following query,

```
select from tscores where ssn=`$"111-11-1111", 0<deltas sc
```

executes significantly faster than,

```
select from tscores where (ssn=`$"111-11-1111")&0<deltas sc
```

We point out that any nested where phrase is logically equivalent to an unnested phrase in which each of the subphrases is joined by &. In our example, the nested query produces the same results as either of the following,

```
select from tscores where (ssn=`$"111-11-1111")&0<deltas sc
```

/ or

```
select from tscores where (0<deltas sc)&ssn=`$"111-11-1111"
```

However, both unnested versions will execute more slowly since the compound criterion is applied against all records in the table.

8.2.9 select[n]

You can return the first or last *n* records of a `select` result using function parameter syntax on the `select`. A positive parameter returns the first records specified by the select body, while a negative parameter returns the last records:

```
        select[2] from kt
eid | name         iq
----|--------------
1001| Dent         42
1002| Beeblebrox   98

        select[-1] from kt
eid | name    iq
----|-----------
1003| Prefect 126
```

8.2.10 fby

It is sometimes desirable to use an aggregate function in the where phrase of select. For example, suppose we are given a table with a foreign key and we wish to determine which key values have more than one entry in the table. A first attempt might be to place a condition in the where phrase that filters on the count being greater than 1. In our example of tdetails, this would be something like:

```
        select distinct eid from tdetails where 1<count eid
eid
----
1003
1001
1002
```

You can see this doesn't work, as the record for eid value 1003 is included even though it has only a single entry in tdetails. What went wrong?

The better question is, what does this where expression actually do? Since count is an aggregate function, it is applied against the list of column values for eid. It cannot select individual rows since it does not return a boolean vector result. Indeed, it returns the scalar 5, the number of items in the column vector.

You could achieve the desired result with a correlated subquery. The inner query counts the records for each key value using aggregation and grouping:

```
        q1:select cnt:count eid by eid from tdetails

        q1
```

```
eid | cnt
----| ---
1001| 2
1002| 2
1003| 1
```

The outer query selects the records with the desired count:

```
        select eid from q1 where 1<cnt
eid
----
1001
1002
```

An easier way to accomplish this result is to use fby in the where phrase. Placing fby in a where subphrase allows an aggregate function to be used to select individual rows. The action is similar to the grouping of by, but with the specified aggregate function applied across the grouped values. (Hence the name **fby**, short for **function by**).

The use of fby is more abstract than other elements of the select template. It is a binary operator of the form,

$(f_{agg}; expr_{col})$ fby c

The left operand is a two-item list comprising an aggregate function f_{agg} and a column expression $expr_{col}$ on which the function will be applied. The right operand c is a symbol containing the name of the column whose values are to be grouped to form lists for the aggregate function.

Inclusion of fby in a where subphrase selects those records whose group passes the subphrase criterion specified by the aggregate function. This means that all records in a group either pass or fail together, depending on the result of the aggregation on the group.

In our example above, we can achieve the desired result with an un-nested select using fby. First, we verify that fby does indeed accomplish what we want. Remember to evaluate the where criterion right-to-left:

```
        select eid from tdetails where 1<(count;eid) fby eid
eid
----
1001
1002
1001
1002
```

Now we eliminate the duplicates:

```
        select distinct eid from tdetails
            where 1<(count;eid) fby eid
eid
----
1001
1002
```

Multiple columns in the right operand of `fby` must be encapsulated in a table. To do this, create an anonymous empty table with the desired column names only:

```
        t:([]sym:`IBM`IBM`MSFT`IBM`MSFT;
           ex:`N`O`N`N`N;
           time:12:10:00.0 12:30:00.0 12:45:00.0 12:50:00.0
           13:30:00.0;
           price:82.1 81.95 23.45 82.05 23.40)

           t
sym  ex  time          price
-----------------------------
IBM  N   12:10:00.000  82.1
IBM  O   12:30:00.000  81.95
MSFT N   12:45:00.000  23.45
IBM  N   12:50:00.000  82.05
MSFT N   13:30:00.000  23.4

        select from t where price=(max;price) fby ([]sym;ex)
sym  ex  time          price
-----------------------------
IBM  N   12:10:00.000  82.1
IBM  O   12:30:00.000  81.95
MSFT N   12:45:00.000  23.45
```

It may take a while to get accustomed to this notation.

8.3 THE UPDATE TEMPLATE

8.3.1 Basic update

The `update` template has the same form as the `select` template:

```
update <p_u> <by p_b> from t_exp <where p_w>
```

The difference is that column assignments in the update phrase p_u represent modifications to columns instead of column name aliases:

```
        t:([] c1:`one`two`three; c2:10 20 30)

        update c1:`third, c2:33 from t where c1=`three
c1    c2
--------
one   10
two   20
third 33
```

> **Important**
>
> In order to modify the contents of t_{exp} you must refer to a table by name.

After execution of the query above, we still find:

```
       t
c1    c2
--------
one   10
two   20
three 30
```

However, t can be modified in place by referring to the table by name:

```
        update c1:`third, c2:33 from `t where c1=`three
`t

       t
c1    c2
--------
one   10
two   20
third 33
```

> **Note**
>
> Unlike updates in SQL, update can add a new column.

```
        t:([] c1:20 10 30 20; c2:`z`y`x`a)

        t
c1 c2
-----
20 z
10 y
30 x
20 a

        update c3:100+c1 from `t
`t

        t
c1 c2 c3
--------
20 z  120
10 y  110
30 x  130
20 a  120
```

8.3.2 update-by

When the by phrase is present, `update` can be used to create new columns from the grouped values. If an aggregate function is used, it is applied to each group of values and the result is assigned to all records in the group:

```
        t:([] n:`a`b`a`c`c`b; p:10 15 12 20 25 14)

        t
n p
----
a 10
b 15
a 12
c 20
c 25
b 14

        update av:avg p by n from t
n p  av
---------
a 10 11
b 15 14.5
a 12 11
c 20 22.5
c 25 22.5
b 14 14.5
```

If a uniform function is used, it is applied across the grouped values and the result is assigned in sequence to the records in the group. With t as above:

```
        update s:sums p by n from t
n p  s
-------
a 10 10
b 15 15
a 12 22
c 20 20
c 25 45
b 14 29
```

8.4 UPSERT

The dyadic function `upsert` is an alternate name for join (,) on tables and keyed tables. For keyed tables, the match is done by key value:

```
        kt:([k:`one`two`three] c:10 20 30)

        kt
k    | c
-----| --
one  | 10
two  | 20
three| 30

        ku:([k:`three`four]; c:300 400)

        ku
k    | c
-----| ---
three| 300
four | 400

        kt upsert ku
k    | c
-----| ---
one  | 10
two  | 20
three| 300
four | 400
```

For (non-keyed) tables, the records are appended:

```
        t:([] c1:`one`two`three; c2:10 20 30)

        t
c1    c2
--------
one   10
two   20
three 30

        u:([] c1:`three`four; c2:30 40)

        u
c1    c2
--------
three 30
four  40

        t upsert u
c1    c2
--------
one   10
two   20
three 30
three 30
four  40
```

> **Note**
>
> The upsert expressions above do not affect the original table. You must refer to the table by name to modify the original.

8.5 DELETE

The syntax of the `delete` template is simpler than `select`, with the added restriction that either p_{cols} or p_w can be present but not both:

```
delete <p_cols> from t_exp <where p_w>
```

If p_{cols} is present as a symbol list of column names, the result is is a table derived from t_{exp} in which the specified columns are removed. If p_w is present, the result is a table derived from t_{exp} in which records meeting the criteria of p_w are removed:

```
        t:([] c1:`a`b`c; c2:`x`y`z)
        t
c1 c2
-----
a  x
b  y
c  z

        delete c1 from t
c2
--
x
y
z

        delete from t where c2=`z
c1 c2
-----
a  x
b  y
```

> **Important**
>
> In order to modify the contents of t_{exp} you must refer to the table by name.

After execution of the last query above, we still find:

```
        t
c1 c2
-----
a  x
b  y
c  z
```

However, t can be modified in place with:

```
        delete from `t where c2=`z
`t
        t
c1 c2
-----
a  x
b  y
```

8.6 GROUPING AND AGGREGATION

Aggregation is the result of applying an aggregate function — one that produces an atom from a list — to a column.

8.6.1 SQL Aggregation

In traditional SQL, aggregation and grouping are limited and cumbersome. Aggregation and grouping are bound together: only columns that appear in the GROUP BY can participate in the SELECT result. Moreover, there is a limited collection of built-in aggregation functions.

In *q*, grouping and aggregation can be used independently or together.

8.6.2 Grouping without Aggregation

Grouping in *q* collects rows having a common value in the group domain. Unlike SQL, any column can participate in the `select` result when grouping. Moreover, the columns in the by phrase are automatically included in the result as keys.

When a column not in the by phrase is explicitly specified in the select phrase, the result of grouping without aggregation has a corresponding column of non-simple type. There will be one item in the value list for each record matching a given group domain value. For example, we can group order quantities by supplier in the `sp.q` script sample tables. Load `\l sp.q`, then:

```
        select qty by s from sp
s  | qty
-- | ---------------------
s1 | 300 200 400 200 100 400
s2 | 300 400
s3 | ,200
s4 | 100 200 300
```

You can group by the result of a function applied to a column. For example, the following query groups all products meeting a certain order quantity threshold:

```
        select distinct p by thrsh:qty>200 from sp
thrsh | p
----- | ------------------
0     | `p$`p2`p4`p5`p6
1     | `p$`p1`p3`p2`p4`p5
```

You can also group by virtual columns from foreign keys:

```
              select sname:s.name, qty by pname:p.name from sp
pname| sname                         qty
-----| ----------------------------------------------
bolt | `smith`jones`blake`clark 200 400 200 200
cam  | `clark`smith                  100 400
cog  | ,`smith                       ,100
nut  | `smith`jones                  300 300
screw| `smith`smith`clark            400 200 300
```

> **Important**
>
> When no columns are explicitly specified in the select phrase, the result of grouping without aggregation has columns of simple type. The value for each result column is obtained by picking the value of the last record matching the group domain value.

For example, the following query,

```
      select by p from sp
p | s  qty
--| ------
p1| s2 300
p2| s4 200
p3| s1 400
p4| s4 300
p5| s1 400
p6| s1 100
```

is equivalent to the following query using the aggregate `last` on each non-grouped column:

```
      select last s, last qty by p from sp
p | s  qty
--| ------
p1| s2 300
p2| s4 200
p3| s1 400
p4| s4 300
p5| s1 400
p6| s1 100
```

One way to obtain all the remaining columns in a grouping without explicitly listing them in a `select` is to use the `xgroup` function. It takes column symbol(s) as the left operand and a table as its right operand. The result is a keyed table that is that same as listing all the non-grouped columns in the comparable `select`. Using the distribution example:

```
        `p xgroup sp
p  | s                 qty
-- | ----------------------------------
p1 | `s$`s1`s2         300 300
p2 | `s$`s1`s2`s3`s4   200 400 200 200
p3 | `s$,`s1           ,400
p4 | `s$`s1`s4         200 300
p5 | `s$`s4`s1         100 400
p6 | `s$,`s1           ,100
```

8.6.3 Aggregation without Grouping

Aggregation can be applied against a column of simple type in any table. The aggregate function can be any function that processes a list of the appropriate form and produces an atom. While *q* has many built-in aggregates, you can also define and use your own.

We calculate the total and average order quantity in the `sp.q` script table sp using the built-in aggregates `sum` and `avg`:

```
        select totq:sum qty, avgq:avg qty from sp
tot q  avg q
-------------
3100   258.3333
```

8.6.4 Grouping with Aggregation

The equivalent of SQL GROUP BY is achieved in *q* by combining aggregation with grouping.

Continuing with the `sp.q` script example, we combine grouping and aggregation to compute the average order quantity by supplier:

```
        select avgqty:avg qty by s.name from sp
name  | avgqty
----- | --------
blake | 200
clark | 200
jones | 350
smith | 266.6667
```

8.6.5 Using Uniform and Aggregate Functions

Any uniform or aggregate functions can be applied directly to columns in aggregation. Again using the `sp.q` distribution example, for each salesperson we can find the cumulative low quantity at the same time with the average and high:

```
        select cumlo:mins qty, av:avg qty, hi:max qty
            by s.name from sp
name  | cumlo                           av        hi
------| -----------------------------------------------
blake | 200                             200       200
clark | 100 100 100                     200       300
jones | 300 300                         350       400
smith | 300 200 200 200 100 100         266.6667  400
```

8.6.6 Using each

If the data in a column is not atomic (that is, the column has a list of values in each row), you must use the `each` modifier to apply an aggregate.

In our `sp.q` example, suppose we define a table of intermediate results as:

```
        o:select qty by p.name from sp
         o
------| ----------------
bolt  | 200 400 200 200
cam   | 100 400
cog   | ,100
nut   | 300 300
screw | 400 200 300
```

We must use `each` to compute the average order size for each product in `o`:

```
        select name, avqty:avg qty from o
'length

        select name, avqty:avg each qty from o
name  avqty
----------
bolt  250
cam   250
cog   100
nut   300
screw 300
```

8.6.7 Using ungroup

The monadic function `ungroup` is a partial inverse to the resultant keyed tables of `select` and `xgroup`. It unwinds the keyed table into a table whose records have the same format as the original table. How closely its output resembles the original table depends on whether information has been collapsed in the grouping. We use the `sp` table from the distribution script for our examples:

```
       sp
s  p  qty
---------
s1 p1 300
s1 p2 200
s1 p3 400
s1 p4 200
s4 p5 100
s1 p6 100
s2 p1 300
s2 p2 400
s3 p2 200
s4 p2 200
s4 p4 300
s1 p5 400
```

```
      `p xgroup sp
p  | s                qty
-- | ----------------------------------
p1 | `s$`s1`s2        300 300
p2 | `s$`s1`s2`s3`s4  200 400 200 200
p3 | `s$,`s1          ,400
p4 | `s$`s1`s4        200 300
p5 | `s$`s4`s1        100 400
p6 | `s$,`s1          ,100
```

Since no aggregation has been performed and all non-key columns are present, the result of `ungroup` is the same as the original table with the rows sorted by the group column(s):

```
    ungroup `p xgroup sp
p  s  qty
---------
p1 s1 300
p1 s2 300
p2 s1 200
p2 s2 400
p2 s3 200
p2 s4 200
```

```
p3 s1 400
p4 s1 200
p4 s4 300
p5 s4 100
p5 s1 400
p6 s1 100
```

If aggregation has been performed or columns have been omitted, then only the selected values will be reflected after the `ungroup`. For example, we omit the `s` column in the following grouping, so it is also missing after the `ungroup`:

```
      select qty by p from sp
p | qty
--| ---------------
p1| 300 300
p2| 200 400 200 200
p3| ,400
p4| 200 300
p5| 100 400
p6| ,100

      ungroup select qty by p from sp
p  qty
------
p1 300
p1 300
p2 200
p2 400
p2 200
p2 200
p3 400
p4 200
p4 300
p5 100
p5 400
p6 100
```

> **Note**
>
> The result of a `select` in which grouping is specified but no columns are explicitly listed is not a keyed table of the proper form for ungroup. You will receive an error if you apply ungroup to the result of such a query.

8.7 SORTING

Recall that tables and keyed tables comprise lists of records and therefore have an inherent order. A table or keyed table can reordered by sorting on the values of any column(s). We use the following table definition in this section:

```
        t:([] c1:20 10 30 20; c2:`z`y`x`a)

        t
c1 c2
-----
20 z
10 y
30 x
20 a
```

8.7.1 xasc

The dyadic `xasc` takes a scalar or list of symbols containing column names as its left argument and a table as its right argument. It returns the records of the table sorted in ascending order of the items in the specified column(s). The order of the column names indicates the sort order, from major to minor:

```
        `c1 xasc t
c1 c2
-----
10 y
20 z
20 a
30 x

        `c2 xasc t
c1 c2
-----
20 a
30 x
10 y
20 z

        `c1`c2 xasc t
c1 c2
-----
10 y
20 a
20 z
30 x
```

> **Important**
>
> In order to modify the contents of a table you must refer to the table by name.

After execution of the expressions above, we still find:

```
     t
c1 c2
-----
20 z
10 y
30 x
20 a
```

However, `t` can be sorted in place with:

```
        `c1`c2 xasc `t
`t

     t
c1 c2
-----
10 y
20 a
20 z
30 x
```

8.7.2 xdesc

The dyadic `xdesc` behaves exactly as `xasc`, except that the sort is performed in descending order:

```
     t
c1 c2
-----
10 y
20 a
20 z
30 x

        `c1`c2 xdesc t
```

```
c1 c2
-----
30 x
20 z
20 a
10 y
```

8.8 RENAMING AND REARRANGING COLUMNS

Since a table is the flip of a column dictionary, its columns are named and ordered by the list of symbols in the dictionary domain. It is sometimes necessary to rename or reorder the columns. This is accomplished using the dyadic functions `xcol` and `xcols`. We use the following table definition in this section:

```
t:([] c1:20 10 30 20; c2:`z`y`x`a;
    c3:101.1 202.2 303.3 404.4)

      t
c1 c2 c3
-----------
20 z  101.1
10 y  202.2
30 x  303.3
20 a  404.4
```

8.8.1 xcol

The dyadic `xcol` takes a scalar or list of symbols containing column names as its left argument (*names*) and a table or keyed table (*source*) as its right argument. The count of *names* must be less than or equal to the number of columns in *source*. The result is a table obtained from *source* by renaming the columns, in order, using the symbols in *names*. For example:

```
       `id`name`val xcol t
id name val
------------
20 z    101.1
10 y    202.2
30 x    303.3
20 a    404.4
```

> **Important**
>
> The function `xcol` does not modify its table operand.

After execution of the expressions above, we still find:

```
          t
c1 c2 c3
-----------
20 z  101.1
10 y  202.2
30 x  303.3
20 a  404.4
```

However, `t` can effectively be renamed with:

```
       t:`id`name`val xcol t

           t
id name val
-------------
20 z    101.1
10 y    202.2
30 x    303.3
20 a    404.4
```

If the count of *names* is less than the number of columns in *source*, the remaining columns are unaffected. Returning to the original definition of `t`:

```
       `id`name xcol t

id name c3
-------------
20 z    101.1
10 y    202.2
30 x    303.3
20 a    404.4
```

8.8.2 xcols

The dyadic `xcols` takes a scalar or list of symbols containing column names as its left argument (*names*) and a table (*source*) as its right argument. The count of *names* must be less than or equal to the number of columns in *source*. It returns a table obtained from *source* by reordering the columns according to the symbols in *names*.

> **Note**
>
> The *source* operand **cannot** be a keyed table.

For example:

```
t:([] c1:20 10 30 20; c2:`z`y`x`a;
    c3:101.1 202.2 303.3 404.4)

    `c3`c2`c1 xcols t
c3    c2 c1
-----------
101.1 z  20
202.2 y  10
303.3 x  30
404.4 a  20
```

> **Important**
>
> The function `xcols` does not modify its *source*.

After execution of the expressions above, we still find:

```
        t
c1 c2 c3
-----------
20 z  101.1
10 y  202.2
30 x  303.3
20 a  404.4
```

However, `t` can effectively be reordered with:

```
t: `c3`c2`c1 xcols t

t
```

```
c3    c2 c1
----------
101.1 z  20
202.2 y  10
303.3 x  30
404.4 a  20
```

If the count of *names* is less than the number of columns in *source*, the specified columns are reordered at the beginning of the column list and the remaining columns are left unchanged. Returning to the original definition of t:

```
      `c3`c1 xcols t
c3    c1 c2
----------
101.1 20 z
202.2 10 y
303.3 30 x
404.4 20 a
```

8.9 Joins

It is common in SQL to reassemble normalized data by joining a table having a foreign key (*source*) to its primary key table along common key values. This situation occurs when the tables have a master-detail relation, or when the values of a field have been factored into a lookup table. Such an inner join with equals in the join criterion is called an *equal join* or an *equijoin*. In an equijoin, the join can be specified in either order, and there will be **exactly one** record in the result for each record in the *source*.

An inner join combines two tables having compatible columns by selecting a subset of the Cartesian product along matching column values. In a *left inner join*, each row from the first table (*source*) is paired with any matching rows from the second table. In a *right inner join*, each row from the second table (source) is paired with any matching rows from the first table. The match columns do not need to be key columns. In an inner join, there may be **no rows or multiple rows** in the result for each row in the source.

SQL also has outer joins, in which each element of one table (*source*) is paired with all matching elements of the other table. The match columns do not need to be key columns. In an outer join, there is at **least one row** in the result for each row in the *source*.

For convenience, we repeat here the definitions of our example tables:

```
kt:([eid:1001 1002 1003] name:`Dent`Beeblebrox`Prefect;
  iq:98 42 126)
```

```
tdetails:([] eid:`kL$1003 1002 1001 1002 1001 1002;
    sc:126 36 92 39 98 42)
```

8.9.1 Equijoin on Foreign Key

Given a primary key table m, foreign key table d and common key column k, an equijoin can be expressed in various SQL notations, among them,

```
m,d WHERE m.k = d.k

m INNER JOIN d ON m.k = d.k
```

A SELECT statement for this join refers to columns in the join by using dot notation based on the constituent tables:

```
SELECT d.col_d, m.col_m FROM m,d WHERE m.k = d.k
```

As we saw in **Chapter 7**, a *q* foreign key is accomplished with an enumeration. An inner join is implicit in the following select on the detail table:

```
select col_d, k.col_m from d
```

This generalizes to the situation where d has multiple foreign keys. Say d has foreign keys k_1, k_2, ..., k_n referring to primary key tables m_1, m_2, ..., m_n. Columns from the n-way join of d to the primary key tables are accessed via a select of the form:

```
select col_d, k_1.col_m1, k_2.col_m2, ..., k_n.col_mn from d
```

For example, in the sp.q distribution script:

```
        select sname:s.name, pname:p.name, qty from sp
sname pname qty
---------------
smith nut   300
smith bolt  200
smith screw 400
smith screw 200
clark cam   100
smith cog   100
jones nut   300
jones bolt  400
blake bolt  200
clark bolt  200
clark screw 300
smith cam   400
```

Multi-way equijoins also arise when m and d are as above and additionally d has a primary key l. If s is a table with a foreign key whose enumeration domain is l, then m, d and s can be joined. In SQL:

```
SELECT m.col_m, d.col_d, s.col_s from m,d,s WHERE m.k=d.k AND d.l=s.l
```

In *q* this is:

```
select l.k.col_m, l.col_d, col_s from s
```

8.9.2 Inner Join

Closely related to the equijoin is the dyadic inner join operator ij. The right operand is a keyed table (*lookup*) and the left operand is a table (*source*) having column(s) that match the key column(s) in *lookup*. In particular, *source* can have a foreign key defined over *lookup*. The inner join ij uses *lookup* to match the records of the appropriate *source* column(s) and upserts *source* with the value column(s) from *lookup*. The matching is done via common column name between *source* and the key column of *lookup* if there is no foreign key relationship.

> **Note**
>
> The inner join only contains records for which a match is found between *source* and *lookup*.

Using our example, all records match:

```
         tdetails ij kt
eid  sc  name         iq
-----------------------
1003 126 Prefect      126
1002 36  Beeblebrox   42
1001 92  Dent         98
1002 39  Beeblebrox   42
1001 98  Dent         98
1002 42  Beeblebrox   42
```

In the following example, the records don't all match and some are omitted from the result:

```
kt:([s:`a`b`c] ex:`N`O`CME)
```

```
        t:([] s:`a`c`d`a; p:121 33.5 42 121.5)

        t ij kt
s p     ex
-----------
a 121   N
c 33.5  CME
a 121.5 N
```

8.9.3 Pseudo Join

It is possible to lookup a table's values in a keyed table even if there is no foreign key relationship defined. One method to achieve this is to perform a dictionary lookup in `select`. There is no requirement for column names to match and the result will be a left outer join.

In the following example, observe that we must transform the column to be looked up into the proper shape:

```
        kt:([k:101 102 103] v:`a`b`c)
        t:([] c1:101 103 104)

        select c1, v:kt[flip enlist c1;`v] from t
c1  v
-----
101 a
103 c
104
```

The function `txf` (see §7.4) can also be used in this situation and it provides a uniform syntax for simple and compound keys. In our simple key example:

```
        select c1, v:txf[kt;c1;`v] from t
c1  v
-----
101 a
103 c
104
```

Here is an example with compound keys:

```
        t:([]c1:`a`b`c; c2:`x`x`z)
        ktc:([k1:`a`b`a; k2:`y`x`x] v:`one`two`three)

        select c1, c2, v:txf[ktc;(c1;c2);`v] from t
```

```
c1 c2 v
----------
a  x  three
b  x  two
c  z
```

8.9.4 Ad hoc Left Join

You can also create a left outer join using the dyadic `lj`. The right operand is a keyed table (*lookup*) and the left operand is a table (*source*) having column(s) that match the key column(s) in *lookup*. In particular, *source* can have a foreign key defined over *lookup*. The ad hoc join `lj` uses *lookup* to map the records of the appropriate *source* column(s) and upserts *source* with the value column(s) from *lookup*. In our example:

```
        tdetails lj kt
eid  sc  name       iq
----------------------
1003 126 Prefect    126
1001 36  Dent       42
1002 92  Beeblebrox 98
1001 39  Dent       42
1002 98  Beeblebrox 98
```

The same result can be obtained with a foreign key join by listing all the columns:

```
        select eid, sc, eid.name, eid.iq from tdetails
eid  sc  name       iq
----------------------
1003 126 Prefect    126
1001 36  Dent       98
1002 92  Beeblebrox 42
1001 39  Dent       98
1002 98  Beeblebrox 42
```

> **Note**
>
> The performance of an equijoin on a key is approximately 2.5 times faster than the equivalent ad hoc left join.

In contrast to the equijoin, an ad hoc left join does not require a column in the *source* table to be defined explicitly as a foreign key into the *lookup* keyed table:

```
td:([] eid:1003 1001 1002 1001 1002; sc:126 92 36 98 39)

        td lj kt
eid  sc  name        iq
-----------------------
1003 126 Prefect     126
1001 92  Dent        98
1002 36  Beeblebrox  42
1001 98  Dent        98
1002 39  Beeblebrox  42
```

> **Note**
>
> If the column(s) for the join are not foreign key(s) into the keyed table, the name(s) must match the key name(s).

Let's examine the general result of lj closely. Say t is the *source* table and kt is the *lookup* keyed table. For each record in t, the result has at least one record. If there are no records in kt whose values in the join column(s) match those in the corresponding column(s) of t, the t columns are present in the result and the remaining columns are null. If there are matching records in kt, for each match the result has a record comprising the catenation of the matching records:

```
kt:([k:1 2 3] b:100 200 300)

     kt
k|  b
-| ---
1| 100
2| 200
3| 300

t:([]k:1 1 2 2 3 4; a:10 11 20 21 30 40)

     t
```

```
k a
----
1 10
1 11
2 20
2 21
3 30
4 40

        t lj kt
k a  b
--------
1 10 100
1 11 100
2 20 200
2 21 200
3 30 300
4 40
```

> **Advanced**
>
> The behavior of lj differs from that of a SQL outer join when there are duplicate columns in the two tables. The SQL left outer join will display both columns, whereas lj upserts the appropriate column items of the *source* table with those of the *lookup* keyed table.

```
        t2:([] k:1 2 3; b:10 20 30)

        t2
k b
----
1 10
2 20
3 30

        kt2:([k:1 2 3 4] b:100 200 300 400)

        kt2
k| b
-| ---
1| 100
2| 200
3| 300
4| 400
```

```
        t2 lj kt2
k b
-----
1 100
2 200
3 300
```

8.9.5 Plus Join

The plus join `pj` is a type of left join that is useful for adding matching values in tables containing numeric data. As with an ad hoc join, the right operand of plus join is a keyed table (*lookup*) and the left operand is a table (*source*) having column(s) that match the key column(s) in *lookup*. The plus join `pj` uses *lookup* to map the records of the appropriate *source* column(s), zero filling nulls in the result from the *lookup* value column(s). It then performs a table add of this interim result into the *source* table. For example:

```
       kt:([k1:1 2; k2:`x`y] a:10 20; b:1.1 2.2)
       t:([]k1:1 2 3; k2:`x`y`z; a:100 200 300)

        t pj kt
k1 k2 a    b
-------------
1  x  110  1.1
2  y  220  2.2
3  z  300  0
```

We examine the result of `pj` more closely. Each record of `t` has a corresponding record in the result.

Along the matching rows, the value columns from *lookup* `kt` are added to those of *source* `t`. In our example, this means that columns a and b are added into `t` on matching rows. Since a exists in both tables, corresponding values are added. According to the rules of table arithmetic, since b does not exist in `t`, it is implicitly assumed to have 0 values in `t` for the addition.

For non-matching rows, the values of the *source* `t` are extended with 0 in the columns of *lookup*.

> **Advanced**
>
> Note that the result in our example can also be obtained by the expression below.

```
          t+0^kt[`k1`k2#t]
k1 k2 a   b
-----------------
1  x  110 1.1
2  y  220 2.2
3  z  300 0
```

8.9.6 Union Join

The union join `uj` combines any two tables. In the result, the rows and columns of the left operand appear before those of the right operand. Column value lists are joined for common columns. For non-common columns, the value lists are extended with nulls so that they are the same length. The column value lists of the left operand have nulls appended, whereas those of the right operand have nulls prepended:

```
          t1:([] c1:1 2 3; c2:101 102 103; c3:`x`y`z)
          t2:([] c2:103 104 105 106; c4:`a`b`c`d)

          t1
c1 c2  c3
---------
1  101 x
2  102 y
3  103 z

          t2
c2  c4
------
103 a
104 b
105 c
106 d

          t1 uj t2
c1 c2  c3 c4
------------
1  101 x
2  102 y
3  103 z
   103    a
   104    b
   105    c
   106    d
```

8.9.7 Asof Join

The asof join is so-named because it is often used to join tables along time columns, but this is not a restriction. There are two forms.

The first is `asof`, which can be used to join the left operand table t_1 to a dictionary or table right operand t_2. The last column of t_1 must match the last key or column of t_2 in name; both must be a time or other type with underlying numeric value. The remaining keys or columns of t_2 must match columns of t_1 in name and type.

More generally, the triadic function `aj` can be used to join two tables along common columns. Significantly, there is no requirement for any of the join columns to be keys. The syntax of an asof join with `aj` is,

```
aj[c₁...cₙ;t₁;t₂]
```

where $c_1 \ldots c_n$ is a symbol list of common column names for the join and t_1 and t_2 are the tables to be joined. The result is a table containing records from the left outer join of t_1 and t_2 along the specified columns.

When t_2 is a dictionary, the result of `asof` is a column dictionary of the matching values in t_1. When t_2 is table, the result of `asof` is a table with last record of t_1 of each match:

```
        t:([] sym:`msft`ibm`ge; qty:100 200 150;
            ti:10:01:01 10:01:03 10:01:04)

        t
sym  qty ti
-----------------
msft 100 10:01:01
ibm  200 10:01:03
ge   150 10:01:04

        d:`sym`ti!(`ibm;10:01:03)

        t asof d
qty| 200

        q1:([] sym:`ibm`msft; ti:10:01:03 10:01:01)

        q1
sym  ti
-------------
ibm  10:01:01
msft 10:01:01
```

```
        t asof q1
qty
---
200
100
```

For each record in t_1, the result of `aj` has one record containing all the items in t_1. If there is no record in t_2 whose values in the specified columns match those in the corresponding columns of t_1, there are no further items in the result record. If there are matching records in t_2, the items of the last (in row order) matching record are appended to those of the t_1 record in the result. With t as above:

```
        q2:([] ti:10:01:01 10:01:01 10:01:01 10:01:01;
            sym:`ibm`msft`msft`ibm; px:100 99 101 98)

         q2
ti         sym   px
-------------------
10:01:01   ibm   100
10:01:01   msft  99
10:01:01   msft  101
10:01:01   ibm   98

         aj[`ti`sym;t;q2]
sym  qty  ti         px
-----------------------
msft 100  10:01:01   98
ibm  200  10:01:01   100
ge   150  10:01:04
```

8.10 PARAMETERIZED QUERIES

Relational databases have the concept of stored procedures, which are programs that operate on tables via SQL statements. The programming languages that extend SQL are not part of the SQL standard, differ across vendors and the capabilities of the programming environments vary greatly.

This situation forces a programmer to make a difficult choice: pay a steep price in programming power to place functionality close to the data, or extract the data into an application server in order to perform calculations. Multi-tier architectures with separate database and application servers have evolved largely to address this problem, but they increase cost and complexity.

This choice is obviated in kdb+, since the *q* programming environment has all the power and performance you need. In fact, *q* is much faster than traditional database programming environments for retrieval and calculations on large time series. Other components of the application can perform their data retrieval and manipulation by making calls to *q*.

Traditional calls to a database are made via stored procedures, which are programs executed by the database manager. Often the stored procedure has parameters that supply specific values to the queries. Such parameters are limited to the basic data types of SQL.

Any *q* program can serve as a stored procedure; there is no distinction between data retrieval and calculations. Any valid *q* expression that operates on tables or dictionaries can be invoked in a function. Function parameters can be used to supply specific values for queries. In particular, the `select`, `exec`, `update` and `delete` templates can be invoked within a function by using parameters to pass specific values to the query. Such a function is called a *parameterized query*.

> **Important**
>
> Parameterized queries have restrictions:
>
> - A column cannot be passed as a parameter.
> - Only a single parameter can be implicit. Multiple parameters must be declared explicitly.

In the following example using our `tdetails` table, we pass a specific value for a foreign key match criterion:

```
getScByEid:{[e] select from tdetails where eid=e}

getScByEid 1003
eid  sc
--------
1003 126
```

This example can be generalized to handle a scalar or list argument:

```
getScByEid:{[e] select from tdetails where eid in ((),e)}

getScByEid 1001
```

```
eid  sc
-------
1001 92
1001 98

        getScByEid 1001 1003
eid  sc
-------
1003 126
1001 92
1001 98
```

The last expression in the revised function definition warrants closer examination. The empty-list join turns a scalar argument into a list and has no effect on a list. It must be enclosed in parentheses because it appears in a phrase in `select`, otherwise the comma is interpreted as a separator.

We could have written the above parameterized queries with an implicit argument x. If we want to pass two parameters, we **must** make them explicit:

```
        getScByEid:{[e;s] select from tdetails where eid=e,sc=s}

        getScByEid[1002;42]
eid  sc
-------
1002 42
```

You can pass a table as a parameter to a stored procedure. Suppose we have multiple trade tables, all having at the columns `px` (price) and `date` in common. The following parameterized query returns the maximum price over a specified date range from any trade table,

```
        maxpx:{[t,range] select max px from t where date within range}
```

Here `t` is a trade table and `range` is a list of two dates in increasing order.

> **Advanced**
>
> You can effectively parameterize column names in two ways. First, you can mimic a common technique from SQL in which the query is created dynamically: build the query text in a string and then pass the string to `value` for execution. There is a performance penalty for this approach. Also, you must remember to escape special characters in the string.

> **Advanced**
>
> The second method is to use the functional form of the query, which has no performance penalty. In the functional form, all columns are referred to by name, so columns names can be passed as symbols.

8.11 VIEWS

In SQL, a view is essentially a stored procedure whose result set is used like a table. Views are used to encapsulate such data transformations as hiding data columns or rows, renaming columns, or simplifying complex queries. q-sql implements a view as an alias to a query.

8.11.1 View

A *view* is a named query created as an alias with the double assignment (::) operator. In the following, the double-colon signifies that v is an alias for the query rather than the current result of the query:

```
t:([] c1:`a`b`c; c2:1 2 3)
v::select c1 from t where c2=2

        v
c1
--
b
```

When the content of the underlying table changes, the result will be reflected in the view. This is not true of the equivalent single assignment:

```
        r:select c1 from t where c2=2

        `t insert (`d;2)
,3

        t
c1 c2
-----
```

```
a  1
b  2
c  3
d  2
```

```
     r
c1
--
b
```

```
     v
c1
--
b
d
```

To find the underlying query of a view, use the function `view` on the symbolic view name:

```
    view `v
"select c1 from t where c2=2"
```

To list all the views in a context, use the function `views` with the context name:

```
    views `.
,`v
```

8.12 FUNCTIONAL FORMS

The functional forms of `select`, `exec`, `update` and `delete` can be used in any situation but are especially useful for programmatically generated queries, such as when column names are dynamically produced. The functional forms are:

```
        ?[t;c;b;a]      / select and exec

        ![t;c;b;a]      / update and delete
```

where `t` is a table, `a` is a dictionary of aggregates, `b` is a dictionary of groupbys and `c` is a list of constraints.

> **Note**
>
> All *q* entities in a, b and c must be referenced by name, meaning they appear as symbols containing the entity names.

The *q* interpreter parses the syntactic forms of `select`, `exec`, `update` and `delete` into their equivalent functional forms, so there is no performance difference. We shall use the sample table below in the following sections:

```
t:( []n:`x`y`x`z`z`y; p:0 15 12 20 25 14)

      t
n p
----
x 0
y 15
x 12
z 20
z 25
y 14
```

> **Advanced**
>
> The function `parse` can be applied to a string containing a query template to produce a parse tree whose items are close to the arguments of the equivalent functional form. See the description of `parse` in **Appendix A** for more details.

8.12.1 Functional select

Let's start with a simple `select` example:

```
select m:max p, s:sum p by name:n from t
    where p>0, n in `x`y
name| m  s
----| -----
x   | 12 12
y   | 15 29
```

Following is the equivalent functional form. Observe the use of `enlist` to create singletons, ensuring that certain entities are lists:

```
        c: ((>;`p;0);(in;`n;enlist `x`y))
        b: (enlist `name)!enlist `n
        a: `m`s!((max;`p);(sum;`p))

        ?[t;c;b;a]
name| m  s
----| -----
x   | 12 12
y   | 15 29
```

Of course, the functional form can be written without the intermediate variables a, b and c. We leave this as an exercise for the macho coder.

The general form of functional `select` is,

```
?[t;c;b;a]
```

where `t` is a table, `c` is a list of where specifications (<u>c</u>onstraints), `b` is a dictionary of grouping specifications (<u>b</u>y phrase), and `a` is a dictionary of `select` specifications (<u>a</u>ggregations).

Each item in `c` is an evaluation list consisting of a boolean or int valued function followed by its argument(s). Each argument is an expression containing column names and other variables. The function is applied to its argument(s), producing a boolean or int vector. The resulting vector selects the rows that yield non-zero results. The selection is performed in the order of the items in `c`, from left to right.

The domain of `b` is a list of symbols that are the key names for the grouping. The range of `b` is a list of column expressions whose results are grouped by common value. The grouping is ordered by the domain items, from major to minor.

The domain of `a` is a list of symbols containing the names of the produced columns. Each element of the range of `a` is an evaluation list consisting of a function and its argument(s), each of which is a column name or another such result list. For each evaluation list, the function is applied to the specified value(s) for each row and the result is returned. The evaluation lists are resolved recursively when operations are nested:

> **Note**
>
> Here are the degenerate cases:
> - For no constraints, make `c` the empty (general) list

- For no grouping make b a boolean 0b
- To produce all colums of the original table in the result, make a the empty list

For example:
```
select from t        / is equivalent to functional form
?[t;();0b;()]        / degenerate case for c, b, a
```

8.12.2 Functional exec

The functional form of `exec` is a simplified form of `select`. Since the constraint parameter is the same as in `select`, we omit it in the following.

In the simplest example of a single result column, the groupby parameter is the empty list and the aggregate parameter is a symbol atom:

```
        exec n from t
`x`y`x`z`z`y

        ?[t;();();`n]        / same as previous exec
`x`y`x`z`z`y
```

In the same query with multiple columns, the groupby parameter is the empty list and the aggregate parameter is a dictionary as it would be in a `select`. Remember that the result is a dictionary rather than a table:

```
        exec n,p from t
n| x y  x  z  z  y
p| 0 15 12 20 25 14

        ?[t;();();`n`p!`n`p]  / same as previous exec
n| x y  x  z  z  y
p| 0 15 12 20 25 14
```

If you wish to group by a single column, specify it as a symbol atom:

```
        exec p by n from t
x| 0  12
y| 15 14
z| 20 25
```

```
        ?[t;();`n;`p]                    / same as previous exec
x|  0  12
y| 15  14
z| 20  25
```

More complex examples of exec seem to reduce to the equivalent select.

8.12.3 Functional update

The functional form of update is completely analogous to functional select, except that ! is used in place of ?. Again observe the use of enlist to create singletons to ensure that appropriate entities are lists:

```
        update p:max p by n from t where p>0
n p
----
x 0
y 15
x 12
z 25
z 25
y 15

        c:enlist (>;`p;0)
        b:(enlist `p)!enlist `p
        a:(enlist `p)!enlist (max;`p)

        ![t;c;b;a]
n p
----
x 0
y 15
x 12
z 20
z 25
y 14
```

> **Note**
>
> The degenerate cases are the same as in functional select.

8.12.4 Functional delete

The functional form of delete is a simplified form of functional update,

```
![t;c;0b;a]
```

where `t` is a table, `c` is a list of where specifications (constraints) and `a` is a list of column names. Either `c` or `a`, but not both, must be present. The list of constraints, which has the same format as in functional `select` and `update`, chooses which rows will be removed. The aggregates argument is a simple list of symbols with the names of columns to be removed.

In the following examples, observe the use of `enlist` to create singletons to ensure that appropriate entities are lists:

```
t:([] c1:`a`b`c; c2:`x`y`z)

/ following is: delete c2 from t
![t;();0b;enlist `c2]
c1
--
a
b
c

/ following is: delete from t where c2 = `y
![t;enlist (=;`c2; enlist `y);0b;`symbol$()]
c1 c2
-----
a  x
c  z
```

8.13 EXAMPLES

In this section we demonstrate many of the capabilities of q-sql using semi-serious examples taken from the world of finance. We create a sample table representing a month's worth of trades for a small set of American stocks. To make things easy, we treat all trades as buys.

8.13.1 The Table Schemas

Our vastly over-simplified trading example involves two tables. The `instrument` table is a reference keyed table that contains basic information about the companies whose financial instruments (stocks in our case) are traded. Its schema has fields for the stock symbol, the name of the company and the industry classification of the company:

```
instrument:([sym:`symbol$()]
    name:`symbol$(); industry:`symbol$())

    instrument
sym| name industry
---| ------------
```

The `trade` table represents a collection of trades. Each trade record comprises: the symbol of the instrument; the date and time of the trade; the quantity — i.e. number of shares traded; and the price of the trade:

```
trade:([] sym:`instrument$(); date:`date$();
    time:`time$(); quant:`int$(); px:`float$())

    trade
sym date time quant px
----------------------
```

> **Note**
>
> In practice, the `trade` table would likely be partitioned by day on disk and only the current day's trades would be stored in memory.

8.13.2 Creating the Tables

Populating the `instrument` reference table is done via simple inserts:

```
`instrument insert (`ibm; `$"International Business Machines";
                    `$"Computer Services")
`instrument insert (`msft; `$"Microsoft"; `$"Software")
`instrument insert (`g; `$"Google"; `$"Internet")
`instrument insert (`intc; `$"Intel"; `$"Semiconductors")
`instrument insert (`gm; `$"General Motors"; `$"Automobiles")
`instrument insert (`ge; `$"General Electric";
                    `$"Diversified Industries")
```

Here is the console display of `instrument`:

```
    instrument
sym | name                          industry
----| --------------------------------------------------
ibm | International Business Machines Computer Services
```

```
msft| Microsoft                Software
g   | Google                   Internet
intc| Intel                    Semiconductors
gm  | General Motors           Automobiles
ge  | General Electric         Diversified Industries
```

In order to populate the trade table with somewhat realistic data, we create an auxiliary function. The `filltrade` function takes the name of the target trade table, a stock symbol, a median price and a count. It populates the named table with simulated trade data for the month of Jan 2007. The trades are randomly distributed across days and times. The quantities occur in multiples of 10. The prices are uniformly distributed around the median price. We do not claim that this represents realistic trade data; only that it is sufficient to serve our query examples:

```
filltrade:{[tname;s;p;n]
    // tname is name of target table
    // s is stock symbol
    // p is median price
    // n is count of items
    //
    / sym column duplicates stock symbol n times
    sc:n#s;
    / date column has n random days in Jan 2007
    dc:2007.01.01+n?31;
    / time column has n random times
    tc:n?24:00:00.000;
    / quantity column has n random multiples of 10
    qc:10*n?1000;
    / price column has n random prices that are
    / distributed uniformly around p
    / prices are in pennies
    pc:.01*floor (.9*p)+n?.2*p*:100;
    / bulk insert columns into target table
    tname insert (sc;dc;tc;qc;pc)
    }

    filltrade[`trade;`ibm;115;10000]
0 1 2 3 4 5 6 7 8 9 10 11 12 13 14 15 16 17 18 19 20 21 22..

    trade
sym date       time              quant  px
-------------------------------------------
ibm 2007.01.15 02:32:54.217      9280   111.59
ibm 2007.01.20 08:56:05.985      9960   110.69
ibm 2007.01.24 19:20:17.727      5970   114.58
..
```

We invoke `filltrade` on each of the remaining instruments:

```
        filltrade[`trade;`msft;30;5000]
10000 10001 10002 10003 10004 10005 10006 10007 10008 10009..

        filltrade[`trade;`g;540;12000]
15000 15001 15002 15003 15004 15005 15006 15007 15008 15009..

        filltrade[`trade;`intc;25;4000]
27000 27001 27002 27003 27004 27005 27006 27007 27008 27009..

        filltrade[`trade;`ge;40;9000]
31000 31001 31002 31003 31004 31005 31006 31007 31008 31009..

        filltrade[`trade;`gm;35;3000]
40000 40001 40002 40003 40004 40005 40006 40007 40008 40009..
```

Finally, we sort `trade` by date and time so that it represents trades as they came in:

```
        `date`time xasc `trade
`trade

        trade
sym   date        time           quant px
---------------------------------------------
intc  2007.01.01  00:00:04.569   5440  26.63
ge    2007.01.01  00:02:24.871   8280  40.11
gm    2007.01.01  00:02:43.419   4280  32.13
ibm   2007.01.01  00:03:06.278   5070  105.73
intc  2007.01.01  00:03:24.229   1740  24.47
gm    2007.01.01  00:04:17.590   830   36.53
gm    2007.01.01  00:04:18.227   5060  33.02
ge    2007.01.01  00:04:18.772   8290  43.73
msft  2007.01.01  00:06:01.424   5170  27.71
..
```

8.13.3 Basic queries

In this section, we demonstrate the use of basic q-sql to query the `trade` and `instrument` tables we have created.

We can count the total number of trades in several ways:

```
        count trade
43000

        select count i from trade
x
-----
43000

        exec count i from trade
43000
```

We can count the number of trades for an individual symbol:

```
        exec count i from trade where sym=`ibm
10000

        count select from trade where sym=`ibm
10000
```

Observe that the former retrieves only a single record from the query whereas the latter retrieves all matching records and then counts them.

We can count the number of trades across all symbols:

```
        select count i by sym from trade
sym | x
----| -----
g   | 12000
ge  | 9000
gm  | 3000
ibm | 10000
intc| 4000
msft| 5000

        () xkey select count i by sym from trade
sym   x
----------
g     12000
ge    9000
gm    3000
ibm   10000
intc  4000
msft  5000
```

Observe that the former retrieves the results as a keyed table and the latter removes the key.

We find one day's trades for GM:

```
        select from trade where sym=`gm, date=2007.01.07
sym date       time          quant px
------------------------------------------
gm  2007.01.07 00:29:31.311 4390  32.24
gm  2007.01.07 00:29:57.886 1270  38.08
gm  2007.01.07 00:30:35.671 3370  35.67
gm  2007.01.07 00:30:43.216 8090  36.77
gm  2007.01.07 00:44:26.336 1800  35.03
..
```

We find all lunch hour trades for GM:

```
        select from trade where sym=`gm,
            time within (12:00:00;13:00:00)
sym date       time          quant px
------------------------------------------
gm  2007.01.01 12:01:32.133 7960  33.61
gm  2007.01.01 12:37:45.021 8480  31.84
gm  2007.01.01 12:39:46.197 5350  32.34
gm  2007.01.01 12:57:13.215 1090  33.34
gm  2007.01.02 12:53:06.764 1080  31.63
..
```

We find the maximum daily price for GE. Due to our simplistic construction, it is statistically constant:

```
        select maxpx:max px by date from trade
            where sym=`ge
date       | maxpx
-----------|------
2007.01.01 | 43.97
2007.01.02 | 43.99
2007.01.03 | 43.99
2007.01.04 | 43.98
..
```

We find the minimum and maximum trade price over the time span for each symbol and display the result by company name. The latter resolves the foreign key to the `instrument` table with an implicit inner join:

```
        select lo:min px, hi:max px by sym.name
            from trade
```

```
name                              | lo     hi
----------------------------------|------------
General Electric                  | 36     43.99
General Motors                    | 31.5   38.49
Google                            | 486    593.99
Intel                             | 22.5   27.49
International Business Machines   | 103.5  126.49
Microsoft                         | 27     32.99
```

We find the total and average trade volume for three symbols. Due to our simplistic construction, the latter are statistically the same:

```
select totq:sum quant,
       avgq:avg quant by sym
       from trade where sym in `ibm`msft`g

sym | tot q      avgq
----|-------------------
g   | 59748830   4979.069
ibm | 49983940   4998.394
msft| 24988910   4997.782
```

We find the daily volume weighted average price for Intel:

```
select vwap:quant wavg px by date from trade
       where sym=`intc

date       | vwap
-----------|--------
2007.01.01 | 24.86849
2007.01.02 | 25.00113
2007.01.03 | 24.82538
2007.01.04 | 24.98049
2007.01.05 | 25.27898
..
```

We find the high, low and close over one minute intervals for Intel:

```
select hi:max px,lo:min px,close:last px
       by date, time.minute from trade where sym=`intc

date       minute| hi    lo    close
-----------------|------------------
2007.01.01 00:12 | 23.3  23.3  23.3
2007.01.01 00:17 | 24.03 24.03 24.03
2007.01.01 00:26 | 24.45 24.45 24.45
```

```
2007.01.01 00:51 | 25.73 25.73 25.73
2007.01.01 00:55 | 25.34 25.34 25.34
..
```

We demonstrate how to use your own functions in queries. Suppose we define a funky average that weights items by their position:

```
favg:{(sum x*1+til count x)%(count x)*count x}
```

Then we can apply this just as we did the built-in *q* function `avg`:

```
       select favgpx:favg px by sym from trade
sym | favgpx
----| --------
g   | 270.0021
ge  | 19.99897
gm  | 17.51145
ibm | 57.53255
intc| 12.48081
msft| 15.00309
```

8.13.4 Meaty Queries

In this section, we demonstrate more interesting q-sql against the `trade` table.

We find the volume weighted average price over 5 minute intervals for intel:

```
        select vwap:quant wavg px by date,
           bucket:5 xbar time.minute from trade where sym=`intc
date       bucket| vwap
-----------------| --------
2007.01.01 00:10 | 23.3
2007.01.01 00:15 | 24.03
2007.01.01 00:25 | 24.45
2007.01.01 00:50 | 25.73
2007.01.01 00:55 | 25.34
..
```

We use `favg` from the previous section to demonstrate that user functions can appear in any phrase of the query:

```
        select from trade where px<2*(favg;px) fby sym
```

```
sym  date       time         quant px
-----------------------------------------
gm   2007.01.01 00:06:02.168 5270  33.6
g    2007.01.01 00:07:36.023 9340  527.71
g    2007.01.01 00:09:46.313 3640  491.6
intc 2007.01.01 00:12:05.909 610   23.3
ibm  2007.01.01 00:12:17.056 6410  112.92
..
```

We find the average daily volume and price for all instruments and store the result for the next example:

```
atrades:select avgqt:avg quant, avgpx:avg px
    by sym, date from trade

       atrades
sym date       | avgqt    avgpx
---------------|------------------
g   2007.01.01| 5098.892 542.3796
g   2007.01.02| 5021.136 538.6672
g   2007.01.03| 5114     539.1208
g   2007.01.04| 4712.385 541.5371
g   2007.01.05| 5202.108 539.6128
..
```

We find the days when the average price went up. Note that we must explicitly exclude the first day because `deltas` is funky on its first value. Observe that the `avpx` column scrolls off the page:

```
select date, avgpx by sym from atrades
    where 0<{0,1_deltas x} avgpx

sym  | date
-----|-------------------------------------------------...
g    | 2007.01.03 2007.01.04 2007.01.06 2007.01.08...
ge   | 2007.01.02 2007.01.04 2007.01.06 2007.01.08...
gm   | 2007.01.02 2007.01.04 2007.01.05 2007.01.07...
ibm  | 2007.01.01 2007.01.03 2007.01.05 2007.01.08...
intc | 2007.01.04 2007.01.05 2007.01.08 2007.01.10...
msft | 2007.01.01 2007.01.02 2007.01.04 2007.01.07...
```

To see a more representative display, take only the first few field values:

```
select 2#date, 2#avgpx by sym from atrades
    where 0<{0,1_deltas x} avgpx
```

```
sym  | date                      avgpx
-----|------------------------------------------
g    | 2007.01.03 2007.01.04 539.1208 541.5371
ge   | 2007.01.02 2007.01.04 39.98092 40.115
gm   | 2007.01.02 2007.01.04 35.13107 35.25371
ibm  | 2007.01.01 2007.01.03 115.1667 115.1036
intc | 2007.01.04 2007.01.05 24.83024 25.18836
msft | 2007.01.01 2007.01.02 29.73195 30.03784
```

We can denormalize `trade` to obtain a keyed table with one row and complex columns for each symbol. We display the first two items of each field to make the structure more evident:

```
dntrades:select date,time,quant,px by sym from trade

select 2#date,2#time,2#quant,2#px by sym from trade

sym  | date                   time                            quant       px
-----|-------------------------------------------------------------------------------
g    | 2007.01.01 2007.01.01 00:09:54.444 00:12:34.851 4670 3080 591.05 523.08
ge   | 2007.01.01 2007.01.01 00:02:24.871 00:04:18.772 8280 8290 40.11  43.73
gm   | 2007.01.01 2007.01.01 00:02:43.419 00:04:17.590 4280 830  32.13  36.53
ibm  | 2007.01.01 2007.01.01 00:03:06.278 00:06:27.951 5070 9740 105.73 117.76
intc | 2007.01.01 2007.01.01 00:00:04.569 00:03:24.229 5440 1740 26.63  24.47
msft | 2007.01.01 2007.01.01 00:06:01.424 00:23:28.908 5170 1370 27.71  29.86
```

In such a complex table or keyed table, you must use `each` to apply a monadic (unary) function across the items in a field:

```
select sym,cnt:count each date,
       avgpx:avg each px from dntrade

/ or the following alternate notation is equivalent

select sym,cnt:each[count] date,
       avgpx: each[avg] px from dntrade

sym   cnt    avgpx
-------------------
g     12000  540.0778
ge    9000   39.99574
gm    3000   34.98716
ibm   10000  114.978
intc  4000   24.96621
msft  5000   29.98583
```

We can also apply our own monadic `favg` function with `each`:

```
        select sym, favgpx:favg each px from dntrades
sym   favgpx
-------------
g     269.94
ge    19.98121
gm    17.48443
ibm   57.49667
intc  12.48413
msft  15.0314
```

We find the volume weighted average price by applying the dyadic `wavg`. In this case we must use the each-both adverb `'`. Observe that our simplistic construction makes the average price and volume weighted average price statistically the same:

```
        select sym, vwap:quant wavg' px from dntrade

        / is equivalent to the alternate notation

        select sym, vwap:wavg'[quant;px] from dntrade
sym   vwap
-------------
g     540.1832
ge    40.00807
gm    34.95398
ibm   114.9836
intc  24.97542
msft  29.96661
```

Note that the latter form generalizes to *n*-adic functions for any *n*>1.

We find the profit of the ideal transaction over the month for each symbol. This is the maximum amount of money that could be made with 20-20 hindsight. In other words, find the largest profit obtainable by buying at any traded price and selling at the highest subsequently traded price. To solve this, we reverse the perspective. For each traded price, we look at the minimum prices that preceeded it. The largest such difference is our answer:

```
        select max px-mins px by sym from trade
sym  | px
-----| ------
g    | 107.99
ge   | 7.99
gm   | 6.99
```

```
ibm  | 22.99
intc | 4.99
msft | 5.99
```

8.13.5 Remote Queries

In this section, we demonstrate how to execute q-sql queries against a remote server. We assume that our sample tables have been created in a *q* instance (the server) that is listening on some port, say 5042. We also assume that we have another *q* process (the client) with an open handle h to the server. See **Chapter 10** for details on how to connect to remote processes in *q*. The following expressions are all executed on the **client**.

We can ask the server to list its tables:

```
        h "tables `."
`dntrades`instrument`trade
```

We can ask the server for the count of its trade table:

```
        h "count trade"
43000
```

We look up a name by sym. Observe the result is a vector:

```
        h "exec sym from instrument where name=`Intel"
,`intc
```

We can look up a sym by name. Observe the necessity of escaping the double quotes inside the dynamic q-sql string:

```
        h "exec name from instrument where name=`$\"General Electric\""
,`General Electric
```

We can construct a query on the client and send it to the server along with parameters to be executed:

```
        qdaily:{[s;d] select from trade where sym=s, date=d}

        h (qdaily;`g;2007.01.12)
```

```
sym date        time         quant px
-----------------------------------------
g   2007.01.12  00:03:24.082  3570  507.44
g   2007.01.12  00:05:31.920  2900  588.99
..
```

We can construct the same query on the server and execute it remotely:

```
        h "qdaily:{[s;d] select from trade where sym=s, date=d}"
        / verify that it's there
        h "qdaily"
{[s;d] select from trade where sym=s, date=d}

        / execute it
        h "qdaily[`msft;2007.01.31]"
sym  date        time         quant px
-----------------------------------------
msft 2007.01.31  00:00:41.237  9940  29.65
msft 2007.01.31  00:01:36.508  580   27.19
..
```

CHAPTER 9
EXECUTION CONTROL

9.0 OVERVIEW

Function evaluation provides sequential execution of a series of expressions. In this chapter, we demonstrate how to achieve non-sequential execution in *q*.

9.1 CONTROL FLOW

In a vector-oriented language such as *q*, the clearest code and best performance is generally obtained by avoiding loops and individual tests. For those times when you simply must write iffy or loopy code, *q* has versions of the usual constructs.

> **Warning**
>
> The constructs in this section all involve branching in the byte code that is generated by the *q* interpreter. The offset of the branch destination is limited (currently to 255 byte codes), which means that the sequence of *q* expressions that can be contained in any part of $, if, do, or while must be short. At some point, insertion of one additional statement will result in a 'branch error, which is *q*'s way of rejecting bloated code. If you insist on writing iffy or loopy code (never a good idea in *q*), factor code blocks into separate functions.

9.1.1 Basic Conditional Evaluation

Languages of C heritage have a form of in-line **if** called conditional evaluation of the form,

   $expr_{cond}$? $expr_{true}$: $expr_{false}$

where $expr_{cond}$ is an expression that evaluates to a boolean (or int in C and C++).

The result of the expression is $expr_{true}$ when $expr_{cond}$ is true (or non-zero) and $expr_{false}$ otherwise.

The same effect can be achieved in *q* using basic conditional evaluation,

```
$[expr_cond; expr_true; expr_false]
```

where $expr_{cond}$ is an expression that evaluates to a boolean or int. The result is $expr_{true}$ when $expr_{cond}$ is not zero and $expr_{false}$ if it is zero:

```
        a:42
        b:98

        $[a>60; `Pass; `Fail]
`Fail

        $[b>60; `Pass; `Fail]
`Pass
```

Observe that a test for zero in $expr_{cond}$ can be abbreviated:

```
        c:0

        $[a; `Nonzero; `Zero]
`Nonzero

        $[b; `Nonzero; `Zero]
`Nonzero

        $[c; `Nonzero; `Zero]
`Zero
```

> **Note**
>
> A null is not acceptable for $expr_{cond}$.

```
        d:0N

        $[d; `NonNull; `Null]
'type
```

9.1.2 Extended Conditional Evaluation

In languages of C heritage, the if-else construct has the form,

```
if (expr_cond) {
    statement_true1;
    .
    .
    .
}
else {
    statement_false1;
    .
    .
    .
}
```

where $expr_{cond}$ is an expression that evaluates to a boolean (or int in C and C++). If the expression $expr_{cond}$ is true (or non-zero) the first sequence of statements in braces is executed; otherwise, the second sequence of statements in braces is executed.

A similar effect can be achieved in *q* using an extended form of conditional evaluation:

```
$[expr_cond; [expr_true1; ...]; [expr_false1; ...]]
```

where $expr_{cond}$ is an expression that evaluates to a boolean or int. When $expr_{cond}$ evaluates to non-zero, the first bracketed sequence of expressions is executed in left-to-right order; otherwise, the second bracketed sequence of expressions is executed:

```
    a1:42
    a2:24

    $[a1<>42; [a:6;b:7;a*b]; [a:`Life;b:`the;c:`Universe;a,b,c]]
`Life`the`Universe

    $[a2<>42; [a:6;b:7;a*b];
    [a:`Life;b:`the;c:`Universe;a,b,c]]
42
```

Languages of C heritage have a cascading form of if-else in which multiple tests can be made:

```
if (expr_cond1) {
    statement_true11;
    .
    .
    .
}
```

```
    else if (expr_condn) {
        statement_truen1;
        .
        .
        .
    }
    .
    .
    .
    else {
        statement_false;
        .
        .
        .
    }
}
```

In this construction, the $expr_{cond}$ are evaluated consecutively until one is true (or non-zero), at which point the associated block of statements is executed and the statement is complete. If none of the expressions passes, the final block of statements, called the *default* case, is executed.

Note that any conditional other than the first is only evaluated if all those prior to it have evaluated to false. In addition, only one of the statement blocks will be executed.

A similar effect can be achieved in *q* with another extended form of conditional execution.

$\$[expr_{cond1}; expr_{true1}; \ldots; expr_{condn}; expr_{truen}; expr_{false}]$

In this form, the conditional expressions are evaluated consecutively until one is non-zero, at which point the associated $expr_{true}$ is evaluated and its result is returned. If none of the conditional expressions evaluates to non-zero, $expr_{false}$ is evaluated and its result is returned. Observe that $expr_{false}$ is distinguished as the last expression following a sequence of paired expressions.

> **Note**
>
> Any conditional other than the first is only evaluated if all those prior to it have evaluated to zero. Otherwise put, a conditional evaluating to non-zero short-circuits the evaluation of subsequent ones.

```
a:42
b:0
c:-42
```

```
        $[a=0;`zero; a>0;`pos; `neg]
`pos

        $[b=0;`zero; b>0;`pos; `neg]
`zero

        $[c=0;`zero; c>0;`pos; `neg]
`neg
```

Finally, the previous extended form of conditional execution can be further extended by substituting a bracketed sequence of expressions for any $expr_{true}$ or $expr_{false}$:

```
    $[expr_cond1;[expr_true11; ...]; ...;
        expr_condn;[expr_truen1; ...];
        [expr_false1; ...]]
```

9.1.3 Vector Conditional Evaluation

Triadic vector-conditional evaluation (?) has the form,

```
    ?[v_b; expr_true; expr_false]
```

where v_b is a simple boolean list and $expr_{true}$ and $expr_{false}$ are of the same type and are atoms or vectors that conform to v_b. The result conforms to v_b and selects from $expr_{true}$ in positions where v_b has 1b and $expr_{false}$ in positions where v_b has 0b.

The following example inserts 42 for odd-valued items of a list:

```
    L:(til 10) mod 3

    L
0 1 2 0 1 2 0 1 2 0

    ?[0=L mod 2; L; 42]
0 42 2 0 42 2 0 42 2 0
```

> **Note**
>
> All arguments of a vector-conditional are fully executed. In other words, there is no short circuiting of the evaluation.

9.1.4 if

The `if` statement conditionally evaluates a sequence of expressions. It has the form,

    if[expr_cond; expr_1; ...; expr_n]

where $expr_{cond}$ is evaluated and if it is non-zero the expressions $expr_1$ thru $expr_n$ are evaluated in left-to-right order. The `if` statement does not have an explicit result. For example:

```
a:42
b:98
z:""

if[a=42; z:"Life the universe and everything"]
z
"Life the universe and everything"

if[b<>42; x:6; y:7; z:x*y]
z
42
```

9.1.5 do

The `do` statement is an iterator of the form,

    do[expr_count; expr_1; ...; expr_n]

where $expr_{count}$ must evaluate to an int. The expressions $expr_1$ thru $expr_n$ are evaluated $expr_{count}$ times in left-to-right order. The `do` statement does not have an explicit result.

For example, the following expression is a loopy computation of n factorial. It iterates n-1 times, decrementing the factor f on each pass:

```
n:5
do[-1+f:r:n; r*:f-:1]
r
120
```

9.1.6 while

The `while` statement is an iterator of the form,

    while[expr_cond; expr_1; ...; expr_n]

where $expr_{cond}$ is evaluated and the expressions $expr_1$ thru $expr_n$ are evaluated repeatedly in left-to-right order as long as $expr_{cond}$ is non-zero. The while statement does not have an explicit result.

Here is the loopy factorial redone with while:

```
        f:r:n:5
        while[f-:1;r*:f]
        r
120
```

Let's examine a nifty example taken from the *q Language Reference Manual*. The following function returns a list in which each null item in the argument list x has been replaced with the item before it:

```
        f:{r:x; r[i]:r[-1+i:where null r]; r}
```

Now observe that the expression,

```
        max null v
```

indicates whether there are any nulls in a list v (why?).

The following expression applies f iteratively until there are no nulls left in v.

```
        while[max null v; v:f v]
```

Effectively, non-null values are propagated forward across nulls:

```
        v:10 -3.1 0n 42 0n 0n 0n 3.4

        while[max null v; v:f v]
        v
10 -3.1 -3.1 42 42 42 42 3.4
```

Do you see the problem with this example? Hint: consider the case where v has one or more initial null items and remember that Ctrl-C terminates execution of a long-running *q* expression. The while expression will iterate forever because there is no value to propagate across the initial item.

When you know v will be of a type having an underlying numeric value, one solution is to prepend a default initial value and remove it afterward. We use a type-matched zero:

```
        v:0n -3.1 0n 42 0n 0n 0n 3.0
```

```
    w:((type v)$0),v

    while[max null w; w:f w]
    1_w
0 -3.1 -3.1 42 42 42 42 3
```

9.1.7 Return and Signal

Normal function execution evaluates each expression in the function and terminates after the last one. There are two mechanisms for ending the execution early: one returns successfully and the other aborts.

To terminate a function's execution successfully and return a value, use an empty assignment, which is assign (:) with a value to its right and no variable to its left. For example, in the following contrived function, execution is terminated and the result is returned after the third expression. The final expression is never evaluated:

```
    c:0

    f:{a:6; b:7; :a*b; c::98}
    f 0
42

    c
0
```

To abort function execution immediately, use *signal*, which is single-quote (') with a value to its right. For example, in the following function, execution will be aborted in the third expression. The final expression that assigns c is never evaluated:

```
    c:0
    g:{a:6; b:7; '`TheEnd;c::98}

    g 0
{a:6;b:7;'`TheEnd;c::98}
'TheEnd

    c
0
```

> **Note**
>
> Unless a function issuing a signal is invoked with protected execution, the signal will cause the calling routine to fail.

You can also use signal within an `if` statement to terminate execution. Compare the following:

```
    a:42
    if[a<50; '`Stop; b:100]
'Stop
```

9.1.8 Protected Evaluation

Languages of C++ heritage have the concept of protected execution using a try-catch. The idea is that an unexpected condition arising from any statement enclosed in the try portion does not abort execution. Instead, control transfers to the catch block, where the exception can be handled or passed up to the caller. This mechanism allows the call stack to be unwound gracefully.

q provides a similar capability using triadic forms of function evaluation (`@`) and (`.`). Triadic `@` is used for monadic functions and triadic `.` is used for multivalent functions. The syntax is the similar for both:

```
@[f_mon; a; expr_fail]

.[f_mul; L_args; expr_fail]
```

Here f_{mon} is a monadic function, `a` is single argument, f_{mul} is a multivalent function, L_{args} is a list of arguments, and $expr_{fail}$ is an expression or function. In both forms, the function `f` is applied to its argument(s). Upon successful application, the protected evaluation returns the result of `f`. Should an error arise, $expr_{fail}$ is evaluated; the error string is passed when $expr_{fail}$ is a function.

> **Note**
>
> If $expr_{fail}$ results in an error, the protected call itself will fail.

These functions are especially useful when processing input received from users. In the following examples, you would replace the unhelpful error message with more useful error handling.

Suppose a user wishes to enter dynamic *q* expressions. You could place the expression in a string and pass it to `value`. The problem with this is that if the user types an invalid *q* expression, it will cause the application to fail. You should instead use protected execution:

```
    s:"6*7"
```

```
        @[value; s; `$"Invalid q expression"]
42

        s:"6x7"
        @[value; s; `$"Invalid q expression"]
`Invalid q expression
```

Similarly, triadic . provides protected execution for multivalent functions:

```
        x:6
        y:7
        .[*; (x;y); `$" Invalid args for *"]
42

        x:6
        y:`7
        .[*; (x;y); `$" Invalid args for *"]
`Invalid args for *
```

9.2 Debugging

Debugging in *q* harkens back to the olden days, before the advent of debuggers and integrated development environments. The *q* gods don't give debugging much consideration because their code always runs correctly the first time. For the rest of us, things aren't quite as bad as inserting print statements, but you are certainly on your own. There is no debugger, nor is there any notion of break points or tracing execution.

When any expression evaluation fails, the console displays an (often cryptic) error message along with a dump of the offending values. Many errors manifest as either 'type or 'length, indicating an incompatibility in function arguments with respect to type or length. The goal is to discover the root cause of the superficial error.

The first step is to examine the dump of the offending arguments. Sometimes, the error will be obvious. A common 'type culprit is violation of type checking by attempting to assign a non-matching value to a simple list (e.g., a table column). Another common 'type offense is attempting to perform an operation on an atom not in the domain of the operation. A common culprit is failure to enlist an argument when a list is expected.

In a technique passed on by Simon Garland, you can get a more useful display of relevant information when a function is suspended. Define a function, say zs, as follows:

```
        zs:{`d`P`L`G`D!(system"d"),v[1 2 3],enlist last v:value x}
```

This function takes another function as its argument and returns a dictionary with entries for the current directory, function parameters, local variables referenced, global variables referenced and the function definition. We demonstrate this with a trivial example:

```
        b:7
        f:{a:6; x+a*b}

        f[100]                      / this is OK
142

        f[`100]                     / this is an error
{a:6;x+a*b}
'type
+
`100
42

        zs f                        / see what's what
d| `.
P| ,`x
L| ,`a
G| ``b
D| "{a:6; x+a*b}"
```

Stopping execution prior to the offending expression is helpful. This can be done be inserting a signal before the expression you wish to examine. You can then evaluate the various items in the offending evaluation. Stopping execution with a signal is a poor man's break point.

However the execution becomes suspended, you can evaluate the expressions of the function by hand from the console. To resume execution with a return value, issue a return (:) with the desired value at the command prompt. To return an error, issue a signal (') from the command line. To terminate execution and clear the call stack, issue (\) from the command line.

9.3 SCRIPTS

A *script* is a *q* program stored in a text file with an extension of *q*. A script can contain any *q* expressions or commands. The contents of the script are executed sequentially from top to bottom. Non-local entities created in the script exist in the workspace after the script is loaded.

9.3.1 Creating and Loading a Script

You can create a script in a text editor and save it with a *q* extension. For example, enter the following lines and save to a file named trades.q in the *q* directory:

```
trades:([] sym:(); ex:(); time:(); price:())

`trades insert (`IBM;`N; 12:10:00.0; 82.1)
`trades insert (`IBM;`O; 12:30:00.0; 81.95)
`trades insert (`MSFT;`N; 12:45:00.0; 23.45)
`trades insert (`IBM;`N; 12:50:00.0; 82.05)
`trades insert (`MSFT;`N; 13:30:00.0; 23.40)
```

Now issue the load command:

```
    \l trades.q
,0
,1
,2
,3
,4
```

You can verify that the trades table has been created and the records have been inserted:

```
    count trades
5
```

A script can be loaded at the start of the *q* session, or at any time during the session using the \l command. The load command can be executed from the console or from another script. See **Chapter 12** for more on commands.

9.3.2 Special Notations

You can comment out a block of code (i.e., multiple lines) in a script by surrounding it with matching / and \ each on its own line. An unmatched \ exits the script.

Here is a script snippet that demonstrates block comments:

```
a:42
b:42
```

```
/
this is a block of
comment text
b:43
and b will not be changed
\
a:43    / this line will be executed
\
nothing from here on will be executed
b:44
and b will still be 42
```

After this script (and no other) is loaded, a will be 43 and b will be 42.

Multi-line expressions are permitted in a script but they have a special form. The first line must **not** be indented — i.e., it begins at the left of the line with no initial whitespace. Any continuation lines **must** be indented, meaning that there is at least one whitespace character at the beginning of the line. Empty lines between expressions are permitted.

Table definition syntax and function definition syntax have the same rule for splitting across multiple lines:

- A table or function can have line breaks after a closing square bracket (]) or after a semicolon separator (;).

9.3.3 Passing Parameters

Parameters are passed to a *q* script at *q* startup similarly to command line parameters in a C or Java program. They are strings that are not explicitly declared and are accessed positionally corresponding to the order in which they are passed.

> **Note**
>
> As of this writing, parameters can be passed when a script is loaded at *q* startup but not when a script is loaded with the \l command.

Specifically, the system variable .z.x is a list of strings, each of wich contains the char representation of an argument present when the script was invoked. For example, the script captureargs.q,

```
/ script that captures its first three arguments
```

```
p0:.z.x 0;
p1:.z.x 1;
p2:.z.x 2;
```

can be loaded during *q* startup,

```
q.exe captureargs.q 42 forty 2.0
```

and in the new *q* session you will find:

```
        p0
"42"

        p1
"forty"

        p2
"2.0"
```

You must cast the string arguments if they are intended to be other data types. For example, if the script `convertargs.q`,

```
/ script that converts its first three arguments
p0:"I"$.z.x 0;
p1:"S"$.z.x 1;
p2:"F"$.z.x 2;
```

is loaded with,

```
q.exe convertargs.q 42 forty 2.0
```

in the new *q* session you will find,

```
        p0
42

        p1
`forty

        p2
2f
```

9.3.4 Example

Here is the commented script text for the sample program from **Overview** at the beginning of the book:

```
/ read px.csv file into table t
t:("DSF"; enlist ",") 0: `:c:/q/data/px.csv;
/ select max Price from t grouped by Date and Sym
tmpx:select mpx:max Price by Date,Sym from t;
/ open connection to q process on port 5042 on aerowing
h:hopen `:aerowing:5042;
/ issue above query against table tpx on remote machine
rtmpx:h "select mpx:max Price by Date, Sym from tpx";
/ close connection
hclose h;
/ append merger of local and remote results to file tpx.dat
.[`:c:/q/data/tpx.dat; (); ,; rtmpx,tmpx]
```

CHAPTER 10
I/O

10.0 OVERVIEW

I/O in *q* is achieved using *handles*, which are symbolic names. An open handle acts as a mapping to an I/O stream, in the sense that retrieving a value from the open handle results in a get and passing a value to the open handle is a set.

10.1 DATA FILES

All *q* entities are automatically serializable to disk. The persistent form is a self-describing version of the in-memory form. A *data file* comprises a *q* entity written to disk.

10.1.1 File Handle

A file handle is a symbol that starts with a colon (:) and has the form,

```
`:[path]fname
```

where the bracketed expression represents an optional path and `fname` is a file name. Both `path` and `fname` must be valid names as recognized by the underlying operating system.

You can convert a raw path (or IP address) string into a valid handle using the `hsym` convenience function:

```
    hsym `$"/q/file name.dat"
`:/q/file name.dat
```

> **Important**
>
> The one caveat is that separators in *q* paths are always represented by the forward slash (/), even for Windows.

10.1.2 Using hcount and hdel

Use `hcount` with a file handle to determine the size of the file in bytes. The result is a long:

```
        hcount `:/q/Life.txt
21210j
```

Use `hdel` with a file handle to delete a file from the file system of the underlying operating system. A return value of the file handle indicates that the deletion was successful. You will get an error message if the file does not exist or if the delete cannot be performed:

```
        hdel `:/q/Life.txt
`:/q/Life.txt
```

10.1.3 Using set and get

A data file is created and a *q* entity written to it in a single step using the binary operator `set`. The left operand is a file handle, the right operand is the entity to be written and the result is the handle of the written file. The file is closed once the write is complete:

```
        `:/q/qdata.dat set 101 102 103
`:/q/qdata.dat
```

> **Note**
>
> The behavior of `set` is to create the file if it does not exist and overwrite it if it does.

A data file can be read using unary `get`, whose argument is a file handle and whose result is the *q* entity contained in the data file:

```
        get `:/q/qdata.dat
101 102 103
```

An alternate way to read a data file is with `value`:

```
        value `:/q/qdata.dat
101 102 103
```

10.1.4 Using hopen and hclose

A data file handle is opened with `hopen`. The result of `hopen` is an int file handle that acts like a function for writing to the file once assigned to a variable:

```
h:hopen `:/q/qdata.dat

h[42]                    / handle used as function

h 1 2 3 4                / juxtaposition notation
```

If the file already exists, opening it with `hopen` appends to it rather than overwriting it.

To close the handle, issue `hclose` on the result of `hopen`. This flushes any data that might be buffered:

```
hclose h
```

After the operations above, we find:

```
        get `:/q/qdata.dat
101 102 103 42 1 2 3 4
```

10.1.5 Using Dot Amend

Fundamentalists can use dot amend to write to data files. To overwrite the file if it exists, use assign (:):

```
    .[`:/q/qdata.dat;();:;1001 1002 1003]
`:/q/qdata.dat

        get `:/q/qdata.dat
1001 1002 1003
```

To append to the file if it exists, use join (,):

```
    .[`:/q/qdata.dat; (); ,; 42 43]
`:/q/qdata.dat

        get `:/q/qdata.dat
1001 1002 1003 42 43
```

10.1.6 Writing Splayed Tables

Writing a table to a data file using the above methods puts it into a single file. For example,

```
        t:([] c1:101 102 103; c2:1.1 2.2 3.3)

        `:/q/data/t.dat set t
`:/q/data/t.dat
```

creates a single file in the data subdirectory of the *q* directory. List the directory on your disk now to verify this.

You can write each column of the table to its own file in the directory specified in the handle; this is especially useful for large tables. A table written in this form is called a *splayed* table. To splay a table, specify the path as a directory — that is, with a trailing slash (/) and no file name:

```
        `:/q/data/t/ set t
`:/q/data/t/

        get `:/q/data/t/
c1   c2
-------
101  1.1
102  2.2
103  3.3
```

If you list the directory in the OS, you will see a new subdirectory named **t**. It contains three files, one file for each column in the original table, as well as a **.d** file containing *q* meta data. The latter describes how to put the columns back together.

> **Important**
>
> For a table to be splayed, each column must be of uniform width. Consequently a splayed table cannot contain any symbol or non-simple columns. A table with symbol column(s) can effectively splayed by enumerating the symbols. Thus, the following fails...

```
        ts:([] c1:`a`b`c`a; c2:10 20 30 40)

        `:/q/data/ts/ set ts
'type
```

Enumerate the symbol column and the write succeeds:

```
        syms:distinct ts.c1

        update c1:`syms$c1 from `ts
`ts

        ts
c1 c2
-----
a  10
b  20
c  30
a  40

        `:/q/data/ts/ set ts
`:/q/data/ts/
```

10.2 SAVE AND LOAD ON TABLES

The `save` and `load` functions simplify the process of writing and reading tables to/from disk files.

In its simplist form, `save` writes a table to a file with the same name as the table. The form,

```
save `:path/tname
```

in which `path` is an optional path name and `tname` is the name of a table in the workspace, is equivalent to,

```
`:path/tname set tname
```

Thus,

```
save `:/q/trade/
```

writes the trade `table` to a file named `trade` in the *q* directory. Similarly,

```
save `:path/tname/
```

splays the table within the directory `tname`.

As you would expect, `load` is the inverse of `save`, in that it reads a table from a file into a variable with the same name as the file. In other words,

```
load `:path/tname
```

is equivalent to,

```
tname:get `:path/tname
```

Thus, the expression,

```
load `:q/trade
```

creates a table variable `trade` and populates it from the file data. As before, appending a / indicates that the table has been splayed. So,

```
load `:path/tname/
```

populates a table `tname` from the directory `tname`. You can also use `save` to write a table as delimited text simply by appending an appropriate file extension. The expression,

```
save `:path/tname.txt
```

writes the table as text records. The expression,

```
save `:path/tname.csv
```

writes the table as csv records. The expression,

```
save `:path/tname.xml
```

writes the table as xml records.

> **Note**
>
> Tables written as .txt or .csv can be read as text files.

As an example, we take the simple table,

```
tsimp:([] c1:`a`b`c; c2:10 20 30)
```

we save it,

```
save `:/q/tsimp
`:/q/tsimp
```

then reload it:

```
        load `:/q/tsimp
`tsimp

        tsimp
c1 c2
-----
a  10
b  20
c  30
```

Next we save it in delimited text formats:

```
        save `:/q/tsimp.txt
`:/q/tsimp.txt

        save `:/q/tsimp.csv
`:/q/tsimp.csv

        save `:/q/tsimp.xml
`:/q/tsimp.xml
```

Let's inspect the files with a text editor. In `tsimp.txt`, we find,

```
c1  c2
a   10
b   20
c   30
```

In `tsimp.csv` we have,

```
c1,c2
a,10
b,20
c,30
```

In `tsimp.xml`, we have,

```
<R>
<r><c1>a</c1><c2>10</c2></r>
<r><c1>b</c1><c2>20</c2></r>
<r><c1>c</c1><c2>30</c2></r>
</R>
```

10.3 TEXT DATA

Importing and exporting data often involves reading and writing text files. The mechanism for doing this in *q* differs from processing *q* data files.

10.3.1 Writing (0:) and Reading (read0) Text Files

The *q* primitive verb denoted 0: takes a file handle as its left argument and a list of *q* strings as it right argument. It writes each string as a line of text in the specified file:

```
    `:/q/Life.txt 0: ("So";"Long")
`:/q/Life.txt
```

Opening the file Life.txt in a text editor will show a file with two lines.

Read a text file with read0. The result is a list of strings, one for each line in the file:

```
    read0 `:/q/Life.txt
"So"
"Long"
```

10.3.2 Using hopen and hclose

A text file handle can be opened with hopen. The result of hopen is a positive int whose **negative** is a file handle that is used to write text to the file:

```
    h:hopen `:/q/Life.txt

    (neg h)["and"]
-152

    (neg h) ("Thanks";"for";"all";"the";"Fish")
-152
```

If the file already exists, opening it with hopen will append to it rather than overwriting it.

To close the handle, issue hclose on the int result of hopen. This flushes any data that might be buffered:

```
    hclose h
```

```
        read0 `:/q/Life.txt
"So"
"Long"
"and"
"Thanks"
"for"
"all"
"the"
"Fish"
```

10.3.3 Prepare Text (0:)

The *q* primitive verb 0: is overloaded to process text. In this use, 0: has left operand a delimiter specified as a char or a special string and right operand a table or list of columns.

In the simplest use, the delimiter is a char. Observe in the second example the use of the *q* built-in constant csv, whch is simply ",":

```
        t:([] c1:`a`b`c; c2:1 2 3)

        "|" 0: t
"c1|c2"
"a|1"
"b|2"
"c|3"

        csv 0: value flip t
"a,1"
"b,2"
"c,3"
```

The primitive 0: can also be used to process text representing key-value pairs. In this situation, the left operand string P_f specifies the pair format. The first char of P_f can be **S** to indicate the key is a string or **I** to indicate the key is an integer. The second char indicates the the key-value separator. The third char indicates the pair delimiter.

The following examples illustrate various combinations in P_f:

```
        "S=;" 0: "one=1;two=2;three=3"
one   two   three
,"1"  ,"2"  ,"3"

        "S:/" 0: "one:1/two:2/three:3"
one   two   three
,"1"  ,"2"  ,"3"
```

```
        "I=;" 0: "1=one;2=two;3=three"
1       2       3
"one"   "two"   "three"
```

10.4 BINARY FILES

It is also useful to read and write data from/to binary files. The mechanism for doing this is similar to that for processing text files. In *q*, a binary record is a simply a list of byte values.

10.4.1 Writing (1:) and Reading (read1)

The *q* primitive verb denoted `1:` takes a file handle as its left argument and a simple byte list as its right argument. It writes each byte in the list as a byte in the specified file:

```
        `:/q/answer.bin 1: 0x2a0607
`:/q/answer.bin
```

Opening the file `answer.bin` in an editor that displays binary data will show a file with three bytes.
    Read a binary file with `read1`. The result is a list of byte:

```
        read1 `:/q/answer.bin
0x2a0607
```

10.4.2 Using hopen and hclose

A binary file handle can be opened with `hopen`. The result of `hopen` is a postive file handle int that can be used to write a list of bytes to the file. Close the file by issuing `hclose` on the handle:

```
        h:hopen `:/q/answer.bin
        h[0x01]
152
```

```
        h 0x020304
152
```

```
    hclose h

    read1 `:/q/answer.bin
0x2a060701020304
```

10.4.3 Reading Text Files as Binary

A text file can also be read as binary data by using `read1`. With `Life.txt` as above:

```
    read0 `:/q/Life.txt
"So"
"Long"
"and"
"Thanks"
"for"
"all"
"the"
"Fish"

    read1 `:/q/Life.txt
0x536f0d0a4c6f6e670d0a616e640d0a5468616e6b730d0a666f720d0...
```

To convert this binary data to char, cast the binary. On a Unix machine, this looks like:

```
    "c"$read1 `:/q/Life.txt
"So\nLong\nand\nThanks\nfor\nall\nthe\nFish\n"
```

On a Windows machine, this looks as follows:

```
    "c"$read1 `:/q/Life.txt
"So\r\nLong\r\nand\r\nThanks\r\nfor\r\nall\r\nthe\r\nFish\r\n"
```

10.5 PARSING FILE RECORDS

Binary forms of `0:` and `1:` parse individual fields of a text or binary record according to data type. Field parsing is based on the following field types:

```
0 1    Type        Width(1)  Format(0)
- --   ----------  --------  --------------------------------
B b    boolean     1         [1tTyY]
X x    byte        1
H h    short       2         [0-9a-fA-F][0-9a-fA-F]
I i    int         4
J j    long        8
E e    real        4
F f    float       8
C c    char        1
S s    symbol      n
M m    month       4         [yy]yy[?]mm
D d    date        4         [yy]yy[?]mm[?]dd or [m]m/[d]d/[yy]yy
Z z    datetime    8         date?time
U u    minute      4         hh[:]mm
V v    second      4         hh[:]mm[:]ss
T t    time        4         hh[:]mm[:]ss[[.]ddd]
blank  skip
  *                          literal chars
```

The column labeled **0** contains the (upper case) field type char for text data. The (lower case) char in column **1** is for binary data. The column labeled **Width(1)** contains the number of bytes that will be parsed for a binary read. The column labeled **Format(0)** displays the format(s) that are accepted in a text read.

> **Note**
>
> The parsed records are presented in column form rather than in row form because *q* considers a table to be a collection of columns.

10.5.1 Fixed Length Records

The binary form of 0: and 1: for reading fixed length files is:

$(L_t; L_w)$ 0: f

$(L_t; L_w)$ 1: f

The left operand is a nested (general) list containing two lists: L_t is a simple list of char containing one letter per field; L_w is a simple list of int containing one int width per field. The sum of the field widths in L_w must equal the width of the record. The result of the function in all cases is a (general) list of lists with an item for each field.

The simplest form of the right operand f is a symbol representing a file handle. For example,

```
("IFC D";4 8 10 6 4) 0: `:/q/Fixed.txt
```

reads a text file containing fixed length records of width 32. The first field is an int of length 4; the second field is a float of width 8; the third field consists of 10 char; the fourth slot of 6 positions is skipped; the fifth field is a date of width 10.

You might think that the widths are superfluous, but they are not. The actual width can be narrower than the default for small values. Alternatively, you may wish to specify a width larger than that required by the corresponding data type to create blanks between fields. If the file in the previous example were rewritten with one additional blank character between fields, the proper left operand to read it would be,

```
("IFC D"; 5 9 11 6 4)
```

For example, we take a file /q/data/Px.txt having the form,

```
1001DBT12345678   98.61002EQT98765432 24.571003CCR00000001121.23
```

The read is:

```
        ("ISF";4 11 6) 0: `:/q/data/Px.txt
1001           1002          1004
DBT12345678 EQT98765432 CCR00000001
98.6           24.75         121.23
```

The second form for the right operand f is,

$(h_{file}; i; n)$

where h_{file} is a symbol containing a file name, i is the offset into the file to begin reading and n is the number of bytes to read. This is useful for large files that cannot be read into memory in one operation.

> **Note**
>
> A read operation must begin and end on a record boundary.

In our trivial example, the following reads the second and third records:

```
          ("ISF"; 4 11 6) 0: (`:/q/data/Px.txt; 21; 42)
1002       1004
EQT98765432 CCR00000001
24.75      121.23
```

10.5.2 Variable Length Records

The binary form of `0:` and `1:` for reading variable length delimited files is,

$(L_t; D)$ `0: f`

$(L_t; D)$ `1: f`

The left operand is a (general) list comprising two items: L_t is a simple list of char containing one type letter per field; D is either a char representing the delimiting character or an enlisted such.

If D is a delimiter char, the result is a general list of lists. Each list in the result is made up of items of type specified by L_t. The simplest form of the right operand `f` is a symbol representing a file handle.

For example, say we have a csv file `/q/data/Px.csv` having records,

```
1001,DBT12345678,98.6

1002,EQT98765432,24.75

1004,CCR00000001,121.23
```

Reading with a simple delimiter char results in a list of column lists:

```
          ("ISF"; ",") 0: `:/q/data/Px.csv
1001       1002       1004
DBT12345678 EQT98765432 CCR00000001
98.6       24.75      121.23
```

Observe that it is possible to retrieve the second field as a string instead of a symbol using "*" as the data type specifier:

```
          ("I*F"; ",") 0: `:/q/data/Px.csv
1001         1002           1004
"DBT12345678" "EQT98765432" "CCR00000001"
98.6         24.75          121.23
```

If D is an enlisted delimiter char, the first record is taken to be a list of column names. Subsequent records are read as data specified by the types in L_t. The result is a table in which each record is formed from a file record.

Say we have a csv file /q/data/pxtitles.csv having records,

```
"Seq","Sym","Px"
1001,"DBT12345678",98.6
1002,"EQT98765432",24.75
1004,"CCR00000001",121.23
```

Reading with an enlisted delimiter results in a table:

```
        ("ISF";enlist ",") 0: `:/q/data/pxtitles.csv
Seq    Sym          Px
------------------------------
1001   DBT12345678  98.6
1002   EQT98765432  24.75
1004   CCR00000001  121.23
```

You can also read this file with an atomic delimiter. The result is a list of lists with nulls in the positions where the header records do not match the specified types:

```
        ("ISF";",") 0: `:c:/q/data/pxtitles.csv
1001         1002         1004
Sym DBT12345678 EQT98765432 CCR00000001
    98.6         24.75        121.23
```

10.6 INTERPROCESS COMMUNICATION

A *q* process can communicate with another *q* process residing anywhere on the network, provided that process is accessible. The process that initiates the communication is the *client*, while the process receiving and processing the request is the *server*. The server process can be on the same machine, the same network, a different network or on the internet. The communication can be synchronous (wait for a result to be returned) or asynchronous (don't wait and no result returned).

The easiest way to examine interprocess communication (IPC) is to start another *q* process on the same machine running your current *q* session. Make sure it is listening on a different port (the default port is 5000). In what follows we shall assume that a server *q* process has been started on the same machine with the command:

```
q -p 5042
```

This means it is listening on port 5042.

10.6.1 Communication Handle

A communication handle is similar to a file handle. It is a symbol that starts with a colon (:) and has the form,

```
`:[server]:port
```

where the bracketed expression represents an optional server machine identifier and *port* is a port number. If the server process is running on the same machine as the client process, you can omit the server identifier. In our case, the communication handle is,

```
`::5042
```

If the server is on the same network as your machine, you can use its machine name. In our case,

```
`:aerowing:5042
```

You can use the IP address of the server,

```
`:198.162.0.2:5042
```

If the server is running on the internet, you can use a url,

```
`:www.yourco.com:5042
```

10.6.2 Connection Handle

Use a communication handle as the argument of hopen to open a connection to the server process. Store the int result of hopen, called the *connection handle*, in a variable. You then issue commands to the server by treating this variable as if it were a function.

For example, if the server process is running on the same machine and is listening on port 5042, the following *q* code opens a connection to the server process. It assigns the value 42 to the variable a on the server and then retrieves the value of a from the server. Finally, the connection is closed:

```
h:hopen `::5042

h "a:42"
h "a"
```
42
```
hclose h
```

> **Note**
>
> Whitespace between h and the quoted string is optional, as it is in function juxtaposition. We include it for readability.

10.6.3 Message Format

The general message format for interprocess communication is a list,

```
(f;arg₁;arg₂;...)
```

Here f is an client-side expression to be sent to the server or a symbol containing the name of a mapping on the server. The client-side expression can contain *q* operators or it can be a function, dictionary or list. The remaining items arg_1, arg_2, ... are optional parameters sent to the server for the evaluation of the map. The parameters are arguments when f is a function, indices when f is a list, or domain items when f is a dictionary. Execution returns the result of the server's evaluation.

This form of remote call is very powerful, in that it can evaluate a mapping that exists on the server or it can send a mapping to the server for evaluation. In particular, the lambda of a function can be transported. In a simple example, say we already have an open handle h to a server. If f is defined on the **client** as,

```
f:{x*x}
```

then executing the following expression on the client,

```
h (f;2)
```

results in f being sent to the server with the argument 2 and then evaluated there. The result is:

```
    h (f;2)
4
```

> **Important**
>
> Exercise caution when sending entities to a remote server. A trivial mistake could place the server into a non-responding state. It is safer to define a function on the server and screen its input internally.

A simplified case of the general message format, which we used in previous sections, is a string containing a *q* expression to be evaluated on the server. For example,

```
"a:6*7"
```

```
"select avg price from t where date>2006.01.01"
```

The connection can also be used to execute a function that has been defined on the server. For example, suppose g is defined on the **server** as:

```
g:{x*x*x}
```

We could execute g and get the result with:

```
    h (`g;2)
8
```

Equivalently, executing the following on the client sends the string "g 2" to the server where it is evaluated. The result is:

```
    h "g 2"
8
```

Compare this with the example above where f is defined on the client.

> **Note**
>
> If the expression in the execution string contains special characters, they must be escaped. For example, to define a string on the server, you must escape the double quotes in the message string:
>
> ```
> "str:\"abc\""
> ```

When the remote function performs an operation on a table, it can be viewed as a remote stored procedure. For example, suppose t and f are defined on the server as:

```
t:([] c1:`a`b`c; c2:1 2 3)

f:{[x] select c2 from t where c1=x}
```

The following expression on the client executes f on the server, selecting rows that match the value `b in c1:

```
     h "f `b"
+(,`c2)!,,2
```

The equivalent of dynamic SQL can be achieved by passing a function definition:

```
     h ({select c2 from t where c1=x}; `b)
+(,`c2)!,,2
```

With this come all the caveats of traditional dynamic SQL.

10.6.4 Synchronous Messages

The messages sent in the previous sections were *synchronous*, meaning that the sending client process waits for a result from the server before proceeding. The result of the operation on the server becomes the return value of the remote call that uses the connection handle.

To send a synchronous message, use the original positive int value of the connection handle as if it were a function. A typical example of sending a synchronous message is executing a `select` expression on the server. In this case, you surely want to wait for the result to return.

For example, suppose a table has been defined on the server as:

```
t:([] c1:`a`b`c; c2:1 2 3)
```

The following message executes a query against t, assuming h is an open connection handle to the server:

```
        h "select from t where c1=`b"
c1 c2
-----
b  2
```

> **Note**
>
> The previous example demonstrates how to perform the equivalent of dynamic SQL against server data.

As another example, send an insert synchronously if you want confirmation of the operation:

```
        h "`t insert (`x;42)"
,3

        h "t"
c1 c2
-----
a  1
b  2
c  3
x  42
```

10.6.5 Asynchronous Messages

It is also possible to send messages *asynchronously*, meaning that the client does not wait and there is no result containing a return value. You would typically send an asynchronous message to kick off a long-running operation on the server. You might also send an asynchronous message if the operation does not have a meaningful result, or if you simply don't care to wait for the result.

To send an asynchronous message, use the negative of the int connection handle returned by hopen. For example, the insert that was sent synchronously in the previous example can also be sent asynchronously:

```
        (neg h) "`t insert (`y;43)"
        h "t"
c1 c2
-----
a  1
b  2
c  3
x  42
y  43
```

Observe that there is no return value from the first message.

> **Advanced**
>
> In the previous example, because the first message is asynchronous, it is possible that the second message leaves the client console before the insert has completed on the server. However, the second message will not execute on the server until the first has completed.

10.6.6 Message Handlers

When a *q* process receives a message via interprocess communication, the default behavior is to evaluate the message, effectively executing the message content. If the message is synchronous, the result is returned to the client.

During message processing on the server, the server connection handle is automatically placed in `.z.w`. This can be used to manage connections on the server. See below for a simple example.

> **Note**
>
> The connection handle on the client side and the connection handle on the server side are assigned independently by their respective *q* processes. In general, their int values are not equal.

The default message processing can be overridden using message filters. Message filters are event-handling functions in the `.z` context. The `.z.pg` message filter processes synchronous requests and `.z.ps` processes asynchronous requests.

> **Advanced**
>
> The names end in **g** and **s** because synchronous processing has **get** semantics and asynchronous processing has **set** semantics.

The following two assignments on the server recreate the default message processing behavior:

```
.z.ps:{value x}
.z.pg:{value x}
```

Message filtering can be used for a variety of purposes. For example, suppose the connection allows a user on the client side to execute dynamic q-sql against the server. You could improve on the default processing by enclosing the evaluation in protected execution:

```
.z.pg:{@[value;x;errHandler x]}
```

Here `errHandler` is a function that recovers from an unexpected error.

A more interesting example is a server that keeps track of the clients connected to it. A simplistic way to do this is to maintain a dictionary of connection handles mapped to client names. The following function on the server registers a new client connection by upserting it to a global dictionary `cp`. Remember that `.z.w` has the connection handle:

```
cp:()!()                                      / server
regConn:{cp[.z.w]::x}                         / server
```

The client could pass its machine name:

```
h:hopen `::5042                               / client
h                                             / client
h "regConn `",string .z.h                     / client
```

After this call, `cp` will contain an entry that reflects the specific handle assigned to the connection on the server. For example:

```
cp                                            / server
4| macpro.local
```

As additional connections are made to the server, `cp` will contain one entry for each connection.

> **Disclaimer**
>
> This simple example is illustrative only. It is not robust and would need serious enhancement to deal with malicious clients.

10.6.7 Handling Close

An open connection can be closed by either the client or the server. The close can be deliberate, meaning it occurs under user or program control, or it can be unanticipated due to a process terminating unexpectedly.

The close handler `.z.pc` can be used to perform processing whenever a connection is closed from the other end. While it will be invoked on any close, it does not know how the close was initiated.

In our example above, we use a close handler to remove the information about a connection once it is closed. Specifically, we create a handler to remove the appropriate entry from `cp`:

```
.z.pc:{cp::cp _ x}                           / server
```

When the client issues an `hclose` on its connection handle,

```
hclose h                                     / client
```

the dictionary `cp` no longer shows the connection:

```
cp                                           / server
_
```

Now that we have established basic close handling on the server, we turn our attention to the client. We want the client to reconnect automatically in the event the server disconnects for any reason. The easiest way to do this is with the timer.

We create a close handler that resets the global connection handle to 0 and issues a command that sets the timer to fire every 2 seconds (2000 milliseconds):

```
.z.pc:{h::0; value"\\t 2000"}
```

The timer handler attempts to re-open the connection. Upon success, it issues a command that turns the timer off:

```
.z.ts:{h::hopen`::5042; if[h>0; value"\\t 0"]}
```

> **Note**
>
> In practice, you should restrict the number of connection retries rather than try forever.

10.6.8 Http Connection Handler

There is also a message handler for http connections, named z.ph. Since http communication is always synchronous, there is only one handler. In contrast to other system handlers, there is a default handler for http, which is used for the *q* web viewer.

The default handler allows a *q* process to be accessed programmatically over the web, similar to a servlet. The ambitious reader could replace this with a handler that processes SOAP, thus enabling *q* to be a web service. (Such a handler would be the object of derision from those who decry SOAP as unnecessary and wasteful.)

CHAPTER 11
WORKSPACE ORGANIZATION

11.0 OVERVIEW

The collection of entities that exist in a *q* session comprises the *workspace*. In other words, the workspace includes all atoms, lists, dictionaries, functions, enumerations, etc., that have been created through the console or via script execution.

Any programming environment of reasonable complexity has the potential for name clashes. For example, should two separate *q* scripts both create a variable called **foobar**, one will overwrite the value of the other. Variable typing is of no help here, since a variable can be reassigned with a different type at any time.

The solution to name clashes and variable limitation is to create namespaces. This is accomplished with a hierarchical naming structure implemented with a separator character, usually a dot or a slash. For example, the name spaces A and B can both have an entity `foobar`, yet `A.foobar` and `B.foobar` are distinct. A familiar example of this is the hierarchical directory/file system used by operating systems.

Namespaces in *q* are called directories or contexts. Contexts provide an organization of the workspace.

11.1 CONTEXTS

The *q* workspace provides a simple namespace structure using dot notation for entity names. Each of the nodes is called a *context*, or a *directory*. The *default* context, also called the *root*, comprises all entities whose names start with an initial alpha character. The variables we have created heretofore have resided in the default context.

11.1.1 Context Notation

A context name has the form of a dot (.) followed by alphnums, starting with an alpha. The following are all valid context names:

```
.a
.q
.z0
.zaphod
```

There is no need to pre-declare the context name. As in the case of variables, a context is created dynamically as required. You specify a variable to a context by prepending the context name to the variable name, separated by a dot (.). The variable `foobar` can be created in various contexts:

```
foobar:42
.aa.foobar:43
.z0.foobar:45
.zaphod.foobar:46
```

Variables of the same name in different contexts are indeed distinct:

```
        foobar
42

        .aa.foobar
43

        .z0.foobar
45

        .zaphod.foobar
46
```

When an entity name includes its full context name, we say the name is *fully qualified*. When an entity name omits the context name, we say the name is *unqualified*.

11.1.2 Reserved Contexts

All contexts of a single letter (both lower and upper case) are reserved for *q* itself. Some of these are listed below:

```
Name    Use
-------------------------------------------
.q      Built-in functions
.Q      Low-level routines used by q
.z      Environmental interaction
```

> **Important**
>
> While *q* will not prevent you from placing entities in the reserved contexts, doing so risks serious problems should you collide with names used by *q*.

11.1.3 Working with Contexts

At any time in a *q* session, there is a *current* or *working* context. When you start a *q* session, the current context is the default context. You change the current context with the \d command. For example, to switch to the files context:

```
\d .files
```

To switch back to the default context:

```
\d .
```

To display the current context:

```
\d
`.
```

Any entity in the current context can be specified using its unqualified name:

```
\d .                  / switch to default contrext
.files.home:`c:
.files.home
`c:

\d .files
home
`c:
```

You can list all the contexts currently defined with key `. In an new *q* session we find:

```
    key `
`q`Q`o`h

    .foo.bar:42
```

```
        key `
`q`Q`o`h`foo
```

11.1.4 A Context is a Dictionary

A context is actually a sorted dictionary whose domain is a list of symbols with the names of the entities defined in the context. Apply the `key` function to the dictionary name to display the names of the entities in the context. Apply `value` to see the entire dictionary mapping:

```
    .new.a:42
    .new.L:1 2 3
    .new.d:`a`b`c!1 2 3

    key `.new
``a`L`d

    value `.new
 | ::
a| 42
L| 1 2 3
d| `a`b`c!1 2 3
```

Observe that *q* places an entry into any non-default context that maps the null symbol to the null item.

You can look up an entity name in the directory to get its associated value. Use a symbol containing the context name to refer to the dictionary:

```
    `.new[`L]
1 2 3
```

> **Note**
>
> In order to access an entity in the default context from another context, you must retrieve the value from the context dictionary. There is no syntactic form.

```
    \d .
`.
    ztop:42
    \d .new
    `.[`ztop]
```

```
42
        `. `ztop
42
```

11.1.5 Expunging from a Context

We have seen that a context is a directory that maps entity names for the context to their values. This means that in order to expunge an entity from a context, we can simply delete it from the dictionary.

For example, if we can define a variable a in the context .new and then remove it from the workspace when it is no longer needed. Observe that we use the symbolic name of the context to ensure that the delete is applied to it by reference:

```
        .new.a:42
        .new
 | ::
a| 42
        /
        / do some work ...
        /
        delete a from `.new
`.new

        .new
 | ::
```

In particular, to expunge a global entity from the default context, use `. as the directory name. In a fresh workspace we find:

```
        a:42
        b:98.6
        c:`life
        \v
`s#`a`b`c

        delete a from `.
`.

        \v
`s#`b`c
```

11.1.6 Functions and Contexts

Function definition presents an issue with respect to global variable references and unqualified names. In the following function, the variable a is an unqualified global variable:

```
f:{a+x}
```

There is a potential ambiguity with respect to the context of a. Is the context resolved at the time f is defined or at the time f is evaluated?

> **Important**
>
> The context of an unqualified global variable in a function is the current context at the time the function is defined, not the context in which it is evaluated.

Thus, we find:

```
        \d .
        a:42

        \d .lib
        f:{a+x}
        f[6]
{a+x}
'a
))\

        a:100
        f[6]
106

        \d .
        .lib.f[6]
106
```

We also find the following result, because even though g lives in the .lib context, it is defined in the default context:

```
        \d .
        .lib.g:{a*x}
        a:42
        g[2]
'g
```

330

```
        \d .lib
        g[3]
126

        a:6
        g[7]
294
```

11.1.7 Saving a Context

Recall that a context is actually a dictionary. You can write an entire context, with all its entities, to a single data file by writing the dictionary. For example, to write out the default context:

```
        `:currentws set value `.
`:currentws
```

11.1.8 Loading a Context

To retrieve a saved context, use `get` with the file handle:

```
        dc:get `:currentws
```

Use `set` with a symbol containing the context name to replace the context:

```
        `. set dc
```

> **Important**
>
> Overlaying the root context replaces all its entities. This is convenient for re-initialization, but be sure of your intent.

11.1.9 Namespaces (Advanced)

It is possible to simulate a multi-level namespace hierarchy by using multiple dots in names:

```
        .lib1.vars.op1:6
        .lib1.vars.op2:7
        .math.fns.f:{x*y}
```

```
        .math.fns.f[.lib1.vars.op1;.lib1.vars.op2]
42
```

In the example above, *q* creates dictionaries at each node of the tree:

```
        value `.lib1.vars
| ::
op1| 6
op2| 7

        value `.math.fns
| ::
f| {x*y}
```

But appearances are deceiving.

> **Important**
>
> As of this writing, *q* does **not** recognize a context tree below the first level. You must use qualified context names if you wish to use deeper contexts.

In our example, you cannot switch to the context .math.fns using the \d command:

```
        \d .math.fns
'.math.fns
```

Instead, you can use an absolulte context name any time or you can use a relative context name from a top level context:

```
        \d .
        .math.fns.f[6;7]
42

        \d .math
        fns.f[6;7]
42
```

332

CHAPTER 12
COMMANDS AND SYSTEM VARIABLES

12.1 COMMAND FORMAT

Commands control aspects of the *q* environment. A command begins with a back-slash (\) and is followed by one or more characters. Some commands have an optional parameter that is separated from the command by whitespace.

> **Important**
>
> Case is significant in the command characters.

To execute a command programmatically, place it in a string and use the `value` function:

```
value "\\p 5042"
```

> **Note**
>
> A backslash in the string must be escaped.

12.1.1 Tables (\a)

The command \a returns a list of symbols with the names of all tables in a context. When used with no parameters, it returns the functions in the current context. For example, in a fresh *q* session:

```
t:([]c1:1 2 3; c2:`a`b`c)
\a
,`t
```

12.1.2 Console (\c)

The command \c (note lower case) controls the size of the *q* virtual console display. The first parameter specifies the number of rows and the second the number of columns. The default setting is 23 by 79:

```
        til 100
0  1  2  3  4  5  6  7  8  9 10 11 12 13 14 15 16 17 18 19 20 21 22
23 24 25 26 27 28 ..


        \c 23 200
        til 1000
0  1  2  3  4  5  6  7  8  9 10 11 12 13 14 15 16 17 18 19 20 21 22
23 24 25 26 27 28 2930 31 32 33 34 35 36 37 38 39 40 41 42
43 44 45 46 47 48 49 50 51 52 53 54 55 56 57 58 59 60 61 62
68 6..
```

12.1.3 Web Console (\C)

The command \C (note upper case) controls the size of the *q* web console display. The first parameter specifies the number of rows and the second the number of columns. The default setting is 36 by 2000.

12.1.4 Change O/S Directory (\cd *path*)

The \cd command affects the current working directory of the underlying operating system. To display the current directory, issue \cd with no argument:

```
        \cd
"/Users/jeffry/bin"
```

The result of \cd is the text string as received from the OS with escapes where applicable. For Windows, the back-slash characters are escaped and are not converted to forward-slashes.

To change the current working directory, issue \cd with the path of the desired directory:

```
        \cd /q
```

If the specified directory does not exist, it will be created.

> **Note**
>
> Since the argument of \cd is not a string, special characters do **not** need to be escaped.

12.1.5 Directory (\d)

The \d command controls the current context (directory). To determine the current context, issue \d with no parameter:

```
    \d
`.
```

To set the current context, issue \d followed by the target context:

```
    \d .tutorial
    \d
`.tutorial
```

> **Note**
>
> If the specified context does not exist, using it in \d will cause its creation.

Issue \d . to set the current working context to the default context:

```
    \d .
    \d
`.
```

12.1.6 Functions (\f)

The \f command returns a sorted list containing the functions in a context (directory). When used with no parameters, it returns the functions in the current context:

```
    \f
`s#`diff`f`g
```

Use \f with the name of a context to list its functions:

```
        \f .debug
`s#``addBPs`break`clearBPs`deleteBPs`stop
```

12.1.7 Load (\l)

A script can be loaded at startup of *q* or during a session. To load the script from the session, issue the \l command with the (optionally qualified) name of the script file.

For example, to load the distribution script sp.q from the current directory:

```
        \l sp.q
+`p`city!(`p$`p1`p2`p3`p4`p5`p6`p1`p2;`london`London
`london`london`london`lon..
(+(,`color)!,`blue`green`red)!+(,`qty)!,900 1000 1200
+`s`p`qty!(`s$`s1`s1`s1`s2`s3`s4;`p$`p1`p4`p6`p2`p2`p4;
300 200 100 400 200 300)
```

12.1.8 Offset (\o)

The \o command shows or sets the offset in hours from GMT used to determine local time. For example:

```
        .z.z
2007.04.12T11:31:13.352

        .z.Z
2007.04.12T07:31:15.365

        \o -2

        .z.z
2007.04.12T11:31:35.954

        .z.Z
2007.04.12T09:31:37.587
```

12.1.9 Port (\p)

The \p command controls which port the kdb+ server listens on. For example,

```
        \p 5001
```

means that it will listen for connections on port 5001.

> **Note**
>
> When you issue the \p commend, kdb+ attempts to open the port. For this to be successful, the security settings of the machine must allow it.

If the port has not been set, you will see:

```
    \p
0
```

This means that no connection to this instance of kdb+ is currently possible because it is not listening on any port. You can also issue \p 0 to stop listening on any port.

12.1.10 Precision (\P)

The precision command \P (note the upper case) shows or sets the display precision for floating point numbers to the specified number of digits.
   The default precision is 7, meaning that the display of float or real values is rounded to the seventh significant digit:

```
    \P
7
    f:1.23456789012345678
    f
1.234568
```

Set the precision with a non-negative int parameter:

```
    \P 12
    f
1.23456789012
```

Set the precision to the maximum available that respects multiplicative tolerance with 0. This is currently the same as using 16:

```
    \P 0
```

```
        f
1.2345678901234567
```

Set the precision to the maximum available with 17:

```
    \P 17
    f
1.2345678901234567
```

12.1.11 Seed (\S)

The \S (note upper case) shows or sets the seed for pseudo-random number generation. The default value is -314159. The argument is an integer:

```
        \S
-314159
        \S 424242
        \S
424242
```

12.1.12 Timer (\t)

The \t command controls the timer. The optional parameter is the number of milliseconds between timer ticks, with 0 signifying that the timer is off. On each timer tick, the function .z.ts is invoked if it has been assigned.

To determine the current timer setting, issue \t with no parameter:

```
      \t
0
```

To set the timer, issue \t with the number of milliseconds. For example, to set the timer to tick once a second:

```
    \t 1000
```

> **Note**
>
> The actual timer tick frequency is determined by the timing granularity supported by the underling operating system. This can be considerably less than a millisecond.

To turn the timer off:

```
\t 0
```

12.1.13 Elapsed Time (\t *expr*)

When the \t command is invoked with an expression as its parameter, the expression is evaluated and its duration of execution is reported. This can be used to profile code execution when tuning an application.

In *q* there are often multiple ways to achieve a desired result, but one may execute significantly faster. This may not matter for small tables or sporadic updates, but for processing very large volumes of data in real time it can be essential. Inserting \t at key points in the program can identify the critical routines that are consuming the most time. By measuring the execution times of alternate expressions for the critical routines, you can determine which is most efficient in your environment.

The following measures the time required to add the first 100,000 integers 10,000 times on the author's laptop:

```
        \t do[10000; sum til 100000]
2553
```

We conclude that adding the first 100,000 integers once requires approximately .25 milliseconds.

If it is actually necessary to add the first 100,000 integers in an application, you could use the formula,

```
    s_n = (n*n-1)%2
```

We time it for n = 100,000:

```
        \t do[10000; (100000*99999)%2]
10
```

As you can see, this is roughly 200 times faster than performing the actual addition. We can do even better by replacing the division with a multiplication,

```
    s_n = .5*n*n-1
```

To see the effects clearly, we increase the counter to 100,000:

```
        \t do[100000; sum til 100000]
25216
```

```
        \t do[100000; (100000*99999)%2]
120
        \t do[100000; .5*100000*99999]
80
```

12.1.14 Timeout (\T)

The `\T` command (note upper case) controls execution timeout. The int parameter is the number of milliseconds any call from a client will execute before it is timed out and terminated. The default value is 0 which means no timeout.

12.1.15 Variables (\v)

The `\v` command returns a sorted list containing the variables in a context (directory). When used with no parameters, it returns the variables in the current context:

```
        \v
`s#`L`h`kt`p`pi`r`sqrt2`t`tdetails`third
```

Use `\v` with the name of a context to list its variables:

```
        \v .debug
`s#`breakPoints`stopPoints
```

12.1.16 Workspace (\w)

The workspace command `\w` (note lower case) displays four integer values that indicate memory usage by the current workspace:

```
        \w
82848 67634176 0 0j
```

The first value indicates the number of bytes currently used. The second indicates the total number of bytes allocated to the kdb+ process. The third indicates the maximum memory available including swap, which is set with the -w command line parameter. The fourth indicates the size of mapped file space.

12.1.17 Week Offset (\W)

The week offset command `\W` (note upper case) shows or specifies the start of week offset. An offset of 0 corresponds to Saturday. The default is 2, which is Monday.

12.1.18 Expunge Handler (\x)

The expunge handler command \x deletes the assignment of a user-specified function to one of the .z.p* event handlers and restores the default behavior. For example, if you have assigned a routine to .z.pc in order to process remote connection close, reset with:

```
\x .z.pc
```

12.1.19 Date Format (\z)

The date format command \z shows or specifies the format for date parsing. A value of 0 corresponds to *mm/dd/yyyy*; a value of 1 corresponds to *dd/mm/yyyy*:

```
        \z
0

        "D"$"12/31/2007"
2007.12.31

        "D"$"31/12/2007"
0Nd

        \z 1
        "D"$"12/31/2007"
0Nd

        "D"$"31/12/2007"
2007.12.31
```

12.1.20 Operating System (*text*)

If a backslash is followed by characters not recognized as a kdb+ command, the text is assumed to be an operating system command and is passed to the O/S for execution. For example, you can issue:

```
        \dir                    / display Windows directory
(" Volume in drive C has no label.";" Volume Serial Number is E89F-3533";..

        \pwd                    / display Unix directory
"/Users/jeffry/bin"
```

Any return value from the O/S is displayed as a list of strings.

12.1.21 Interrupt (Ctrl-C)

You can terminate a long-running routine by pressing the Ctrl-C combination.

12.1.22 Terminate (\)

The terminate command, denoted by a single backslash (\), exits one level of the *q* interpreter. This is useful when debugging a failed function evaluation. In the following console shot, we do not suppress the *q* prompt:

```
q)f:{x*y}
q)f[2;`3]
{x*y}
'type
*
2
`3

q))\
q)_
```

Here the underscore denotes the blinking cursor.

> **Advanced**
>
> If you issue \ at the q) prompt, you drop into a *k* session.

```
q)\
    _
```

Again, the underscore denotes the blinking cursor. Because *k* is *q*'s underlying implementation language, some *q* expressions will execute as expected in the *k* session but most will not. Explanation of *k* is beyond the scope of this manual.

To return to the *q* console from a *k* session and see the q) prompt again, enter a single \ at the prompt:

```
    \
q)
```

12.1.23 Exit q (\\)

To exit the *q* process, enter a double backslash (\ \) :

```
\\
```

> **Important**
>
> There is no confirmation prompt for \ \. The *q* session is terminated with extreme prejudice.

12.2 SYSTEM VARIABLES

Variables in certain reserved contexts provide useful *q* environmental interaction.

12.2.1 IP Address (.z.a)

The variable .z.a is an int representing the IP address of the current running *q* instance. To see the usual four-integer IP address, decode the int using base 256. For example, on the author's laptop:

```
    .z.a
-1442929031

     `int$0x00 vs .z.a
169 254 166 121
```

12.2.2 Dependencies (.z.b)

The systen variable .z.b is a dictionary that represents variable dependencies. Recall that non-local assignment with : : establishes a dependency between the variable and variables in the expression assigned to it. These dependencies are recorded in the dictionary .z.b that maps a variable name to a list of the names of variables that depend on it. For example, in a new *q* session, we find:

```
    a:42
    b:98
    c::a+b
    .z.b
```

```
a| c
b| c
```

12.2.3 Global Date (.z.d)

The variable `.z.d` retrieves the date component of Greenwich Mean Time (GMT) and is eqivalent to,

```
`date$.z.z
```

12.2.4 Local Date (.z.D)

The variable `.z.D` retrieves the local date component from the local datetime and is eqivalent to,

```
`date$.z.Z
```

12.2.5 Startup File (.z.f)

The system variable `.z.f` is a symbol representing the name of the file or directory provided on the command line when the running instance of *q* was invoked. For example, if *q* is invoked from the O/S console with,

```
q.exe convertargs.q 42 forty 2.0
```

we find:

```
    .z.f
`convertargs.q

    .z.x
("42";"forty";"2.0")
```

12.2.6 Host (.z.h)

The variable `.z.h` is a symbol representing the name of the host running the *q* instance:

```
    .z.h
`macpro.local
```

12.2.7 Process ID (.z.i)

The system variable `.z.i` is an int representing the process id of the running *q* instance:

```
        .z.i
8615
```

> **Note**
>
> As of this writing, `.z.i` is not yet implemented on Windows.

12.2.8 Release Date (.z.k)

The system variable `.z.k` is a date value representing the release date of the running *q* instance:

```
        .z.k
2006.06.01
```

12.2.9 Release Major Version (.z.K)

The system variable `.z.K` is a float value representing the major version of the running *q* instance:

```
        .z.K
2.4
```

12.2.10 License Information (.z.l)

The variable `.z.l` is a list of strings containing information about the license of the running kdb+ instance. The most useful are the items in positions 1 and 2 which represent the expiry date and update date, respectively:

```
        .z.l
" "
"2007.07.01"
"2007.07.01"
```

```
,"1"
,"1"
,"1"
,"0"
```

12.2.11 O/S (.z.o)

The system variable `.z.o` is a symbol representing the underlying operating system. For example, this tutorial is being written on a 64 bit Mac system:

```
    .z.o
`m64
```

12.2.12 Process Close (.z.pc)

The variable `.z.pc` is a *q* function representing an event handler that is executed whenever a connection to the current *q* process is closed. See **§10.6** for a discussion.

To reset the `.z.pg` to the default behavior, issue the command:

```
    \x .z.pc
```

12.2.13 Process Get (.z.pg)

The variable `.z.pg` is a *q* function representing an event handler that is executed whenever a client *q* process makes a synchronous call to the current *q* process. The name derives from the fact that an asynchronous call has get semantics. See **§10.6** for a discussion.

To reset the `.z.pg` to the default setting, issue the command:

```
    \x .z.pg
```

12.2.14 Process HTTP Get (.z.ph)

The variable `.z.ph` is a *q* function representing an event handler that is executed whenever an HTTP get is routed to the current *q* process. See **§10.6** for a discussion.

To reset the `.z.ph` to the default setting, issue the command:

```
    \x .z.ph
```

12.2.15 Process Input (.z.pi)

The variable `.z.pi` is a *q* function representing an event handler that is executed when *q* echoes the result of user input to the console. You can make the console display mimic that of **2.3** by assigning:

```
.z.pi:{-1 .Q.s1 value x}
```

You can make the console display mimic that of **2.4** by assigning:

```
.z.pi:{-1 .Q.s value x}
```

To reset the `.z.pi` to the default setting, issue the command:

```
\x .z.pi
```

12.2.16 Process Open (.z.po)

The variable `.z.po` is a *q* function representing an event handler that is executed whenever a connection to the current *q* process is opened. See **§10.6** for a discussion.

To reset the `.z.po` to the default setting, issue the command:

```
\x .z.pot
```

12.2.17 Process HTTP Post (.z.pp)

The variable `.z.pp` is a *q* function representing an event handler that is executed whenever an HTTP post is routed to the current *q* process.

To reset the `.z.pp` to the default setting, issue the command:

```
\x .z.pp
```

12.2.18 Process Set (.z.ps)

The variable `.z.ps` is a *q* function representing an event handler that is executed whenever a client *q* process makes an asynchronous call to the current *q* process. The name derives from the fact that an asynchronous call has set semantics. See **§10.6** for a discussion.

To reset the `.z.ps` to the default setting, issue the command:

```
\x .z.ps
```

12.2.19 Self (.z.s)

The variable `.z.s` represents the current function during function evaluation. This can be useful when writing recursive functions. For example, here is factorial using `.z.s`:

```
    {$[x>1;.z.s[x-1]*x;1]}[5]
120
```

It is also useful for debugging a failed function since it is then defined as the function whose execution is suspended. Here it is combined with the utility function of **§9.2** to inspect the currently suspended function:

```
    zs:{`d`P`L`G`D!(system"d"),v[1 2 3],enlist last v:value x}

    f:{a:6; x+a*b}
    f[`100]
{a:6; x+a*b}
'b

q))show zs .z.s
d| `.
P| ,`x
L| ,`a
G| ``b
D| "{a:6; x+a*b}"
```

12.2.20 Global Time (.z.t)

The variable `.z.t` retrieves the time component of Greenwich Mean Time (GMT) and is equivalent to,

```
    `time$.z.z
```

12.2.21 Local Time (.z.T)

The variable `.z.T` retrieves the time component of local time and is equivalent to,

```
    `time$.z.Z
```

12.2.22 Timer Expression (.z.ts)

The variable `.z.ts` is a *q* function representing an event handler that is executed on every timer tick (see the command `\t`). For example, the following displays local time to the console approximately every two seconds:

```
        .z.ts:{0N!`time$.z.Z}
        \t 2000

17:52:38.896
17:52:40.896
17:52:42.896
17:52:44.896
...
```

12.2.23 User (.z.u)

The variable `.z.u` is a symbol representing the user id that invoked the running *q* instance:

```
        .z.u
`Jeffry
```

12.2.24 Value Set (.z.vs)

The variable `.z.vs` is a *q* function representing an event handler that is executed whenever **any** variable is assigned in *q*. You could use `.z.vs`, for example, to monitor who is modifying certain variables.

The signature of the handler is,

```
    {[v;i]...}
```

where `v` represents a symbol with the name of the variable being assigned and `i` is the index for which the assignment is applied. The following trivial handler displays `v` and `i` to the console:

```
        .z.vs:{[v;i]0N!v;0N!i;}
        a:42
`a
()

        a:til 5
`a
()
```

```
        a[2]:42
`a
,2

        a[0 3]:6
`a
,0 3
```

Since the granularity of .z.s is all or nothing, you'd need to write your own logic to monitor only certain variables, for instance.

To remove the handler, issue the command \x .z.vs:

```
    \x .z.vs
    a:42
```

12.2.25 Handle (.z.w)

The variable .z.w contains an int with the connection handle (i.e., "who") during synchronous or asynchronous request processing. See **§10.6** for a discussion.

12.2.26 Command Line Parameters (.z.x)

The system variable .z.x is a list of strings representing the command line parameters provided after the name of the file or directory on the command line when the running instance of *q* was invoked. For example, if *q* is invoked from the O/S console with,

```
    q.exe convertargs.q 42 forty 2.0
```

we find:

```
    .z.f
`convertargs.q

    .z.x
("42";"forty";"2.0")
```

12.2.27 GMT (.z.z)

The variable .z.z is a datetime value representing the current Greenwich Mean Time (GMT) as reported by the operating system:

```
    .z.z
2007.02.02T15:24:28.156
```

12.2.28 Local Date and Time (.z.Z)

The variable `.z.Z` is a datetime value representing the current local time as known to the operating system:

```
    .z.Z
2007.02.02T10:24:30.820
```

> **Note**
>
> The `-o` startup option or `\o` command override the default time zone offset as determined by the operating system. This is useful when you want to adjust time manually, such as for daylight savings time.

12.3 COMMAND LINE PARAMETERS

We describe here the options of a *q* session that can be set via command line parameters. A command line parameter is denoted by a dash (-) and a single character, followed by whitespace and then the value(s) of the parameter. Multiple command line characters are separated by whitespace and can be entered in any order.

> **Note**
>
> The case of the command line character is significant.

Most command line parameters have equivalent workspace commands denoted by the same character. See **§12.1** for detailed descriptions and examples.

12.3.1 Console (-c)

The *console* parameter is a pair of ints that specify the size of the *q* virtual console display. The first specifies the number of rows and the second the number of columns. The default setting is 23 by 79. This parameter corresponds to the command \c.

12.3.2 Web Browser Console (-C)

The *web console* parameter (note upper case) is a pair of ints the specify the size of the *q* web console display. The first parameter specifies the number of rows and the second the number of columns. The default setting is 36 by 2000. This parameter corresponds to the command \C.

12.3.3 Offset (-o)

The *offset* parameter is an int that sets the offset in hours from GMT used to determine local time in .z.Z. This parameter corresponds to the command \o.

12.3.4 Port (-p)

The *port* parameter is an int that specifies the port number on which the kdb+ server listens. This parameter corresponds to the command \p.

12.3.5 Print Digits (-P)

The *print digits* parameter is an int that specifies the display precision for floating point numbers to the specified number of digits. The default precision is 7, meaning that the display of float or real values is rounded to the seventh significant digit. This parameter corresponds to the command \P.

12.3.6 Timer (-t)

The *timer* parameter is an int that specifies the number of milliseconds between timer ticks, with 0 signifying that the timer is turned off. This parameter corresponds to the command \t.

12.3.7 Timeout (-T)

The *timeout* parameter (note upper case) is an int that specifies the number of milliseconds any call from a client will execute before it is timed out and terminated. The default value is 0 which means no timeout. This parameter corresponds to the command \T.

12.3.8 Workspace Size (-w)

The *workspace* parameter is an int that specifies the maximum workspace size in megabytes. The default value is twice the amount of RAM on the machine. A value of 0 means an unlimited workspace.

12.3.9 Week Offset (-W)

The *week offset* parameter (note upper case) is an int that specifies the start of week as an offset from Saturday. For example,

```
q -W 2
```

starts a *q* session in which Monday is considered the beginning of the week.

12.3.10 Date Format (-z)

The *date format* parameter is a boolean value that specifies the format expected in date parsing. A value of 0 corresponds to *mm/dd/yyyy*; a value of 1 corresponds to *dd/mm/yyyy*. This parameter corresponds to the command \z .

APPENDIX A
BUILT-IN FUNCTIONS

A.0 OVERVIEW

The collection of built-in functions in *q* is rich and powerful. In this chapter, we group functions by form. A *string function* takes a string and returns a string. An *aggregate function* takes a list and returns an atom. A *uniform function* takes a list and returns a list of the same count. A mathematical function takes numeric arguments and returns a numeric argument derives by some numerical calculation.

Note that these categories are not mutually exclusive. For example, some mathematical functions are also aggregate functions.

A.1 STRING FUNCTIONS

The basic string functions perform the usual string manipulations on a list of char. There are also powerful functions that are unique to *q*.

A.1.1 like

The dyadic `like` performs pattern-matching on its first string argument (*source*) according to the pattern in its string second argument (*pattern*). It returns a boolean result indicating whether *pattern* is matched. The pattern is expressed as a mix of regular characters and special formatting characters. The special chars are ?, *, the pair [and], and ^ enclosed in square brackets.

The special char ? represents an arbitrary single character in the pattern:

```
        "fan" like "f?n"
1b

        "fun" like "f?n"
1b

        "foP" like "f?p"
0b
```

The special char * represents an arbitrary sequence of characters in the pattern.

> **Note**
>
> As of this writing, only a single occurence of * is allowed in the pattern, except that a * can occur at both the beginning and end of the pattern.

```
      "how" like "h*"
1b

      "hercules" like "h*"
1b

      "wealth" like "*h"
1b

      "flight" like "*h*"
1b

      "Jones" like "J?ne*"
1b

      "Joynes" like "J?ne*"
0b

      "Joynes" like "J*ne*"
'nyi
```

The special character pair [and] encloses a sequence of alternatives for a single character match:

```
      "flap" like "fl[ao]p"
1b

      "flip" like "fl[ao]p"
0b

      "459-0609" like "[0-9][0-9][0-9]-0[0-9][0-9][0-9]"
1b

      "459-0609" like "[0-9][0-9][0-9]-1[0-9][0-9][0-9]"
0b
```

The special character ^ is used in conjunction with [and] to indicate that the enclosed sequence of characters is disallowed. For example, to test whether a string ends in a numeric character:

```
        "M26d" like "*[^0-9]"
1b

        "Joe999" like "*[^0-9]"
0b
```

A.1.2 lower

The monadic `lower` takes a char, string or symbol argument and returns the result of converting any alpha characters to lower case:

```
        lower `A
`a

        lower "a Bc42De"
"a bc42de"
```

A.1.3 ltrim

The monadic `ltrim` takes a string argument and returns the result of removing leading blanks:

```
        ltrim "   abc  "
"abc  "
```

You can also apply `ltrim` to a non-blank char:

```
        ltrim "a"
"a"
```

A.1.4 rtrim

The monadic `rtrim` takes a string argument and returns the result of removing trailing blanks:

```
        rtrim "   abc  "
"   abc"
```

You can also apply `rtrim` to a non-blank char:

```
        rtrim "a"
"a"
```

A.1.5 ss

The dyadic `ss` (**string search**) performs the same pattern matching as `like` against its first string argument (*source*), looking for matches to its string second argument (*pattern*). However, the result of `ss` is a list containing the position(s) of the matches of the pattern in *source*. See **§A.1.1** for a discussion of `like`:

```
        "Now is the time for all good men to come to" ss "me"
13 29 38

        "fun" ss "f?n"
,0
```

If no matches are found, an empty int list is returned:

```
        "aa" ss "z"
`int$()
```

> **Note**
>
> You cannot use * to match with `ss`.

A.1.6 ssr

The triadic `ssr` (**string search and replace**) extends the capability of `ss` with replacement. The result is a string based on the first string argument (*source*) in which all occurrences of the second string argument (*pattern*) are replaced with the third string argument:

```
        ssr["suffering succotash";"s";"th"]
"thuffering thuccotathh"
```

> **Note**
>
> You cannot use * to match with `ssr`.

A.1.7 string

The monadic `string` can be applied to any *q* entity to produce a textual representation of the entity. For scalars, lists and functions, the result of `string` is a list of char that does not contain any *q* formatting characters. Following are some examples:

```
        string 42
"42"

        string 6*7
"42"

        string 42422424242j
"42422424242"

        string `Zaphod
"Zaphod"

        f:{[x] x*x}
        string f
"{[x] x*x}"
```

The next example demonstrates that `string` is not atomic, because the result of applying it to an atom is a *list* of char:

```
        string "4"
,"4"
```

The following example may be surprising:

```
        string 0x42
"42"
```

To see why, recall from **§5.1.6** that a string can be parsed into *q* data using $ with the appropriate upper-case type domain character. Now, converting to a string and parsing from a string should be inverse maps, in that their composite returns the original input value. That is, we should find:

```
        "X"$string 0x42
0x42
```

Thus, the behavior of `string` is determined by that of parse:

```
        "X"$"42"
0x42
```

Comparing these two results, we see that the result of `string` on a `byte` must not contain the format characterless. This reasoning works for other types as well.

Although `string` is not atomic (it returns a list from an atom), it does act like an atomic function in that its application is extended item-wise to a list:

```
        string 42 98
"42"
"98"

        string 1 2 3
,"1"
,"2"
,"3"

        string "Beeblebrox"
,"B"
,"e"
,"e"
,"b"
,"l"
,"e"
,"b"
,"r"
,"o"
,"x"

        string(42; `life; ("the"; 0x42))
"42"
"life"
((,"t";,"h";,"e");"42")
```

Considering a list as a mapping, we see that `string` acts on the range of the mapping. Viewing a dictionary as a generalized list, we conclude that the action of `string` on a dictionary should also apply to its range:

```
        d:1 2 3!100 101 102

        string d
1| "100"
2| "101"
3| "102"
```

A table is the flip of a column dictionary, so we expect `string` to operate on the range of the column dictionary:

```
        t:([] a:1 2 3; b:`a`b`c)
```

```
         string t
a    b
---------
,"1" ,"a"
,"2" ,"b"
,"3" ,"c"
```

Finally, a keyed table is a dictionary, so we expect `string` to operate on the value table:

```
      kt:([k:1 2 3] c:100 101 102)
      string kt
k| c
-| -----
1| "100"
2| "101"
3| "102"
```

A.1.8 sv

The basic form of dyadic `sv` (**string from vector**) takes a char as its left operand and a list of strings (*source*) as its right operand. It returns a string that is the concatenation of the strings in *source*, separated by the specified char:

```
      "," sv ("Now";"is";"the";"time";"")
"Now,is,the,time,"
```

When `sv` is used with an empty symbol as its left operand and a list of symbols as its right operand (*source*), the result is a symbol in which the items in *source* are concatenated with a separating dot:

```
      ` sv `qalib`stat
`qalib.stat
```

This is useful for *q* context names.

When `sv` is used with an empty symbol as its left operand and a symbol right operand (*source*) whose first item is a file handle, the result is a symbol in which the items in *source* are concatenated with a separating forward-slash. This is useful for fully qualified path names:

```
      ` sv `:`q`tutorial`draft1
`:/q/tutorial/draft1
```

When `sv` is used with an empty symbol as its left operand and a list of strings as the right operand, it catenates the strings, inserting a new line character after each:

```
    ` sv ("abc";"de")
"abc\nde\n"
```

When `sv` is used with an int left operand (*base*) that is greater than 1, together with a right operand of a simple list of place values expressed in *base*, the result is an int representing the converted base 10 value:

```
    2 sv 101010b
42
    10 sv 1 2 3 4 2
12342
    256 sv 0x001092
4242
```

Advanced

More precisely, the last version of `sv` evaluates the polynomial,

    (d[n-1]*b exp n-1) + ... +d[0]

where d is the list of digits, n is the count of d, and b is the base.

Thus, we find:

```
    10 sv 1 2 3 11 2
12412

    -10 sv 2 1 5
195
```

A.1.9 trim

The monadic `trim` takes a string argument and returns the result of removing leading and trailing blanks:

```
    trim "   abc   "
"abc"
```

> **Note**
>
> The function `trim` is equivalent to the following, below.

```
        {ltrim rtrim x}
```

You can also apply `trim` to a non-blank char:

```
        trim "a"
"a"
```

A.1.10 upper

The monadic `upper` takes a char, string or symbol argument and returns the result of converting any alpha characters to upper case:

```
        upper `a
`A

        upper "a Bc42De"
"A BC42DE"
```

A.1.11 vs

The dyadic `vs` (**vector from string**) takes a char as its left operand and a string (*source*) as its right operand. It returns a list of strings containing the tokens of *source* as delimited by the specified char:

```
        " " vs "Now is the time "
"Now"
"is"
"the"
"time"
" "
```

When `vs` is used with an empty symbol as its left operand and a symbol right operand (*source*) containing separating dots, it returns a simple symbol list obtained by splitting *source* along the dots:

```
        ` vs `qalib.stat
`qalib`stat
```

When `vs` is used with an empty symbol as its left operand and a symbol representing a fully qualified file name as the right operand, it returns a simple list of symbols in which the first item is the path and the second item is the file name:

```
        ` vs `:/q/tutorial/draft
`:/q/tutorial`draft
```

Note that in the last usage, `vs` is not quite the inverse of `sv`.

When `vs` is used with a null of binary type as the left operand and an value of integer type as the right operand (*source*), it returns a simple list whose items comprise the digits of the corresponding binary representation of *source*:

```
        0x00 vs 4242
0x00001092

        10h$0x00 vs 8151631268726338926j
"q is fun"

        0b vs 42
00000000000000000000000000101010b
```

The last form can be used to display the internal representation of special values:

```
        0b vs 0W
01111111111111111111111111111111b

        0b vs -0W
10000000000000000000000000000001b
```

A.2 MATHEMATICAL FUNCTIONS

The mathematical functions perform the mathematical operations for basic calculations. Their implementations are efficient.

A.2.1 acos

The monadic `acos` is the mathematical inverse of `cos`. For a float argument between -1 and 1, `acos` returns the float between 0 and π whose cosine is the argument:

```
        sqrt2:1.414213562373095
```

```
        acos 1
0f

        acos sqrt2
0n

        acos -1
3.1415926535897931

        acos 0
1.5707963267948966
```

A.2.2 asin

The monadic `asin` is the mathematical inverse of `sin`. For a float argument between -1 and 1, `asin` returns the float between $-\pi/2$ and $\pi/2$ whose sine is the argument:

```
        sqrt2:1.414213562373095

        asin 0
0f

        asin sqrt2%2
0.7853982

        asin 1
1.570796

        asin -1
-1.5707963267948966
```

A.2.3 atan

The monadic `atan` is the mathematical inverse of `tan`. For a float argument, `atan` returns the float between $-\pi/2$ and $\pi/2$ whose tangent is the argument:

```
        sqrt2:1.414213562373095

        atan 0
0f

        atan sqrt2
```

```
0.95531661812450919

        atan 1
0.78539816339744828
```

A.2.4 cor

The dyadic `cor` takes two numeric lists of the same count and returns a float equal to the mathematical correlation between the items of the two arguments:

```
        23 -11 35 0 cor 42  21 73 39
0.9070229
```

> **Note**
>
> The function `cor` is equivalent to the following, below.

```
        {cov[x;y]%dev[x]*dev y}
```

A.2.5 cos

The monadic `cos` takes a float argument and returns the mathematical cosine of the argument:

```
        pi:3.141592653589793

        cos 0
1f

        cos pi%3
0.5

        cos pi%2
6.123032e-17

        cos pi
-1f
```

A.2.6 cov

The dyadic `cov` takes a numeric atom or list in both arguments and returns a float equal to the mathematical covariance between the items of the two arguments. If both arguments are lists, they must have the same count:

```
        98 cov 42
0f

        23 -11 35 0 cov 42  21 73 39
308.4375
```

> **Note**
>
> The function `cov` is equivalent to the following, below.

```
{avg[x*y]-avg[x]*avg y}
```

A.2.7 cross

The binary `cross` takes atoms or lists as arguments and returns their Cartesian product — that is, the set of all pairs drawn from the two arguments:

```
        1 2 cross `a`b`c
1 `a
1 `b
1 `c
2 `a
2 `b
2 `c
```

> **Note**
>
> The `cross` operator is equivalent to the function:

```
{raze x,\:/:y}
```

A.2.8 inv

The monadic `inv` returns the inverse of a float matrix:

```
        m:(1.1 2.1 3.1; 2.3 3.4 4.5; 5.6 7.8 9.8)

        inv m
-8.165138  16.51376  -5
12.20183   -30.18349 10
-5.045872  14.58716  -5
```

> **Note**
>
> An integer argument will cause an error, so cast it to float.

A.2.9 lsq

The dyadic matrix function `lsq` returns the matrix X that solves the following matrix equation, where A is the float matrix left operand, B is the float matrix right operand and · is matrix multiplication:

```
    A = X·B
```

For example:

```
        A:(1.1 2.2 3.3;4.4 5.5 6.6;7.7 8.8 9.9)
        B:(1.1 2.1 3.1; 2.3 3.4 4.5; 5.6 7.8 9.8)

        A lsq B
1.211009   -0.1009174  2.993439e-12
-2.119266  2.926606    -3.996803e-12
-5.449541  5.954128    -1.758593e-11
```

Observe that the result of `lsq` can be obtained as:

```
        A mmu inv B
1.211009   -0.1009174  1.77991e-12
-2.119266  2.926606    -5.81224e-12
-5.449541  5.954128    -1.337952e-11
```

> **Note**
>
> Integer arguments will cause an error, so cast them to float.

A.2.10 mmu

The dyadic matrix multiplication function mmu returns the matrix product of its two float vector or matrix arguments, which must be of the correct shape:

> **Note**
>
> Integer arguments will cause an error, so cast them to float.

Here is an example of multiplying a matrix and its transpose:

```
        m1:(1.1 2.2 3.3;4.4 5.5 6.6;7.7 8.8 9.9)
        m2:flip m2

        m1 mmu   m2
36.3    43.56    50.82
79.86   98.01    116.16
123.42  152.46   181.5
```

The $ operator is overloaded to yield matrix multiplication when its arguments are float vectors or matrices:

```
        1 2 3f mmu 1 2 3f
14f

        1 2 3f$1 2 3f
14f
```

A.2.11 sin

The monadic sin takes a float argument and returns the mathematical sine of the argument:

```
        pi:3.141592653589793

        sin 0
```

```
        0f
            sin pi%4
0.7071068
            sin pi%2
1f
            sin pi
1.224606e-016
```

A.2.12 tan

The monadic `tan` takes a float argument and returns the mathematical tangent of the argument.

> **Note**
>
> The value `tan x` is `(sin x)%cos x`.

```
            pi:3.141592653589793
            tan 0
0f
            tan pi%8
0.4142136
            tan pi%4
1f
            tan pi%2
1.633178e+16
            tan pi
-1.224606e-16
```

A.2.13 var

The monadic `var` takes a scalar or numeric list and returns a float equal to the mathematical variance of the items:

```
            var 42
```

```
0f
        var 42 45 37 38
10.25
```

> **Note**
>
> The function `var` is equivalent to the following, below.

```
        {(avg[x*x]) - (avg[x])*(avg[x])}
```

A.2.14 wavg

The dyadic `wavg` takes two numeric lists of the same count and returns the average of the second argument weighted by the first argument. The result is always of type float:

```
        1 2 3 4 wavg 500 400 300 200
300f
```

> **Note**
>
> The expression `w wavg b` is equivalent to the following, below.

```
        (sum w*a)%sum w
```

In our example:

```
        (sum (1 2 3 4)*500 400 300 200)%sum 1 2 3 4
300f
```

It is possible to apply `wavg` to a nested list provided all sublists of both arguments conform. In this context, the result conforms to the sublists and the weighted average is calculated recursively across the sublists:

```
        (1 2;3 4) wavg (500 400; 300 200)
350 266.6667
```

```
        ((1;2 3);(4;5 6)) wavg ((600;500 400);(300;200 100))
360f
285.7143 200
```

A.2.15 wsum

The dyadic `wsum` takes two numeric lists of the same count and returns the sum of the second argument weighted by the first argument. The result is always of type float:

```
        1 2 3 4 wsum 500 400 300 200
3000f
```

> **Note**
>
> The expression `w wsum b` is equivalent to the following, below.

```
        sum w*a
```

In our example:

```
        sum (1 2 3 4)*500 400 300 200
3000
```

It is possible to apply `wsum` to a nested list provided all sublists of both arguments conform. In this context, the result conforms to the sublists and the weighted sum is calculated recursively across the sublists:

```
        (1 2;3 4) wsum (500 400;300 200)
1400 1600
        ((1;2 3);(4;5 6)) wsum ((600;500 400);(300;200 100))
1800
2000 1800
```

A.3 Aggregate Functions

An aggregate function operates on a list and returns an atom. Aggregates are especially useful with grouping in `select` expressions.

A.3.1 all

The monadic `all` takes a scalar or list of numeric type and returns the result of `&` applied cumulatively across the items:

```
        all 1b
1b
        all 100100b
0b
        all 10 20 30
10
```

A.3.2 any

The monadic `any` takes a scalar or list of numeric type and returns the result of `|` applied cumulatively across the items:

```
        any 1b
1b
        any 100100b
1b
        any 2001.01.01 2006.10.13
2006.10.13
```

A.3.3 avg

The monadic `avg` takes a scalar, list, dictionary or table of numeric type and returns the arithmetic average. The result is always of type float:

```
        avg 42
42f
        avg 1 2 3 4 5
3f
        avg `a`b`c!10 20 40
3.33333
```

It is possible to apply `avg` to a nested list provided the sublists conform. In this context, the result conforms to the sublists and the average is calculated recursively on the sublists:

```
        avg (1 2;100 200;1000 2000)
367 734f

        avg ((1 2;3 4);(100 200;300 400))
50.5    101
151.5   202
```

For tables, the result is a dictionary that maps each column name to the average of its column values:

```
        t:([]c1:1.1 2.2 3.3 4.4; c2:5 4 3 2)

        t
c1  c2
------
1.1 5
2.2 4
3.3 3
4.4 2

        avg t
c1| 2.75
c2| 3.5
```

A.3.4 dev

The monadic `dev` takes a scalar, list, or dictionary of numeric type and returns the standard deviation. The result is a float:

```
        dev 42
0f

        dev 42 45 37 38
3.201562

        dev `a`b`c!10 20 40
12.47219
```

> **Note**
>
> The function `dev` is equivalent to the following, below.

```
        {sqrt[var[x]]}
```

A.3.5 max

The monadic max takes a scalar or list of numeric type and returns the result of | applied cumulatively across the items:

```
        max 42
42
        max 100100b
1b
        max 2001.01.01 2006.10.13
2006.10.13
```

A.3.6 med

The monadic med takes a list, dictionary or table of numeric type and returns the statistical median.

For lists and dictionaries, the result is a float:

```
        med 42 21 73 39
40.5
        med `a`b`c!10 20 40
23.33333
```

> **Note**
>
> The function med is equivalent to the following, below.

```
        {$[n:count x;.5*sum x[rank x]@floor .5*n-1 0;0n]}
```

For tables, the result is a dictionary mapping each column name to the median of its column values:

```
        t:([]c1:1.1 2.2 3.3 4.4; c2:5 4 3 2)
        t
c1  c2
------
1.1 5
2.2 4
3.3 3
4.4 2
```

```
        med t
c1| 2.75
c2| 3.5
```

A.3.7 min

The monadic `min` takes a scalar or list of numeric type and returns the result of `&` applied cumulatively across the items:

```
        min 42
42

        min 100100b
0b

        min 10 20 30
10
```

A.3.8 prd

The monadic `prd` takes a scalar, list, dictionary or table of numeric type and returns the arithmetic product.

For scalars, lists and dictionaries the result has the type of its argument:

```
        prd 42
42

        prd 1.1 2.2 3.3 4.4 5.5
193.2612

        prd `a`b`c!10 20 40
8000
```

It is possible to apply `prd` to a nested list provided the sublists conform. In this case, the result conforms to the sublists and the product is calculated recursively on the sublists:

```
        prd (1 2; 100 200; 1000 2000)
100000 800000

        prd ((1 2;3 4); (100 200;300 400))
100 400
900 1600
```

For tables, the result is a dictionary that maps each column name to the product of its column values:

```
        t:([]c1:1.1 2.2 3.3 4.4; c2:5 4 3 2)
        t
c1  c2
------
1.1 5
2.2 4
3.3 3
4.4 2

        prd t
c1| 35.1384
c2| 120
```

A.3.9 sum

The monadic sum takes a scalar, list, dictionary or table of numeric type and returns the arithmetic sum.

For scalars, lists and dictionaries the result has the type of its argument:

```
        sum 42
42
        sum 1.1 2.2 3.3 4.4 5.5
16.5
        sum `a`b`c!10 20 40
70
```

It is possible to apply sum to a nested list provided the sublists conform. In this case, the result conforms to the sublists and the sum is calculated recursively on the sublists:

```
        sum (1 2;100 200;1000 2000)
1101 2202
        sum ((1 2;3 4);(100 200;300 400))
101 202
303 404
```

For tables, the result is a dictionary that maps each column name to the sum of its column values:

```
        t:([]c1:1.1 2.2 3.3 4.4; c2:5 4 3 2)
        t
c1  c2
------
1.1 5
2.2 4
3.3 3
4.4 2

        sum t
c1| 11f
c2| 14
```

A.4 Uniform Functions

Uniform functions operate on lists and return lists of the same shape. They are useful in `select` expressions.

A.4.1 deltas

The uniform `deltas` takes as its argument (*source*) a scalar, list, dictionary or table of numeric type and returns the difference of each item from its predecessor:

```
        deltas 42
42
        deltas 1 2 3 4 5
1 1 1 1 1
        deltas 96.25 93.25 58.25 73.25 89.50 84.00 84.25
96.25 -3 -35 15 16.25 -5.5 0.25
        deltas `a`b`c!10 20 40
a| 10
b| 10
c| 20
        t:([]c1:1.1 2.2 3.3 4.4; c2:5 4 3 2)
        t
c1  c2
------
```

```
1.1 5
2.2 4
3.3 3
4.4 2

       deltas t
c1  c2
------
1.1  5
1.1 -1
1.1 -1
1.1 -1
```

> **Important**
>
> As the third example shows, the initial item of the result of deltas is the initial item of source. This may be inconsistent with the behavior of similar functions in other languages or libraries that return 0 in the initial position. The alternate behavior can be achieved with the expression:
>
>   0,1_ deltas

In our example above:

```
       0,1_ deltas 96.25 93.25 58.25 73.25 89.50 84.00 84.25
0
-3f
-35f
15f
16.25
-5.5
0.25
```

A.4.2 differ

The uniform differ takes as its argument (*source*) a list and returns a boolean list whose item in position i is the result of match (~) applied to the item at position i and the item at position i-1. The result of differ on a scalar is 0b:

> **Note**
>
> The item at position 0 in the result is always 1b.

```
      differ 1 1 2
101b

      differ 0N 0N 1 1 2
10101b

      differ "mississippi"
11101101101b

      differ (1 2; 1 2; 3 4 5)
101b
```

One use of differ is to locate runs of repreated items in a list:

```
      L:0 1 1 2 3 2 2 2 4 1 1 3 4 4 4 5

      L where nd|next nd:not differ L
1 1 2 2 2 1 4 4 4
```

A.4.3 fills

The uniform fills takes as its argument (*source*) a scalar, list, dictionary or table of numeric type and returns a copy of the *source* in which non-null items are propagated forward to fill nulls:

```
      fills 42
42

      fills 1 0N 3 0N 5
1 1 3 3 5

      fills `a`b`c`d`e`f!10 0N 30 0N 0N 60
a| 10
b| 10
c| 30
d| 30
e| 30
f| 60
```

```
        tt:([] c1:1 0N 3 0N; c2:`a`b``d)
        tt
c1 c2
-----
1  a
   b
3
   d

        fills tt
c1 c2
-----
1  a
1  b
3  b
3  d
```

> **Note**
>
> Initial nulls are not affected by `fills`.

```
        fills 0N 0N 3 0N 5
0N 0N 3 3 5
```

A.4.4 mavg

The uniform dyadic `mavg` takes as its first argument an int (*length*) and as its second argument (*source*) a numeric list. It returns the moving average of *source*, obtained by applying `avg` over *length* consecutive items. For positions less than *length*-1, `avg` is applied only through that position.

In the following example, the first item in the result is the average of itself only; the second result item is the average of the first two source items; all other items reflect the average of the item at the position along with its two predecessors:

```
        3 mavg 10 20 30 40 50
10 15 20 30 40f
```

For *length* 1, the result is the source converted to `float`. For *length* less than or equal to 0 the result is all nulls:

> **Note**
>
> As of release **2.4**, mavg ignores null values.

```
        3 mavg 10 20 0N 40 50 60 0N
10 15 15 30 45 50 55f
```

A.4.5 maxs

The uniform maxs takes as its argument (*source*) a scalar, list, dictionary or table and returns the cumulative maximum of the *source* items:

```
        maxs 42
42

        maxs 1 2 5 4 10
1 2 5 5 10

        maxs "Beeblebrox"
"Beeelllrrx"

        maxs `a`b`c`d!10 30 20 40
a| 10
b| 30
c| 30
d| 40

        t:([]c1:1.1 2.2 3.3 4.4; c2:5 4 3 2)

        t
c1  c2
------
1.1 5
2.2 4
3.3 3
4.4 2

        maxs t
c1  c2
------
1.1 5
2.2 5
3.3 5
4.4 5
```

A.4.6 mcount

The uniform dyadic `mcount` takes as its first argument an int (*length*) and as its second argument (*source*) a numeric list. It returns the moving count of *source*, obtained by applying `count` over *length* consecutive items. For positions less than *length*-1, `count` is applied only through that position.

This function is useful in computing other moving quantities. For example:

```
      3 mcount 10 20 30 40 50
1 2 3 3 3
```

For *length* less than or equal to 0 the result is all zeroes.

> **Note**
>
> As of release **2.4**, `mcount` ignores null values.

```
      3 mcount 10 20 0N 40 50 60 0N
1 2 2 2 2 3 2
```

A.4.7 mdev

The uniform dyadic `mdev` takes as its first argument an int (*length*) and as its second argument (*source*) a numeric list. It returns the moving standard deviation of *source*, obtained by applying `dev` over *length* consecutive items. For positions less than *length*-1, `dev` is applied only through that position.

In the following example, the first item in the result is the standard deviation of itself only; the second result item is the standard deviation of the first two source items; all other items reflect the standard deviation of the item at the position along with its two predecessors:

```
      3 mdev 10 20 30 40 50
0 5 8.164966 8.164966 8.164966
```

For *length* less than or equal to 0 the result is all nulls.

A.4.8 mins

The uniform `mins` takes as its argument (*source*) a scalar, list, dictionary or table and returns the cumulative minimum of the *source* items:

```
        mins 42
42

        mins 10 4 5 1 2
10 4 4 1 1

        mins "Beeblebrox"
"BBBBBBBBBB"

        mins `a`b`c`d!40 10 30 20
a| 40
b| 10
c| 10
d| 10

        t:([]c1:1.1 2.2 3.3 4.4; c2:5 4 3 2)

        t
c1   c2
-------
1.1  5
2.2  4
3.3  3
4.4  2

        mins t
c1   c2
-------
1.1  5
1.1  4
1.1  3
1.1  2
```

A.4.9 mmax

The uniform dyadic mmax takes as its first argument an int (*length*) and as its second argument (*source*) a numeric list. It returns the moving maximum of *source*, obtained by applying max over *length* consecutive items. For positions less than *length*-1, max is applied only through that position.

In the following example, the first item in the result is the maximum of itself only; the second result item is the maximum of the first two source items; all other items reflect the maximum of the item at the position along with its two predecessors:

```
        3 mmax 20 10 30 50 40
20 20 30 50 50
```

For *length* less than or equal to 0 the result is *source*.

A.4.10 mmin

The uniform dyadic mmin takes as its first argument an int (*length*) and as its second argument (*source*) a numeric list. It returns the moving minimum of *source*, obtained by applying min over *length* consecutive items. For positions less than *length*-1, min is applied only through that position.

In the following example, the first item in the result is the minimum of itself only; the second result item is the minimum of the first two source items; all other items reflect the minimum of the item at the position along with its two predecessors:

```
        3 mmin 20 10 30 50 40
20 10 10 10 30
```

For *length* less than or equal to 0 the result is *source*.

A.4.11 msum

The uniform dyadic msum takes as its first argument an int (*length*) and as its second argument (*source*) a numeric list. It returns the moving sum of *source*, obtained by applying sum over *length* consecutive items. For positions less than *length*-1, sum is applied only through that position.

In the following example, the first item in the result is the sum of itself only; the second result item is the sum of the first two source items; all other items reflect the sum of the item at the position along with its two predecessors:

```
        3 msum 10 20 30 40 50
10 30 60 90 120
```

For *length* less than or equal to 0 the result is all zeroes.

A.4.12 next

The uniform next takes as its argument (*source*) a list or table of numeric type and returns the *source* shifted one position to the left with no wrapping. For lists and dictionaries, the last item of the result is a null matching the type of *source*. For tables, the last record of the result is a row of nulls:

```
        next 1 2 3 4 5
2 3 4 5 0N

        t:([]c1:1.1 2.2 3.3 4.4; c2:5 4 3 2)

        t
c1  c2
------
1.1 5
2.2 4
3.3 3
4.4 2

        next t
c1  c2
------
2.2 4
3.3 3
4.4 2
```

A.4.13 prds

The uniform sums takes as its argument (*source*) a scalar, list, dictionary or table of numeric type and returns the cumulative product of the *source* items:

```
        prds 42
42

        prds 1 2 3 4 5
1 2 6 24 120

        prds `a`b`c!10 20 40
a| 10
b| 200
c| 8000

        t:([]c1:1.1 2.2 3.3 4.4; c2:5 4 3 2)

        t
c1  c2
------
1.1 5
2.2 4
3.3 3
4.4 2

        prds t
```

```
c1       c2
-----------
1.1      5
2.42     20
7.986    60
35.1384  120
```

A.4.14 prev

The uniform `prev` takes as its argument (*source*) a scalar, list, dictionary or table. It returns the *source* shifted one position forward with initial null filling:

```
        prev 42
42

        prev 1 2 3 4 5
0N 1 2 3 4

        prev `a`b`c!10 20 40
a|
b| 10
c| 20

        t:([]c1:`a`b`c;c2:10 20 40)

        t
c1 c2
-----
a  10
b  20
c  40

        prev t
c1 c2
-----
   
a  10
b  20
```

A.4.15 rank

The uniform `rank` takes as its argument (*source*) a list, dictionary or table whose values are sortable. It returns a list of int containing the order of each item in the *source* under an ascending sort.

For dictionaries, the operation is against the range:

```
        rank 5 2 3 1 4
4 1 2 0 3

        rank `a`b`c`e`f! 5 2 3 1 4
4 1 2 0 3
```

For tables and keyed tables, the result is a list with the rank of the records under ascending sort of the first column or the key column:

```
        ttt:([] c1:2.2 1.1 3.3 5.5 4.4; c2:1 2 3 4 5)

        ttt
c1  c2
------
2.2 1
1.1 2
3.3 3
5.5 4
4.4 5

        rank ttt
1 0 2 4 3

        kt:([k:103 102 101 105 104] d:1 2 3 4 5)

        kt
k   | d
----| -
103 | 1
102 | 2
101 | 3
105 | 4
104 | 5

        rank kt
2 1 0 4 3
```

A.4.16 ratios

The uniform `ratios` takes as its argument (*source*) a scalar, list, dictionary or table of numeric type and returns the float ratio of each item to its predecessor:

```
        ratios 42
42
```

```
        ratios 1 2 3 4 5
1 2 1.5 1.333333 1.25

        ratios 96.25 93.25 58.25 73.25 89.50 84.00 84.25
96.25 0.9688312 0.6246649 1.257511 1.221843 0.9385475 1.002976

        deltas `a`b`c!10 20 40
a| 10
b| 10
c| 20

        t:([]c1:1.1 2.2 3.3 4.4; c2:5 4 3 2)

        t
c1  c2
------
1.1 5
2.2 4
3.3 3
4.4 2

        ratios t
c1        c2
------------------
1.1       5
2         0.8
1.5       0.75
1.333333  0.6666667
```

> **Important**
>
> As the second example shows, the initial item of the result of `ratios` is the initial item of source. This may be inconsistent with the behavior of similar functions in other languages or libraries that return 1 in the initial position. The alternate behavior can be achieved with the expression,
>
> ```
> 1,1_ ratios
> ```

In our example above:

```
        1,1_ ratios 96.25 93.25 58.25 73.25 89.50 84.00 84.25
1
0.9688312
0.6246649
```

```
1.257511
1.221843
0.9385475
1.002976
```

A.4.17 rotate

The uniform dyadic `rotate` takes as its first argument an int (*length*) and as its second argument (*source*) a numeric list or table. It returns the source shifted *length* positions to the left with wrapping if *length* is positive, or *length* positions to the right with wrapping if *length* is negative. For *length* 0, it returns the source:

```
        2 rotate 1 2 3 4 5
3 4 5 1 2

        -2 rotate 1 2 3 4 5
4 5 1 2 3

        t:([]c1:1.1 2.2 3.3 4.4; c2:5 4 3 2)

        t
c1  c2
------
1.1 5
2.2 4
3.3 3
4.4 2

        2 rotate t
c1  c2
------
3.3 3
4.4 2
1.1 5
2.2 4
```

A.4.18 sums

The uniform `sums` takes as its argument (*source*) a scalar, list, dictionary or table of numeric type and returns the cumulative sum of the *source* items:

```
        sums 42
42

        sums 1 2 3 4 5
```

```
1 3 6 10 15

        sums `a`b`c!10 20 40
a| 10
b| 30
c| 70

        t:([]c1:1.1 2.2 3.3 4.4; c2:5 4 3 2)

        t
c1  c2
------
1.1 5
2.2 4
3.3 3
4.4 2

        sums t
c1  c2
------
1.1 5
3.3 9
6.6 12
11  14
```

A.4.19 xbar

The uniform dyadic xbar takes as its first argument a non-negative numeric atom (*width*) and a second argument (*source*) that is a numeric list, dictionary or table. It returns an entity that conforms to *source*, in which each item of *source* is mapped to the largest multiple of the *width* that is less than or equal to that item. The type of the result is that of the *width* parameter:

```
        3 xbar 2 7 12 17 22
0 6 12 15 21

        5.5 xbar 59.25 53.75 81.00 96.25 93.25 58.25 73.25 89.50
55 49.5 77 93.5 88 55 71.5 88 82.5 82.5

        15 xbar `a`b`c!10 20 40
a| 0
b| 15
c| 30

        t:([]c1:1.1 2.2 3.3 4.4; c2:5 4 3 2)

        t
```

```
c1   c2
------
1.1  5
2.2  4
3.3  3
4.4  2

     select by 2 xbar c1 from t
c1|  c2
--|  --
0 |  5
2 |  3
4 |  2
```

Since xbar is atomic in its second argument it can be applied to a nested list:

```
       5 xbar ((11;21 31);201 301)
10    20 30
200   300
```

A.4.20 xprev

The dyadic xprev takes an int as its first argument (*shift*) and is uniform in its second argument (*source*), which can be a list a dictionary or a table. It returns a result that conforms to *source*. When *shift* is 0 or positive, each entity in *source* is shifted *shift* positions forward in the result, with the initial *shift* entries null filled:

```
       2 xprev 10 20 30 40
0N 0N 10 20

       d:`a`b`c`d!10 20 40 80
       (2 xprev key d)!(2 xprev value d)
 |
 |
a| 10
b| 20

       t:([]c1:`a`b`c`d;c2:10 20 30 40)
       t
c1 c2
-----
a  10
b  20
c  30
d  40
```

```
        2 xprev t
c1 c2
-----


a  10
b  20
```

When *shift* is negative, the result is a copy of *source* with the initial *shift* entries null filled:

```
        -2 xprev 10 20 30 40
0N 0N 30 40
```

A.4.21 xrank

The binary `xrank` is uniform in its right operand (*source*), which is a list, dictionary, table or keyed table whose values are sortable. The left operand is a positive int (*quantile*). It returns a list of int containing the quantile of the source distribution to which each item of *source* belongs. The analysis is applied to the range of a dictionary and the first column of a table.

For example, by choosing *quantile* to be 4, `xrank` determines into which quartile each item of *source* falls:

```
        4 xrank 30 10 40 20 90
1 0 2 0 3

        4 xrank `a`b`c`d`e!30 10 40 20 90
1 0 2 0 3

        t:([] c1:30 10 40 20 90; c11:`a`b`c`d`e)

        t
c1 c11
------
30 a
10 b
40 c
20 d
90 e

        4 xrank t
1 0 2 0 3
```

Choosing *quantile* to be 100 gives percentile ranking.

A.5 MISCELLANEOUS FUNCTIONS

We collect here the built-in functions that don't fit neatly into any of the previously defined categories.

A.5.1 Conditional Append (?)

The left operand of conditional append (?) is a symbol representing the name of a list of symbols (*target*) and the right operand is a symbol, the right operand is appended to *target* if and only if it is not in *target*. There is no effect when the right operand is already in *target*. The result is the enumeration of the right operand in *target*:

```
        v:`a`b`c

        `v?`z
`v$`z

        v
`a`b`c`z

        `v?`b
`v$`b

        v
`a`b`c`z
```

> **Note**
>
> While conditional append is normally used with a target list of unique items, this is not a requirement.

A.5.2 asc

The monadic function `asc` operates on a list or a dictionary (*source*). The result of `asc` on a list is a list comprising the items of *source* sorted in increasing order with the s# attribute applied. The result of `asc` on a dictionary is an equivalent mapping with the range items sorted in increasing order and with the s# attribute applied:

```
        asc 3 7 2 8 1 9
`s#1 2 3 7 8 9
```

```
        asc `b`c`a!3 2 1
a| 1
c| 2
b| 3
```

A.5.3 bin

The dyadic `bin` takes a simple list of items (*target*) in strictly increasing order as its first argument and is atomic in its second argument (*token*). Loosely speaking, the result of bin is the position at which *token* would fall in *target*.

More precisely, the result is -1 if *token* is less than the first item in *target*. Otherwise, the result is the position of the right-most item of *target* that is less than or equal to *token*; this reduces to the found position if the token is in *target*. If *token* is greater than the last item in *target*, the result is the count of *target*.

> **Note**
>
> For large sorted lists, the binary search performed by `bin` is generally more efficient than the linear search algorithm used by `in`.

Some examples with simple lists:

```
        1 2 3 4 bin 3
2

        "xyz" bin "a"
-1

        1.0 2.0 3.0 bin 0.0 2.0 2.5 3.0
-1 1 1 2
```

Observe that the type of *token* must **strictly** match that of *target*:

```
        1 2 3 bin 1.5
`type
```

We can apply `bin` to a dictionary to perform reverse lookup, provided the dictionary domain is in increasing order. When *source* is a dictionary, `bin` takes a *token* whose type matches that of the dictionary range. The result is null if *token* is less than every item of the range. Otherwise, the result is the right-most domain element whose corresponding range element is less than or equal to *token*. Loosely put, when *token* is not found, the result is the domain item after which you would make an insertion to place it into the dictionary in proper order.

Note that the result reduces to the corresponding domain item if *token* is found in *target*, and is the last domain item if *token* is greater than every range item:

```
        d:10 20 30!`first`second`third

        d bin `second
20

        d bin `missing
10

        d bin `zero
30

        d bin `aaa
0N
```

Because a table is a list of records, we expect bin to return the row number of a record:

```
        t:([] a:1 2 3; b:`a`b`c)

        t
a b
---
1 a
2 b
3 c

        t bin `a`b!(2;`b)
1
```

As always, the record can be abbreviated to the list of row values:

```
        t bin (1;`a)
0

        t bin (2;`a)
0N

        t bin (2;`z)
1
```

Observe that the result is null if the record could not fall in the (presumably sorted) list of table records and the insert position if it could.

Finally, since a keyed table is a dictionary, `bin` will perform a reverse lookup on a record of the value table, which can be abbreviated to a list of row values:

```
        kt:([k:1 2 3] c:100 101 102)

        kt
k| c
-| ---
1| 100
2| 101
3| 102

        kt bin (enlist `c)!enlist 101
k| 2

        kt bin 101
k| 2
```

> **Warning**
>
> While the items of the first argument of `bin` should be in strictly increasing order for the result to meaningful, this condition is not enforced. The results of `bin` when the first argument is not strictly increasing are predictable but not particularly useful.

A.5.4 count

The monadic `count` returns a non-negative int representing the number of entities in its argument. Its domain comprises scalars, lists, dictionaries, tables and keyed tables:

```
        count 3
1
        count 10 20 30
3
        count `a`b`c`d!10 20 30 40
4
```

```
        count ([] a:10 20 30; b:1.1 2.2 3.3)
3

        count ([k:10 20] c:`one`two)
2
```

> **Note**
>
> You cannot use `count` to determine whether an entity is a scalar or list since scalars and singletons both have count 1.

```
        count 3
1

        count enlist 3
1
```

This test is accomplished instead by testing the sign of the type of the entity:

```
        0>type 3
1b

        0>type enlist 3
0b
```

> **Aside**
>
> Do you know why they call it count? Because it loves to count! Nyah, ha, ha, ha, ha. Vun, and two, and tree, and ...

A.5.5 cut

The binary operator `cut` is related to the `_` operator. It is the same as `_` when the right operand is a list or dictionary and the left operand is a list of items from the map domain:

```
        d:1 2 3!`a`b`c
        (enlist 2) cut d
1| a
3| c
```

However, for a list right operand *source* and an int left operand *size*, `cut` returns a new list created by collecting the items of *source* into sublists of count *size*:

```
        5 cut til 13
0 1 2 3 4
5 6 7 8 9
10 11 12
```

> **Advanced**
>
> The `cut` function is equivalent to:
>
>   {$[0>type x; x*til neg floor neg(count y)mod x; x]_y}

A.5.6 cut (_)

The symbol _ is overloaded to have several meanings depending on the signature of its operands. See also drop.

> **Note**
>
> When _ is used as an operator, whitespace is required to the left if the left operand is a name. This is because _ is a valid non-initial name chaacter. Whitespace is permitted but not required to the right.

When the first argument of dyadic (_) is a list of non-negative int and the second argument (*source*) is a list, it produces a new list obtained by breaking *source* into sublists at the positions indicated in the first argument. An example will make this clear:

```
        0 3_100 200 300 400 500
100 200 300
400 500
```

Each sublist includes the items from the beginning cut position up to, but not including, the next cut position. The final cut includes the items to the end of *source*. Observe that if the left argument does not begin with 0, the initial items of *source* will **not** be included in the result:

```
            2 4_2006.01 2006.02 2006.03 2006.04 2006.05 2006.06
2006.03 2006.04
2006.05 2006.06
```

When the right operand of _ is a dictionary (*source*) and the left operand is a list of key values whose type matches *source*, the result is a dictionary obtained by removing the specified key-value pairs from the target. For example:

```
        d:1 2 3!`a`b`c

        (enlist 42) _ d
1| a
2| b
3| c

        (enlist 2) _ d
1| a
3| c

        1 3 _ d
2| b

        1 2 3 _ d
```

> **Note**
>
> The operand must be a list, so a single key value must be enlisted.

This construct can also be used to remove columns by name from a table:

```
        t:([]a:1 2 3;b:`a`b`c;c:1.1 2.2 3.3)

        `a`c _ t
b
-
a
b
c
```

When the first argument of dyadic cut (_) is a list or a dictionary (*source*) and the second argument is a position in the list or an item in the domain of the dictionary, the result is a new entity obtained by deleting the specified item from the *source*:

```
        L: 101 102 103 104 105

        L _ 2
101 102 104 105

        d:`a`b`c`d!101 102 103 104

        d _ `b
a| 101
c| 103
d| 104
```

Since a table is a list, cut can be applied by row number:

```
        t:([] c1:1 2 3; c2:101 102 103; c3:`x`y`z)

        t
c1 c2  c3
---------
1  101 x
2  102 y
3  103 z

        t _ 1
c1 c2  c3
---------
1  101 x
3  103 z
```

Since a keyed table is a dictionary, cut can be applied by key value:

```
        kt:([k:101 102 103] c:`one`two`three)

        kt
k  | c
---| -----
101| one
102| two
103| three

        kt _ 102
k  | c
---| -----
101| one
103| three
```

A.5.7 desc

The monadic function `desc` operates on a list or a dictionary (*source*). The result of `desc` on a list is a list comprising the items of *source* sorted in decreasing order with the s# attribute applied. The result of `desc` on a dictionary is an equivalent mapping with the range items sorted in decreasing order and with the s# attribute applied:

```
        desc 3 7 2 8 1 9
9 8 7 3 2 1

        desc `b`c`a!3 2 1
b| 3
c| 2
a| 1
```

A.5.8 distinct

The monadic function `distinct` returns the distinct entities in its argument. For a list, it returns the distinct items in the list, in order of first occurrence:

```
        distinct 1 2 3 2 3 4 6 4 3 5 6
1 2 3 4 6 5
```

For a table, `distinct` returns a table comprising the distinct records of the argument, in the order of first occurrence:

```
        tdup:([]a:1 2 3 2 1;
            b:`washington`adams`jefferson`adams`wasington)

        tdup
a b
------------
1 washington
2 adams
3 jefferson
2 adams
1 washington

        distinct tdup
a b
------------
1 washington
```

```
2 adams
3 jefferson
1 wasington
```

Observe that all fields of the records must be identical for the records to be considered identical. Otherwise put, if any field differs, the records are distinct.

When applied to an int n, `distinct` produces a random int between 0 (inclusive) and n (exclusive):

```
        distinct 42
37

        distinct 42
39
```

A.5.9 drop (_)

The symbol _ is overloaded to have several meanings depending on the signature of its operands. See also delete.

> **Note**
>
> When _ is used as an operator, whitespace is **required** to the left if the left operand is a name. This is because _ is a valid non-initial name character. Whitespace is permitted but not required to the right.

When the first argument of the dyadic _ is an int and the second argument (*source*) is a list, the result is a new list created via removal from *source*. Positive int in the first argument indicates that the removal occurs from the beginning of the *source*, whereas a negative int in the first argument indicates that the removal occurs from the end of the *source*.

The *source* can be a list, a dictionary, a table or a keyed table:

```
        2_10 20 30 40
30 40

        -3_`one`two`three`four`five
`one`two

        2_`a`b`c`d!10 20 30 40
c| 30
d| 40
```

```
        -1_([] a:10 20 30 40; b:1.1 2.2 3.3 4.4)
a b
------
10 1.1
20 2.2
30 3.3


        2_([k:10 20 30] c:`one`two`three)
k | c
--|-----
30| three
```

The result of drop is of the same type and shape as *source* and is never a scalar:

```
        1_42 67
,67
```

Observe that for nested lists, the deletion occurs at the top-most level:

```
        1_(100 101 102;103 104 105)
103 104 105
```

In the degenerate case, the result is an empty entity derived from *source*:

```
        4_10 20 30 40
`int$()

        4_`a`b`c`d!10 20 30 40

        4_([] a:10 20 30 40; b:1.1 2.2 3.3 4.4)
a b
---

        3_([k:10 20 30] c:`one`two`three)
k| c
-| -
```

A.5.10 eval

The monadic eval evaluates a list that represents a valid *q* parse tree, which can be produced by parse or by hand (if you know what you're doing). A discussion of parse trees is beyond the scope of this manual.

```
        show pt:parse "a:6*7"
```

```
        :`a
(*;6;7)

        eval pt
42

        a
42
```

A.5.11 except

The dyadic `except` takes a simple list or a dictionary whose range is a simple list as its first argument (*target*) and returns a list containing the items of *target* excluding those that are in its second argument, which can be a scalar or a list. The returned items are in the order of their first occurrence in *target*:

```
        1 2 3 4 3 2 except 2
1 3 4 3

        1 2 3 4 3 2 except 1 2 10
3 4 3

        "Now is the time_" except "_"
"Now is the time"

        d:`a`c`d`e!1 2 1 2

        d except 1
2 2
```

The result of `except` is never a scalar:

```
        1 2 except 1
,2

        1 2 except 2 1
`int$()

        d except 1 2
`int$()
```

A.5.12 exit

The monadic `exit` takes an int as its argument and executes the system command \\ with the specified parameter.

> **Warning**
>
> Exit does not prompt for a confirmation.

A.5.13 fill (^)

The dyadic fill (^) takes an atom as its first argument and a list, dictionary, table or keyed table (*target*) as its second argument. For a list, it returns a list obtained by substituting the first argument for every occurrence of null in *target*. It operates on the range of a dictionary:

```
        42^1 2 3 0N 5 0N
1 2 3 42 5 42

        ";"^"Now is the time"
"Now;is;the;time"

        `NULL^`First`Second``Fourth
`First`Second`NULL`Fourth

        d:`a`b`c`d!100 0N 200 0N

        42^d
a| 100
b| 42
c| 200
d| 42
```

Observe that the action of fill is recursive — i.e., it is applied to sublists of the target:

```
        42^(1;0N;(100;200 0N))
1
42
(100;200 42)
```

For a dictionary, fill operates on the range. For a table of keyed table, it operates on the columns:

```
        d:`a`b`c!1 0N 3

        42^d
```

```
a| 1
b| 42
c| 3

        t:([]c1:1.0 2.0 0n; c2:0N 2 0N)

        0^t
c1 c2
-----
1  0
2  2
0  0
```

A.5.14 find (?)

When the first argument (*target*) of find (?) is a simple list, find is atomic in the second argument (*source*) and returns the positions in *target* of the initial occurrence of each item of *source*.
  The simplest case is when *source* is a scalar:

```
        100 99 98 87 96?98
2

        "Now is the time"?"t"
7
```

If *source* is not found in *target*, find returns the count of *target* — i.e., the position one past the last element:

```
        `one`two`three?`four
3
```

In this context, find is atomic in its second argument, so it is extended item-wise to a *source* list:

```
        "Now is the time"?"the"
7 8 9
```

Note that find always returns the position of the **first** occurrence of each atom:

```
        "Now is the time"?"time"
7 4 13 9
```

When the first argument (*target*) of find is a general list, find considers both elements to be general lists and attempts to locate the second argument (*source*) in the target, returning the position where it is found or the count of *target* if not found:

```
    (1 2;3 4)?3 4
1
```

Observe that find only compares items at the top level of the two arguments and does not look for nested items:

```
    ((0;1 2);3 4;5 6)?1 2
3

    ((0;1 2);3 4;5 6)?(1;(2;3 4))
3
```

When the first argument (*target*) of find is a dictionary, find represents reverse lookup and is atomic in the second argument (*source*). In other words, find returns the domain item mapping to *source* if *source* is in the range, or a null appropriate to the domain type otherwise:

```
    d:1 2 3!100 101 102

    d?101
2

    d?99
0N

    d?102 100
3 1
```

When the first argument (*target*) of find is a table and the second argument (*source*) is a record of the target, find returns the position of *source* if it is in *target*, or the count of *target* otherwise:

```
    t:([] a:1 2 3; b:`a`b`c)

    t
a b
---
1 a
2 b
3 c
```

```
        t?`a`b!(2;`b)
1
```

As usual with records, you can abbreviate the record to its row value list:

```
        t?(3;`c)
2
```

When the first argument of find is a keyed table, which is a dictionary, find performs a reverse lookup on a record from the value table:

```
        kt:([k:1 2 3] c:100 101 102)

        kt
k| c
-| ---
1| 100
2| 101
3| 102

        kt?`c!101
k| 2
```

Again, a record of the value table can be abbreviated to its row values:

```
        kt?102
k| 3
```

A.5.15 flip

The monadic function `flip` takes a rectangular list, a column dictionary or a table as its argument (*source*). The result is the transpose of *source*.

When *source* is a rectangular list, the items are rearranged, effectively reversing the first two indices in indexing at depth. For example:

```
        L:(1 2 3;(10 20;100 200;1000 2000))

        L
1          2          3
10  20     100  200   1000 2000

        L[1;0]
10 20

        fL:flip L
```

```
        fL
1 10   20
2 100  200
3 1000 2000

        fL[0;1]
10 20
```

When *source* is a singleton list whose item is a simple list, `flip` creates a vertical list:

```
        flip enlist 101 103
101
103
```

This idiom is used to index multiple key values into keyed tables:

```
        kt:([k:101 102 103] c:`one`two`three)

        kt flip enlist 101 103
c
-----
one
three
```

When *source* is a column dictionary, the result is a table with the given column names and values. Row and column access are effectively reversed, but no data is rearranged:

```
        d:(`a`b`c!(1 2 3;1.1 2.2 3.3;("one";"two";"three")))

        d
a| 1     2     3
b| 1.1   2.2   3.3
c| "one" "two" "three"

        d[`b;0]
1.1

        t:flip d

        t
a b   c
----------
1 1.1 "one"
2 2.2 "two"
3 3.3 "three"
```

When *source* is a table, the result is the underlying column dictionary. Row and column access are effectively reversed, but no data is rearranged:

```
        t:([]a:1 2 3;b:1.1 2.2 3.3;c:("one";"two";"three"))

        t
a b   c
-----------
1 1.1 "one"
2 2.2 "two"
3 3.3 "three"

        t[1;`c]
"two"

        d:flip t

        d
a| 1     2     3
b| 1.1   2.2   3.3
c| "one" "two" "three"

        d[`c;1]
"two"
```

A.5.16 getenv

The monadic function `getenv` takes a symbol argument representing the name of an O/S environment variable and returns the value (if any) of that environment variable:

```
        getenv `SHELL
"/bin/bash"
```

A.5.17 group

The monadic function `group` operates on a list (*source*) and returns a dictionary in which each distinct item in *source* is mapped to a list of the indices of its occurrences in *source*. The items in the domain of the result are in the order of their first appearance in *source*:

```
        group "i miss mississippi"
i| 0 3 8 11 14 17
 | 1 6
m| 2 7
```

```
s| 4 5 9 10 12 13
p| 15 16
```

This can be used to extract specific information about the occurrences, such as:

```
     dm:group "i miss mississippi"

     count each dm
i| 6
 | 2
m| 2
s| 6
p| 2

     first each dm
i| 0
 | 1
m| 2
s| 4
p| 15
```

A.5.18 iasc

The monadic function `iasc` operates on a list or a dictionary (*source*). Considering *source* as a mapping, the result of `iasc` is a list comprising the domain items arranged in increasing order of their associated range items. Otherwise put, retrieving the items of *source* in the order specified by `iasc` sorts *source* in ascending order:

```
     L:3 7 2 8 1 9

     iasc L
4 2 0 1 3 5

     L[iasc L]
1 2 3 7 8 9

     d:`b`c`a!3 2 1

     iasc d
`a`c`b

     d[iasc d]
1 2 3
```

A.5.19 identity

The monadic function denoted by double colon (::) is the identity function, meaning that the return value is the same as the argument:

```
        ::[42]
42

        ::[`zaphod]
`zaphod

        ::["Life the Universe and Everything"]
"Life the Universe and Everything"
```

> **Note**
>
> The identity function cannot be used with juxtaposition or @. Its argument must be enclosed in brackets.

```
        :: 42
'::
```

A.5.20 idesc

The monadic function `idesc` operates on a list or a dictionary (*source*). Considering *source* as a mapping, the result of `idesc` is a list comprising the domain items arranged in decreasing order of their associated range items. Otherwise put, retrieving the items of *source* in the order specified by `idesc` sorts *source* in descending order:

```
        L:3 7 2 8 1 9

        idesc L
5 3 1 0 2 4

        L[idesc L]
9 8 7 3 2 1

        d:`b`c`a!3 2 1
```

```
        idesc d
`b`c`a

        d[idesc d]
3 2 1
```

A.5.21 in

The dyadic function in is atomic in its first argument (*source*) and takes a second argument (*target*) that is an atom or list. It returns a boolean result that indicates whether *source* appears in *target*. The comparison is strict with regard to type:

```
        3 in 8
0b

        42 in 0 6 7 42 98
1b

        "cat" in "abcdefg"
110b

        `zap in `zaphod`beeblebrox
0b

        2 in 0 2 4j
'type

        42 43 in 0 6 7 42 98
10b
```

A.5.22 inter

The dyadic inter can be applied to lists, dictionaries and tables. It returns an entity of the same type as its arguments, containing those elements of the first argument that appear in the second argument:

```
        1 1 2 3 inter 1 2 3 4
1 1 2 3

        "ab cd " inter " bc f"
"b c "
```

> **Note**
>
> Lists are not sets and the operation of `inter` on lists is not identical to intersection of sets. In particular, the result of `inter` does not comprise the **distinct** items common to the two arguments.
>
> One consequence is that the expression,
>
>   (x inter y)~y inter x
>
> is **not** true in general.

When applied to dictionaries, `inter` returns the set of common range items that are mapped from the common domain items:

```
d1:1 2 3!100 200 300
d2:2 4 6!200 400 600

d1 inter d2
,200
```

Tables that have the same columns can participate in `inter`. The result is a table with the records that are common to the two tables:

```
     t1
a b
--------
1 first
2 second
3 third

     t2
a b
--------
2 second
4 fourth
6 sixth

     t1 inter t2
a b
--------
2 second
```

A.5.23 join (,)

The dyadic join (,) can take many different combinations of arguments.

When both operands are either lists or atoms, the result is a list with the item(s) of the left operand followed by the item(s) of the right operand:

```
        2,3
2 3

        `a,`b`c
`a`b`c

        "xy","yz"
"xyyz"

        1.1 2.2,3 4
1.1
2.2
3
4
```

Observe that the result is a general list unless all items are of homogeneous type.

When both operands are dictionaries, the result is the merge of the dictionaries using upsert semantics. The domain of the result is the (set theoretic) union of the two domains. Range assignment of the right operand prevails on common domain items:

```
        d1:1 2 3!`a`b`c
        d2:3 4 5!`cc`d`e

        d1,d2
1| a
2| b
3| cc
4| d
5| e
```

When both operands are tables having the same column names and types, the result is a table in which the records of the right operand are appended to those of the left operand:

```
        t1:([] a:1 2 3; b:`x`y`z)

        t1
a b
---
```

```
1 x
2 y
3 z

        t2:([] a:3 4; b:`yy`z)

        t2
a b
----
3 yy
4 z

        t1,t2
a b
----
1 x
2 y
3 z
3 yy
4 z
```

When both operands are keyed tables having the same key and value columns, the result is a keyed table in which the records of the left operand are upserted with those of the right operand:

```
        kt1:([k:1 2 3] v:`a`b`c)

        kt1
k| v
-| -
1| a
2| b
3| c

        kt2:([k:3 4] v:`cc`d)

        kt2
k| v
-| --
3| cc
4| d

        kt1,kt2
k| v
-| --
1| a
2| b
3| cc
4| d
```

A.5.24 join-each (, ')

The verb join (,) can be combined with the adverb monadic each (') to yield join-each (, ') which can be used on lists, dictionaries or tables.

List operands must have the same count:

```
        L1:1 2 3
        L2:`a`b`c

        L1,'L2
1 `a
2 `b
3 `c
```

As always with dictionaries, the operation occurs along the common domain items, with null extension elsewhere:

```
        d1:1 2 3!10 20 30

        d2:2 3 4!`a`b`c

        d1,'d2
1| 10  `
2| 20  `a
3| 30  `b
4| 0N  `c
```

For two tables with the same count of records, join-each results in a column join (see §7.6.5), in which columns with non-common names are juxtaposed and overlapping columns are upserted:

```
        t1:([] c1:1 2 3; c2:1.1 2.2 3.3)

        t1
c1 c2
------
1  1.1
2  2.2
3  3.3

        t2:([] c2:`a`b`c; c3:100 200 300)

        t2
c2 c3
------
```

```
a  100
b  200
c  300

         t1,'t2
c1 c2 c3
--------
1  a  100
2  b  200
3  c  300
```

> **Note**
>
> When join-each is used in a `select`, it must be enclosed in parentheses to avoid the comma being interpreted as a separator.

```
      select j:(c1,'c2) from t1
j
-----
1 1.1
2 2.2
3 3.3
```

A.5.25 list

The function `list` takes a variable number of arguments and returns a list whose items are the arguments. It is useful for creating lists programmatically.

> **Note**
>
> Unlike user-defined functions, the number of arguments to `list` is not restricted to eight.

For example:

```
      list[6;7;42;`Life;"The Universe"]
6
7
42
```

```
`Life
"The Universe"

        list[1;2;3;4;5;6;7;8;9;10]
1 2 3 4 5 6 7 8 9 10
```

A.5.26 md5

The monadic function md5 computes the MD5 (Message Digest Algorithm 5) 128-bit hash of a string:

```
        md5 "Life the Universe and Everything"
0x0e9a5631e4db880d43808504d05348df
```

A.5.27 null

The atomic function null takes an atom or a list (*source*) and returns a boolean comprising the result of testing each item in *source* against null:

```
        null 1 2 3 0N 5 0N
000101b
        null `a`b``d```f
0010110b
```

Since null is atomic, it is applied recursively to sublists:

```
        null (1 2;3 0N)
00b
01b
```

It is useful to combine where with null to obtain the positions of the null items:

```
        where null 1 2 3 0N 5 0N
3 5
```

When applied to a dictionary (*source*), null returns a dictionary in which each item in the *source* range is replaced with the result of testing the item against null:

```
        null 1 2 3!100 0N 300
1| 0
2| 1
3| 0
```

The action of `null` on a table (*source*) is explained by recalling that the table is a flipped column dictionary. Based on the action of `null` on a dictionary, we expect the result of `null` on a table will be a new table in which each column value in the source is replaced with the result of testing the value against null:

```
        tnull:([]a:1 0N 3; b:0N 200 300)

        null tnull
a b
---
0 1
1 0
0 0
```

Similarly, we expect `null` to operate on a keyed table by returning a result keyed table whose value table entries are the result of testing those of the argument against null:

```
        ktnull:([k:101 102 103] v:`first``third)

        null ktnull
k  | v
---| -
101| 0
102| 1
103| 0
```

A.5.28 parse

The monadic function `parse` takes a string argument containing a valid *q* expression and returns a list containing the corresponding parse tree. Applying the function `eval` to the result will evaluate it. A discussion of *q* parse trees is beyond the scope of this tutorial.

```
        parse "a:6*7"
:
`a
(*;6;7)

        eval parse "a:6*7"
42
```

> **Note**
>
> It is useful to apply `parse` to a query template in order to discover its functional form. The result is not always exactly the functional form, especially for `exec`, but a little experimenting will lead to the correct form.

```
        t:([]c1:`a`b`a; c2:1 2 3)

        select c2 by c1 from t
c1| c2
--| ---
a | 1 3
b | ,2

        parse "select c2 by c1 from t"
?
`t
()
(,`c1)!,`c1
(,`c2)!,`c2

        ?[t;();(enlist `c1)!enlist `c1;(enlist `c2)!enlist `c2]
c1| c2
--| ---
a | 1 3
b | ,2

        exec c2 by c1 from t
a| 1 3
b| ,2

        parse "exec c2 by c1 from t"
?
`t
()
,`c1
,`c2

        ?[t;();`c1;`c1]
a| `a`a
b| ,`b
```

A.5.29 random (?)

The dyadic function rand (?) is overloaded to have multiple meanings. In the case where both arguments are numeric scalars, ? returns a list of random numbers. More specifically, the first argument must be of integer type, and the second argument can by any numeric value. In this context, ? returns a list of pseudo-random numbers of count given by first argument.

In case the second argument is a positive number of floating point type and the first argument is positive, the result is a list of random float selected **with** replacement from the range between 0 (inclusive) and the second argument (exclusive):

```
    5?4.2
3.778553 1.230056 1.572286 0.517468 0.07107598

    4?1.0
0.5274765 0.5435815 0.4611484 0.7493561
```

In case the second argument is of integer type and the first argument is a positive int, the result is a list of random integers selected **with** replacement from the range between 0 (inclusive) and the second argument (exclusive):

```
    10?5
1 2 0 3 4 4 0 3 1

    10?5
0 2 1 0 2 4 2 3 4 0

    1+10?5
4 2 3 3 3 2 1 1 5 3
```

The last example shows how to select random integers between 1 and 5. More generally, for integers i and j, where i<j, and any integer n, the idiom,

```
i+n?j+1-i
```

selects n random integers between i and j inclusive:

```
    i:3
    j:7
    n:10

    i+n?j+1-i
3 4 5 7 7 5 4 4 7 4
```

In case the second argument is of integer type and the first argument is negative, the result is a list of random integers selected **without** replacement from the range between 0 (inclusive) and the second argument (exclusive). Since the selected values are not replaced, the absolute value of the first argument cannot exceed the second argument:

```
        -3?5
2 3 0

        -5?5
4 1 2 0 3

        -6?5
'length
```

In the case the first argument is an integer *n* and the second is a list *L*, the result is a list of *n* randomly selected items from *L*. When *n* is positive, the selection is done with replacement. When *n* is negative, the selection is done without replacement. The last example shows how to shuffle a list:

```
        L:10+til 10
10 11 12 13 14 15 16 17 18 19

        3?L
11 19 16

        10?L
16 14 12 12 14 15 11 12 12 11

        -10?L
10 14 16 18 17 11 13 19 12 15
```

In case the first argument is a positive integer *m* and the second argument is a symbol of the form `` `n `` where *n* is a positive integer no greater than eight, the result is a random list of m symbols, each comprising exactly *n* characters:

```
        3?`1
`o`m`h

        4?`8
`mdeghofn`olclfpfo`ncbmhcfp`fkdfagkl
```

A.5.30 raze

The monadic `raze` takes a list or dictionary (*source*) and returns the entity derived from the source by eliminating the top-most level of nesting:

```
        raze (1 2;`a`b)
1
2
`a
`b
```

One way to envision the action of `raze` is to write the source list in general form, then remove the parentheses directly beneath the outer-most enclosing pair:

```
        raze ((1;2);(`a;`b))
1
2
`a
`b
```

Observe that `raze` only removes the top-most level of nesting and does **not** apply recursively to sublists:

```
        raze ((1 2;3 4);(5;(6 7;8 9)))
1 2
3 4
5
(6 7;8 9)
```

If *source* is not nested, the result is the source:

```
        raze 1 2 3 4
1 2 3 4
```

When `raze` is applied to an atom, the result is a list:

```
        raze 42
,42
```

When `raze` is applied to a dictionary, the result is `raze` applied to the range:

```
        dd:`a`b`c!(1 2; 3 4 5;6)
        raze dd
1 2 3 4 5 6
```

A.5.31 reshape (#)

When the first argument of the dyadic reshape (#) is a list (*shape*) of two positive int, the result reshapes the source into a rectangular list according to *shape*. Specifically, the count of the result in dimension *i* is given by the item in position *i* in *shape*. The elements are taken from the beginning of the source. A simple example makes this clear:

```
      2 3#1 2 3 4 5 6
1 2 3
4 5 6
```

As in the case of take, if the number of elements in the source exceeds what is necessary to form the result, trailing elements are ignored:

```
      2 2#`a`b`c`d`e`f`g`h
a b
c d
```

Similarly, if the number of elements in the source is less than necessary to form the result, the extraction resumes from the initial item of the source; this process is repeated until the result is complete:

```
      5 4#"Now is the time"
"Now "
"is t"
"he t"
"imeN"
"ow i"
```

It is possible create a ragged array of any number of rows or columns with the reshape operator (#). Using 0N as the number of rows with a specified number of columns we get:

```
      0N 3#til 10
0 1 2
3 4 5
6 7 8
,9
```

Using 0N as the number of columns with a specified number of rows we get:

```
      3 0N#til 10
```

```
0 1 2 3
4 5 6 7
8 9
```

A.5.32 reverse

The monadic `reverse` inverts the order of the constituents of its argument. In the case of an atom, it simply returns the argument:

```
        reverse 42
42
```

In the case of a list, the result is a list in which the items are in reverse order of the argument:

```
        reverse 1 2 3 4 5
5 4 3 2 1
```

For nested lists, the reversal takes place only at the topmost level:

```
        reverse (1 2 3;"abc";`Four`Score`and`Seven)
`Four`Score`and`Seven
"abc"
1 2 3
```

In the case of an empty list, `reverse` returns the argument:

```
        reverse ()
```

In the case of a dictionary, `reverse` inverts both the domain and range lists:

```
        reverse`a`b`c!1 2 3
c| 3
b| 2
a| 1
```

Since a table is a list of records, `reverse` inverts the order of the records:

```
        t:([] c1:`a`b`c; c2:1 2 3)

        t
```

```
c1 c2
-----
a  1
b  2
c  3

    reverse t
c1 c2
-----
c  3
b  2
a  1
```

Since a keyed table is a dictionary, `reverse` inverts both the domain and range tables, effectively inverting the row order:

```
    t:([k:1 2 3] c:100 200 300)

    kt
k| c
-| ---
1| 100
2| 101
3| 102

    reverse kt
k| c
-| ---
3| 102
2| 101
1| 100
```

A.5.33 setenv

The dyadic function `setenv` takes a symbol left argument representing the name of an O/S environment variable and a string right argument. It calls the underlying O/S to set the named environment variable to the specified string value:

```
    `SHELL setenv "/bin/bash"
```

A.5.34 sublist

The dyadic function `sublist` retrieves a sublist of contiguous items from a list. The left operand is a simple list of two ints: the first item is the starting index (*start*); the second item is the number of items to retrieve (*count*). The right operand (*target*) is a list or dictionary.

If *target* is a list, the result is a list comprising *count* items from *target* beginning at index *start*:

```
        L:1 2 3 4 5

        1 3 sublist L
2 3 4
```

If *target* is a dictionary, the result is a dictionary whose domain comprises *count* items from the *target* domain beginning at index *start*, and whose range is the corresponding items in *target*:

```
        d:`a`b`c`d`e!1 2 3 4 5

        1 3 sublist d
b| 2
c| 3
d| 4
```

Since a table is a list of records, `sublist` applies to the rows of a table:

```
        t:([] c1:`a`b`c`d`e; c2:1 2 3 4 5)

        1 3 sublist t
c1 c2
-----
b  2
c  3
d  4
```

Since a keyed table is a dictionary, `sublist` is applied to the key table:

```
        kt:([k:`a`b`c`d`e] c1:1 2 3 4 5)

        1 3 sublist kt
k| c1
-| --
b| 2
c| 3
d| 4
```

A.5.35 system

The monadic `system` takes a string argument and executes it as a *q* command, if recognized, or an O/S command otherwise. The function system is convenient in situations such as remote or programmatic execution in which the backslashes must be escaped.

The following changes the current working directory to its parent directory:

```
system "cd .."
```

A.5.36 take (#)

When the left operand of take (#) is an int atom, it creates a new entity via extraction from its right operand (*source*) as specified by the first operand. A positive integer in the first operand indicates that the extraction occurs from the beginning of the *source*, whereas a negative integer in the first operand indicates that the extraction occurs from the end of the *source*.

The *source* can be an atom, a list, a dictionary, a table or a keyed table:

```
        2#3
3 3

        -1#10 20 30 40
,40

        -2#`a`b`c`d!10 20 30 40
c| 30
d| 40

        3#([] a:10 20 30 40; b:1.1 2.2 3.3 4.4)
a  b
-----
10 1.1
20 2.2
30 3.3

        1#([k:10 20 30] c:`one`two`three)
k | c
--| ---
10| one
```

The result of take is of the same type and shape as the *source*, except the result is never a scalar:

```
        1#42
,42
```

If the number of elements in *source* exceeds what is necessary to form the result, trailing elements are ignored:

```
        4#`a`b`c`d`e`f`g`h
(`a`b`c`d)
```

If the number of elements in *source* is less than necessary to form the result, the extraction resumes from the starting point of the *source* list; this process is repeated until the result is filled:

```
        5#98 99
98 99 98 99 98

        -7#`a`b`c
`c`a`b`c`a`b`c
```

In the degenerate case, the result is an empty entity with the same type as the source. This is an effective way to obtain the schema of a *q* dictionary or list:

```
        0#42
`int$()

        0#10 20 30 40
`int$()

        0#`a`b`c`d!10 20 30 40

        0#([] a:10 20 30 40; b:1.1 2.2 3.3 4.4)
a b
---

        0#([k:10 20 30] c:`one`two`three)
k| c
-| -
```

> **Note**
>
> Since the result of 0# is always a list, we can use this construct as shorthand to initialize an empty value column with a definite type in a table definition. This ensures that only values of the specified type can be inserted into the column.

For example,

```
        ([] a:0#0; b:0#`)
a b
---
```

defines an empty table whose first column is of type int and whose second column is of type symbol.

When the left operand of # is a list of symbol column names and the right operand is a table, the result is the table obtained by extracting the specified columns from t:

```
        t:([] c1:`a`b`c; c2:1 2 3; c3:1.1 2.2 3.3)

        `c1`c3#t
c1 c3
------
a  1.1
b  2.2
c  3.3
```

When the left operand of # is a table (*keys*) and the second operand is a keyed table whose key table contains *keys*, the result is the keyed table corresponding to those values in *keys*:

```
        ktc:([lname:`Dent`Beeblebrox`Prefect;
              fname:`Arthur`Zaphod`Ford] iq:98 42 126)

            ktc
lname       fname  | iq
-------------------| ---
Dent        Arthur | 98
Beeblebrox  Zaphod | 42
Prefect     Ford   | 126

        K:([] lname:`Dent`Prefect; fname:`Arthur`Ford)

        K#ktc
lname    fname  | iq
----------------| ---
Dent     Arthur | 98
Prefect  Ford   | 126
```

A.5.37 til

The monadic `til` returns a list of the integers from 0 to *n*-1, where its argument *n* is a non-negative integer:

```
        til 4
0 1 2 3
```

The result of til is always a list of int. So:

```
        til 1
,0

        til 0
`int$()
```

Generating sequences is simple with til:

```
        2*til 10                    / evens
0 2 4 6 8 10 12 14 16 18

        1+2*til 10                  / odds
1 3 5 7 9 11 13 15 17 19

        20+til 5
20 21 22 23 24

        0.5*til 10
0 0.5 1 1.5 2 2.5 3 3.5 4 4.5
```

The function til is useful for extracting a sublist from a list. The idiom,

```
    L[i+til n]
```

extracts from the list L the sublist of length n starting with the element in position i. For example:

```
        L:10 20 30 40 50 60 70
        i:2
        n:3

        L[i+til n]
30 40 50
```

Similarly, the idiom,

```
    L[i+til j+1-i]
```

extracts the sublist from positions i through j, inclusive. With L and i as above:

```
        i:2
        j:5

        L[i+til j+1-i]
30 40 50 60
```

> **Note**
>
> In the second idiom, omitting the increment-by-one retrieves one less item than you probably intend. This is an easy error to make.

These idioms are useful for extracting substrings:

```
        s:"abcdefg"
        i:1
        n:2
        j:4

        s[i+til n]
"bc"

        s[i+til j+1-i]
"bcde"
```

> **Note**
>
> You can use the built-in function `sublist` to retrieve substrings.

The expression,

```
    n = count til n
```

is true for every $n \geq 0$. Similarly, the expression,

```
    L~L[til count L]
```

is true for every list L. Both expressions remain valid in the degenerate case of the empty list.

A.5.38 ungroup

The monadic `ungroup` can be applied to a keyed table that is the result of a `select` with grouping or of the `xgroup` function. The result will have the selected records in the same format as the original table but they may be in a different order since they will be sorted by the grouping column(s).

Using the distribution example:

```
         sp
s  p  qty
---------
s1 p1 300
s1 p2 200
s1 p3 400
s1 p4 200
s4 p5 100
s1 p6 100
s2 p1 300
s2 p2 400
s3 p2 200
s4 p2 200
s4 p4 300
s1 p5 400


         ungroup select s, qty by p from sp
p  s  qty
---------
p1 s1 300
p1 s2 300
p2 s1 200
p2 s2 400
p2 s3 200
p2 s4 200
p3 s1 400
p4 s1 200
p4 s4 300
p5 s4 100
p5 s1 400
p6 s1 100
```

> **Note**
>
> You can apply ungroup to a keyed table that did not arise from a group operation, but it must have the correct form or an error will result.

A.5.39 union

The dyadic `union` can be applied to lists and tables. It returns an entity of the same type as its arguments containing the distinct elements from both arguments:

```
        1 union 2 3
1 2 3

        1 2 union 2 3
1 2 3

        1 1 3 union 1 2 3 1
1 3 2

        "a good time" union "was had by all"
"a godtimewshbyl"
```

Observe that the items of the first argument appear first in the result.

Tables that have the same columns can participate in `union`. The result is a table with the distinct records from the combination of the two tables:

```
        t1:([] a:1 2 3 4; b:`first`second`third`fourth)

        t2:([] a:2 4 6; b:`dos`cuatro`seis)

        t1
a b
--------
1 first
2 second
3 third
4 fourth

        t2
a b
--------
2 dos
4 cuatro
6 seis

        t1 union t2
a b
--------
1 first
```

```
2 second
3 third
4 fourth
2 dos
4 cuatro
6 seis
```

> **Note**
>
> As of this writing, `union` does not apply to dictionaries or keyed tables.

A.5.40 value

The function `value` has two uses. When applied to a dictionary, `value` returns the range of the dictionary:

```
        d:`a`b`c!1 2 3

        value d
1 2 3
```

Logically enough, for a keyed table, `value` returns the value table:

```
        kt:([k:101 102 103] c1:`a`b`c)

        kt
k  | c1
---| --
101| a
102| b
103| c

        value kt
c1
--
a
b
c
```

When `value` is applied to a string, it passes the string to the *q* interpreter and returns the result:

```
        value "6*7"
42

        value "{x*x} til 10"
0 1 4 9 16 25 36 49 64 81

        z:98.6

        value"z"
98.6

        value "a:6;b:7;c:a*b"

        a
6

        b
7

        c
42
```

> **Note**
>
> This use of the value function is a powerful feature that allows *q* code to be written and executed on the fly. If abused, it can quickly lead to unmaintainable code.
>
> (The spellchecker suggests *unmentionable* instead of *unmaintainable*. How did it know?)

A common use of value is to convert a symbol or string containing the name of a *q* entity into the value associated with the entity:

```
        a:42
        s:`a

        value `a
42

        value s
42

        value "a"
42
```

A.5.41 where

The monadic `where` has multiple uses, depending on the type of its argument.

When the argument is a boolean list, `where` returns a list of int comprising the positions in the argument having value `1b`:

```
        where 00110101b
2 3 5 7
```

This is useful when the boolean list is generated by a test on a list:

```
        L:"Now;is;the;time"

        where L=";"
3 6 10

        L[where L=";"]:" "

        L
"Now is the time"
```

> **Note**
>
> The behavior of the `where` phrase in the `select` template is related to the `where` function on a boolean list. The former limits the selection to table rows in those positions where the value of the `where` expression is not zero. Since the expression involves test(s) on column value(s), the `where` phrase effectively selects the rows satisfying its column condition, just as in SQL. See **§8.2.2** for more on the `where` phrase.

When the argument s of `where` is a list of non-negative int, the result is a list of int comprising the items 0, ... , -1+count s, in which i is repeated $s[i]$ times. For example:

```
        where 2 1 3
0 0 1 2 2 2

        where 4 0 2
0 0 0 0 2 2

        where 4#1
0 1 2 3
```

When the argument *s* is a dictionary whose range is a list of non-negative int, `where` returns a list comprising items of the domain of *s*, in which the item at position *i* is repeated *s[i]* times. For example:

```
        where `a`b`c!2 1 3
`a`a`b`c`c`c

        where `a`b`c!4 0 2
`a`a`a`a`c`c
```

> **Note**
>
> The behavior of `where` on a dictionary is consistent with its behavior on a list by considering a list L as a mapping whose implicit domain is `til count L`.

A.5.42 within

The dyadic function `within` is atomic in its first argument (*source*) and takes a second argument that is a list of two items that have underlying numeric values. It returns a boolean value representing whether *source* is between the two items of the second argument (inclusive):

```
        3 within 2 5
1b

        100 within 0 100
1b

        "c" within "az"
1b

        2006.11.19 2007.07.04 2008.08.12 within 2007.01.01 2007.12.31
010b
```

Observe that `within` is type tolerant provided both arguments have underlying numeric values, meaning that the types of its arguments do not need to match:

```
        0x42 within (30h;100j)
1b
```

```
        100 within "aj"
1b
```

It is also possible to apply within to symbols since they have lexicographic order:

```
        `ab within `a`z
1b
```

> **Note**
>
> The expression,
>
>   x within (a;b)
>
> is equivalent to,
>
>   (a<=x)&x<=b
>
> Thus, if the items of the second argument are not in increasing order, the result of within will always be 0b. See below.

```
        5 within 6 2
0b
```

Appendix B
Error Messages

B.1 Runtime Errors

Error	Example	Description
access		Attempt to read files above directory, run system commands or failed usr / pwd
assign	cos:12	Attempt to reuse a reserved word
conn		Too many incoming connections (1022 maximum)
domain	til -1	Argument out of domain
fail	`s#3 2	Invalid attribute setting
glim		`g# limit, kdb+ currently limited to 99 concurrent `g#'s
length	(til 2)+til 3	Incompatible list lengths
limit		Attempt to create list longer than allowable maximum
loop	a::b::a	Circular reference loop
mismatch		Columns cannot be aligned for operation
mlim		More than 999 nested columns in splayed table
nyi		Not yet implemented
os		Operating system error
pl		peach can't handle parallel lambdas (**2.3** only)
Q7		Unimplemented op on file nested array
rank	+[2;3;4]	Invalid rank or valence
splay		Unimplemented op on splayed table
stack		Exhausted stack space
stop		User interrupt (ctrl-c) or time limit (-T)
stype	'42	Invalid type used to signal
type	til 4.2	Wrong type
value		Missing value
vd1		Attempted multithread update
wsfull		malloc failed, ran out of swap (or addressability on 32bit), or hit -w limit
xxx	'xxx	*xxx* undefined

B.2 Parse Errors

Error	Example	Description

(
)
[
]
{
}
"
		Unpaired item

branch		A branch (if;do;while;$[.;.;.]) more than 255 byte codes away
char		Invalid character
constants		Too many constants (max 96)
globals		Too many global variables (255 maximum)
locals		Too many local variables (24 maximum)
params		Too many parameters (8 maximum)

B.3 System Errors

Error	Example	Description
xxx:yyy		*xxx* is a kdb+ message *yyy* is the OS message

		xxx can be
		  addr
		  close
		  conn
		  p (from –p)
		  snd
		  rcv
		  filename (invalid)

B.4 LICENSE ERRORS

Error	Example	Description
cpu		Exceeded number of licensed cpus
exp		Expiry date passed
host		Unlicensed host
k4.lic		k4.lic file not found, check *q* HOME/QLIC
os		Unlicensed OS
srv		Attempt to use client-only license in server mode
upd		Attempt to use version of kdb+ more recent than update date
user		Unlicensed user
wha		Invalid system date

REFERENCES

KDB+ Database and q Language Primer, Dennis Shasha
http://kx.com/q/d/primer.htm

Kdb+ Database Reference Manual, Don Orth
http://kx.com/q/d/kdb+1.htm

q Language Reference Manual, Don Orth
http://kx.com/q/d/q1.htm

Abridged Kdb+ Database Manual, Arthur Whitney
http://kx.com/q/d/kdb+.htm

Abridged q Language Manual, Arthur Whitney
http://kx.com/q/d/q.ht

INDEX

Reserved symbols

:: (alias assignment) · 94
    (view assignment) · 267
': (each-previous) · 123
' (each-both) · 116
' (signal) · 293
- (subtract) · 71
! (functional delete) · 272
! (functional update) · 272
! (xkey) · 153
(attribute) · 211
(reshape) · 425
(take) · 200, 429
$ (cast) · 139
$ (enumeration) · 147
$ (matrix multiplication) · 368
% (divide) · 71
& (min) · 75
( ) as list delimiters · 29
( ) grouping in expressions · 63
( ) in table definition · 177
\ (scan) · 123
\ (terminate) · 342
* (multiply) · 71
,' (column join) · 205
, (join) · 41, 164, 415
    on dictionaries · 164
    on tables · 202
, as subphrase separator in select · 226
,/:\: (Cartesian Product) · 120
,' (join-each) · 417
. (in contexts) · 325
. (protected evaluation (· 294
. (quartic for dyadic functions) · 134
. (triadic for monadic functions) · 135
. (verb) · 128
.q (context) · 326
.Q (context) · 326
.z (context) · 326
.z.pc (close handler) · 323
.z.pg (process synchronous request) · 321
.z.ph (http handler) · 324
.z.ps (process asynchronous request) · 321
.z.x (parameters) · 298
/ \ (comment delimiters in script) · 297
/ (comment) · 8

/ (over) · 122
/ (path delimiter in file handle) · 301
/ (writing splayed file) · 304
/: (each-right) · 120
: (amend) · 106
\: (each-left) · 120
: (return) · 293
:: (global variable assignment) · 105
:: (identity function) · 102, 412
; (separator in script) · 298
; as list item separator · 29
? (conditional append) · 393
? (conditional evaluation) · 287
? (find) · 53, 161, 201, 406
? (functional exec) · 271
? (functional select) · 270
? (rand) · 422
? (vector conditional evaluation) · 290
@ (protected evaluation) · 294
@ (quartic for dyadic functions) · 131
@ (triadic for monadic functions) · 133
@ (verb) · 127
[ ] in function definition · 99
[ ] in keyed table definition · 188
[ ] in table definition · 177
[ ] used in list indexing · 36
[ ] with select · 234
\\ (exit) · 343
^ (coalesce) · 204
^ (fill) · 405
_ (cut) · 398, 399
    on dictionary · 162
_ (delete)
    on dictionary · 162
_ (drop) · 402
_ in name · 6
` (symbol identifier) · 18
`: (file handle) · 301
`: communication handle) · 316
`g (grouped attribute) · 215
`p (parted attribute) · 213
`s (sorted attribute) · 211
`u (unique attribute) · 213
{}in function definition · 98
| (max) · 75
~ (match) · 64
+ (add) · 71
< (less than) · 69

<= (less or equal) · 69
<> (not equal) · 66
= (equal) · 66
> (greater than) · 69
>= (greater or equal) · 69
0: (processing text) · 309
0: (reading text file) · 308
0: (writing fixed length records) · 312
0: (writing variable length records) · 314
0x (type identifier) · 16
1: (readig variable length rcords) · 314
1: (reading fixed length records) · 312
1: (writing a binary file) · 310
\a (command) · 333
b (type identifier) · 16
blank as list item separator · 31
\c (command) · 334
\C (command) · 334
\cd (command) · 334
Ctrl-C (break) · 342
\d (command) · 327, 335
dd (temporal constitutent) · 23
e (scientific notation) · 15
e (type identifier) · 15
\f (command) · 335
f (type identifier) · 14
h (type identifier) · 14
j (type identifier) · 14
\l (command) · 336
m (type identifier) · 21
mm (temporal constituent) · 23
NaN · 25
\o (command) · 336
\p (command) · 336
\P (command) · 337
\S (command) · 338
\t (command) · 338
\T (command) · 340
\t (timer) · 339
\v (command) · 340
\w (command) · 340
\W (command) · 340
\x (command) · 341
year (temporal constituent) · 23
\z (command) · 341

A

abs (operator) · 81
absolute value · 81
acos (function) · 363
ad hoc
    left join · 258

ad hoc left join · 258
    no foreign key requirement · 259
    performance vs equijoin · 258
adverb · 116
aggregation · 245
    using each · 246
    using uniform and aggregate functions · 246
    with grouping · 245
aj (function) · 263
    syntax · 263
alias · 94
all (function) · 372
amend
    and type checking · 107
    list · 107
    overview · 106
    simple · 106
and (operator) · 76
any (function) · 372
apply
    for dyadic functions · 131
    for monadic functions · 133
arithmetic operations
    domain · 72
    item-wise extension · 74
    on binary types · 72
    on dictionaries · 166
    on floating point · 73
    on integer types · 73
    on nulls and infinities · 88
    on temporal values · 82
    overflow · 73
    type compatibility · 72
arithmetic operators · 71
asc (function) · 393
asin (function) · 364
asof (function) · 263
asof join · 263
    syntax · 263
assign
    as return · 293
assignment
    value · 9
association · See dictionary
asynchronous message · 320
atan (function) · 364
atom · 12
atomic functions
    item-wise extension · 61, 112
attribute
    grouped · 215
    parted · 213
    sorted · 211
    syntax · 211

unique · 213
attributes · 210
    are descriptive · 210
avg (function) · 372

B

bin (function) · 394
binary
    operator · 71
binary data · 16
    is numeric · 17
binary file · 310
    read · 310
    writing · 310
block comment · 297
boolean · 16
built-in functions · 354
by phrase · 224, 228
    omission · 228
by subphrase · 228
byte · 16

C

cardinals · 85
cartesian product · 120
cast (operator) · 139
    source · 139
    target · 139
    with symbolic name · 140
    with type char · 140
ceiling (operator) · 81
    domain · 81
char · 17
    null · 28
character data · 17
coalesce (operator)
    on keyed tables · 204
coercing type · 143
collision
    local and global variable · 105
cols (function)
    on dictionary · 154
column
    default value · 178
column dictionary · 169
    accessing values · 170
    definition · 169
    flip of flip · 173
    rows and columns · 171
    simple · 169

simple example · 169
transpose · 172
with single column · 171
column join · 205
command
    \ · 342
    break · 342
    \cd · 334
    console · 334
    \d · 335
    exit (\\) · 343
    \f · 335
    format · 333
    \l · 336
    \o · 336
    operating system · 341
    \p · 336
    \P · 337
    programmatic execution · 333
    \S · 338
    \t · 338
    \T · 340
    tables · 333
    \v · 340
    \w · 340
    \W · 340
    web console · 334
    \x · 341
    \z · 341
command line parameter
    -c · 351
    -C · 352
    -o · 352
    -p · 352
    -P · 352
    -t · 352
    -w · 353
    -W · 353
    -z · 353
command line parameters (system variable) · 350
commands · 333
comment · 8
communication handle · 316
complex column values · 206
composite function · 5
compound column operations · 208
compound foreign key · 209
    multiple types · 210
    schema · 210
compound key · 194
compound keyed table
    empty · 195
    retrieval by key · 195
    retrieval by table of keys · 195

conditional append (function) · 393
conditional evalation
   vector · 290
conditional evaluation · 286
   basic · 286
   extended · 287
connection handle · 316
console · 8
console (command line parameter) · 351
context
   and function definition · 329
   changing current · 327
   current · 327
   default · 327
   displaying · 327
   expunging from · 329
   is a dictionary · 328
   loading · 331
   name · 325
   notation · 325
   reserved · 326
   saving · 331
   working · 327
contexts · 325
   listing · 327
control flow · 286
cor (function) · 365
cos (function) · 365
count (function) · 396
   on dictionary · 154
   on table · 181
cov (function) · 366
create delimited text · 309
cross (function) · 366
cross product · 120
cut (operator) · 163, 397
   on dictionary · 162

D

data file
   definition · 301
   handle · 303
data file handle · 301
date · 19
   integral part · 82
date and time arithmetic · 83
date format (command line parameter) · 353
datetime · 20
day count · 83
debugging · 295
default value
   column · 178

delete
   functional form · 268
delete (operator)
   on dictionary · 162
delete template · 241
   modifying original table · 242
   syntax · 241
deltas (function) · 377
dependencies (system variable) · 343
depth · 43
desc (function) · 401
dev (function) · 373
dictionary
   amend · 160
   arithmetic operations · 166
   as generalization of a list · 156
   definition · 153
   domain · 153
   extension via index assignment · 160
   extracting sub-dictionary by key · 159
   flip · 173
   is not a list · 156
   join · 164
   keys · 153
   lookup · 155
   lookup by key list · 156
   non simple domain or range · 158
   operations · 163
   order is significant · 155
   range · 153
   remove entry · 162
   reverse lookup · 161
   simple example · 154
   type of · 153
   uniqueness of domain items · 154, 158
   values · 154
dictionary join · 164
   disjoint · 164
   non disjoint · 165
   upsert semantics · 165
differ (function) · 378
distinct
   in exec · 231
   in select · 231
   in select vs. exec · 232
distinct (function) · 401
   with table · 231
div (operator) · 78
division
   result is float · 72
do · 291
domain
   dictionary · 153
   function · 3
dot

for dyadic functions · 134
for monadic functions · 135
dot amend · 303
    append to file · 303
    overwrite file · 303
dot notation
    temporal constituents · 22
double assignment
    alias · 94
dyadic · 5

E

each
    both · 116
    in where phrase · 232
    left · 120
    monadic · 118
    previous · 123
    right · 120
elided indices · 53
    matrix · 53
    using verb . · 129
empty
    table · 183
empty list
    typed · 143
empty table
    column type · 184
    general · 183
    with specific column types · 184
enumerated value · 147
enumeration
    adding to · 149
    definition · 147
    example · 147
    resolving · 151
    traditional · 144
    type of · 151
    updating · 149
    uses cast · 147
equal (operator) · 66
equijoin · 255
    n-way · 255
eval (function) · 403
evolution of q · 1
except (function) · 404
exec
    difference from select · 229
    functional form · 268
    result of multi-column · 230
    single column · 230
exec template · 224
    syntax · 229
exit (function) · 404
exp (operator) · 76
expunging · 329
expunging a global entity · 329

F

fby · 235
    on multiple columns · 237
    syntax · 236
file deletion
    using hdel · 302
file handle · 301
fill (function) · 405
fills (function) · 379
find
    in a list · 53
    on dictionary · 161
    using with enumeration · 148
find (operator) · 406
    on keyed table · 201
    on table · 201
first (function)
    on table · 200
fixed length records · 312
fkeys (function) · 198
flip
    on rectangular list · 56
flip (operator) · 408
    on dictionary · 173
flipped column dictionary
    is list of records · 181
float · 14
floating point data · 14
floor (operator) · 80
    domain · 80
    using to truncate decimals · 80
foreign key · 197
    and relation · 199
    compound · 209
    definition · 197
    example · 197, 199
    in table syntax · 198
    resolving · 198
function · 3
    aggregate · 354
    anonymous · 102
    atomic · 60
    composite · 5
    definition · 98
    identity · 102
    notation · 60, 99

projection · 108
return value · 100
specification · 98
string · 354
uniform · 354
valence · 100
functional amend · 131
functional delete · 268
functional exec · 268
    multi-column · 271
    single column · 271
    with by · 271
functional select · 268
    syntax · 270
functional update · 268
    degenerate case · 272
    syntax · 272
functions
    built-in · 354
    introduction · 60

G

general list
    type of · 138
get
    on data file · 302
getenv (function) · 410
global date (system variable) · 344
global time (system variable) · 348
global variable · 104
    assignment · 105
graph
    function · 4
greater or equal (operator) · 69
greater than (operator) · 69
greenwich mean time (system variable) · 350
group (function) · 410
grouping · 243
    with aggregation · 245
    without aggregation · 229

H

handle
    communication · 316
    text file · 308
handle (system variable) · 350
hclose
    on data file handle · 303
    on text file · 308
hdel (function) · 302

hopen
    on binary file · 310
    on communication handle · 316
    on data file · 303
    on existing file · 303
    on text file · 308
host name (system variable) · 344
hsym (function) · 301
http connection
    default handler · 324
    handler · 324

I

I/O · 301
iasc (function) · 411
identity (function) · 102
idesc (function) · 412
if · 291
ij (function) · 256
in (function) · 413
index · 36
    domain · 38
    empty · 38
    empty list · 39
    is offset · 36
    notation · 36
    out of bounds · 38, 114
index assignment
    and type checking · 37
indexed assignment · 37
indexing
    by general list · 50
    by list · 48
    by simple list · 49
    juxtaposition · 52
    list assignment · 51
indexing a depth
    and positional retrieval · 113
    and ragged arrays · 112
indexing and evaluationverb form · 126
indexing at depth · 46
    notation · 47
infinities · 25
    producing · 86
infinity · 25
    type of · 138
inner join · 256
input and output · 301
insert · 217
    and type matching · 218
    as operator · 219
    basic · 217

bulk · 220
  into empty table · 218, 221
  keyed table · 220
  of duplicate key · 221
  of record · 219
  projected · 219
  repeated · 219
  with foreign key · 222
int · 13
integer data · 13
inter (function) · 413
interprocess communication · 315
  message format · 317
inv (function)
  matrix inverse · 367
ip address (system variable) · 343
item indexing · 37
  repeated · 46

J

join (operator) · 415
  append a record · 202
  on dictionaries · 164
  on keyed table · 203
  on tables · 203, 254
join-each (function) · 417
joining lists · 41
juxtaposition
  with indexing · 52

K

adverbs · 124
key (function)
  on dictionary · 154
key lookup
  txf · 196
keyed table · 186
  converting to table · 192
  empty · 188
  key lookup · 188
  multiple record retrieval · 189
  multiple value reverse lookup · 190
  retrieval by table of keys · 189
  reverse lookup · 190
  simple example · 187
  specification · 188
keys
  of dictionary · 153
keyword
  do · 291

from · 224
if · 291
select · 224
while · 291

L

last (function)
  on table · 200
least squares
  lsq · 367
left inner join · 254
left join
  ad hoc · 258
left of right evaluation · 63
  gotcha · 63
length · 57
less or equal (operator) · 69
less than (operator) · 69
license information (system variable) · 345
like (function) · 354
list · 29
  as map · 42
  assignment · 29
  count · 30
  definition · 29
  general · 29
  general empty · 34
  indexing · 36
  item order · 30
  mixed temporal · 34
  notation · 29
  rectangular · 56
  simple · 29, 31
  simple binary · 32
  simple char · 33
  simple floating point · 31
  simple integer · 31
  simple symbol · 33
  singleton · 35
list (function) · 418
list of records
  is converted to flipped column dictionary · 182
lj (function) · 258
  compared to SQL outer join · 260
load
  splayed table · 306
  table · 305
loading a script · 297
local date (system variable) · 344
local date and time (system variable) · 351
local time (system variable) · 348

local variable · 103
   lifespan · 104
   maximum number · 104
log (operator) · 77
long · 13
lookup
   in dictionary · 155
loookup
   with @ · 157
lower (function) · 356
lsq (function)
   least squares · 367
ltrim (function) · 356

M

major version (system variable) · 345
map · *See* function
   list and function as · 111
mapping · 3
match
   is not identity · 65
match (operator) · 64
matrices · 57
matrix
   columns · 57
   rows · 57
   three dimensional · 58
   two-dimensional · 57
   type · 57
matrix inverseinv · 367
mavg (function) · 380
max (function) · 374
max (operator) · 75
maximum workspace size · 340
maxs (function) · 381
mcount (function) · 382
md5 (function) · 419
mdev (function) · 382
med (function) · 374
message
   asynchronous · 320
   filter · 321
   handler · 321
   synchronous · 319
message filter · 321
meta
   and non-simple column · 180
meta (function)
   on table · 179
metadata · 179
min (function) · 375
min (operator) · 75

mins (function) · 382
minute · 21
mmax (function) · 383
mmin (function) · 384
mmu (function)
   matrix multiplcation · 368
mod (operator) · 79
monadic · 5
monadic each · 118
   adverbs · 124
month · 21
msum (function) · 384

N

namespace · 325
   advanced topics · 331
NaN
   producing · 87
neg (operator) · 74, 92
negate
   is not - · 74
nesting · 43
   depth · 43
   examples · 44
   pictorial representation · 43
next (function) · 384
niladic · 5
no operator precedence · 64
non-simple column
   in meta · 180
normalization
   using enumeration · 145
not (operator) · 67, 91
not equal (operator) · 66
not zero · 67
null · 26
   binary · 27
   character · 28
   numeric · 27
   temporal · 27
   values · 26
null (function) · 419
null item · 39
   forces general list · 40
   type · 39
nulls and infinities
   comparison · 92
   equality · 89
   match · 91
   max and min · 94
   neg · 92
   not · 91

operating on · 86
type promotion · 89

O

offset (command line parameter) · 352
open
    text file · 308
operating system (system variable) · 346
operations
    on dictionaries · 163
operator precedence · 62
    traditional · 62
or (operator) · 76
ordering · 69
    compatibility · 69
    item-wise extensions · 70
ordinals · 85
outer join · 254
over · 122

P

parameterized query · 264
    definition · 265
    restrictions · 265
parameters
    implicit · 101
parse
    using to obtain functional form · 421
parse (function) · 420
parse order · 10
parsing
    file records · 311
parsing strings · 142
pj (function) · 261
plus join · 261
port (command line parameter) · 352
prd (function) · 375
prepare text · 309
prev (function) · 386
primary key · 186
    compound · 194
primitive operators · 61
print digits (command line parameter) · 352
process close(system variable) · 346
process get (system variable) · 346
process http get (system variable) · 346
process http post (system variable) · 347
process id (system variable) · 345
process input (system variable) · 347
process key-value pairs · 309

process open (system variable) · 347
process set (system variable) · 347
projection
    and index elision · 114
    function · 108
    multiple · 110
    verb · 109
protected evaluation · 294
    monadic function · 294
    multivalent fucntion · 294
pseudo join · 257

Q

q console · 6
q script · 296
q-sql · 216

R

ragged array · 113
    creating with # · 113
rand (function) · 422
range
    dictionary · 153
    function · 3
rank (function) · 386
ratios (function) · 387
raze (function) · 423
reading
    binary data · 310
    text as binary · 311
real · 15
reciprocal (operator) · 79
record
    definition of · 181
records
    table · 181
rectangular list · 56
recursive function · 5
referential integrity · 223
relational operators · 66
release date (system variable) · 345
remote call
    function defined on server client · 318
    function sent from client · 317
remote stored procedure · 319
reshape (function) · 425
return · 293
return value · 100
reverse (function) · 426
reverse lookupkeyed table · 190

right inner join · 254
rotate (function) · 389
row value list · 181
rtrim (function) · 356

S

sample q program · 10
save
    splayed table · 305
    table · 305
    table as csv · 306
    table as text · 306
    table as xml · 306
scalar · 57
scan · 123
schema · 184
    obtaining · 430
script · 296
    block comments · 297
    casting parameters · 299
    example · 300
    exit · 297
    multiline expressions · 298
    passing parameters · 298
    table definition · 298
second · 22
select
    basic form · 184
    comma separators · 226
    first or last result records · 234
    functional form · 268
    result is table · 185
    subphrase · 226
    using join in · 226
select phrase · 224, 227
    and repeated columns · 227
    naming convention · 227
select template · 224
self (system variable) · 348
set
    on data file · 302
setenv (function) · 427
short · 13
sideways join · 118
signal · 293
signum (operator) · 79
simple list
    type of · 138
sin (function) · 368
sorting
    a dictionary · 393, 401
    a dictionary via lookup · 411, 412

    a list · 393, 401
    a list via index · 411, 412
    a table · 249
splayed table · 304
    creating · 304
    enumerate symbol column · 304
    writing · 304
SQL aggregation · 243
sqrt (operator) · 76
ss (function) · 357
ssr (function) · 357
startup file (system variable) · 344
stored procedure
    remote · 319
string · 33
    from data · 115
string (function) · 357
string from vector · 360
string search · 357
string search and replace · 357
sublist (function) · 427
sum (function) · 376
sums (function) · 385, 389
sv (function) · 360
symbol · 18
    creating symbol from string · 141
    null · 28
synchronous
    message · 319
system (function) · 428
system variable
    .z.a · 343
    .z.b · 343
    .z.d · 344
    .z.D · 344
    .z.f · 344
    .z.h · 344
    .z.i · 345
    .z.k · 345
    .z.K · 345
    .z.l · 345
    .z.o · 346
    .z.pc · 346
    .z.pg · 346
    .z.ph · 346
    .z.pi · 347
    .z.po · 347
    .z.pp · 347
    .z.ps · 347
    .z.s · 348
    .z.t · 348
    .z.T · 348
    .z.ts · 349
    .z.u · 349
    .z.vs · 349

.z.w · 350
.z.x · 350
.z.z · 350
.z.Z · 351

T

table
    accessing items · 176
    converting to keyed table · 191
    display · 176
    empty · 183
    is flip of colukmn dictionary · 175
    joins · 254
    metadata · 179
    rearranging columns · 251
    records · 181
    renaming columns · 251
    schema · 184
    sorting · 249
    type of · 175
table definition
    default column value · 177
    example · 177
    syntax · 177
    using variables · 177
table save and load
    example · 306
table syntax
    pf keyed table · 188
tables · 175
tables (function) · 180
take (operator)
    on dictionary with keys · 159
    on table · 200
    with int arg · 429
    with keys arg · 431
tan (function) · 369
temporal
    cardinals · 86
    ordinals · 86
temporal data · 19
temporal types
    basic operations · 83
    internal format · 82
text file · 308
    close · 308
    handle · 308
    read as binary · 311
    writing · 308
til (function) · 431
time · 20
    internal format · 82

time count · 83
time expression (system variable) · 349
timeout (command line parameter) · 352
timer (command line parameter) · 352
transpose
    of column dictionary · 172
trim (function) · 361
txf (function)
    creating a pseudo join · 257
    in select · 257
    key lookup · 196
type
    summary table · 137
type (function) · 137
type promotion
    integer · 14

U

uj (function) · 262
unary
    operator · 71
ungroup (function) · 434
    after by phrase · 229
    using · 247
union (function) · 435
union join · 262
update
    adding new columns with · 238
    by phrase · 239
    functional form · 268
    syntax · 237
update template · 237
    modify original table · 238
upper (function) · 362
upper case type char
    and non-simple column · 180
upsert
    on dictionary · 161
    on keyed table · 240
    on non-keyed table · 240
upsert (function) · 240
user (system variable) · 349
shuffle · 423

V

valence · 5, 100
    maximum allowed · 100
value (function) · 436
    on dictionary · 154
values

dictionary · 154
var (function) · 369
variable · 6
   assignment · 6
   name · 6
variable length records · 314
variable set (system variable) · 349
vector · 31, 57
vector conditional evaluation · 290
vector from string · 362
verb
   projection · 109
verb . · 128
   and elided indices · 129
   and niladic functions · 129
   and whitespace · 128
verb @ · 127
   on dictionary · 157
verbose programming · 1
verbs · 60
view · 267
view (function) · 268
views (function) · 268
virtual column · 199
   i · 227
vs (function) · 362

using with enumeration · 148
where phrase · 224, 226
   compared to where · 438
   nested · 233
   order of execution · 226
   subphrases · 226
   using each · 232
while · 291
whitespace · 7
   and comment · 8
within (function) · 439
workspace · 325
workspace size (command line parameter) · 353
writing
   binary data · 310
   text · 308
wsum (function) · 371

W

wavg (function) · 370
web browser console (command line parameter) · 352
week offset (command line parameter) · 353
where (function) · 438

X

xasc (function) · 249
xbar (function) · 390
xcol (function) · 251
xcols (function) · 252
xdesc (function) · 250
xexp (operator) · 77
xgroup (function) · 244
xkey (operator)
   on keyed table · 192
   on table · 191
   to define dictionary · 153
xlog (operator) · 78
xprev (function) · 391
xrank (function) · 392